Heroic Desire

Lesbian Identity and Cultural Space

Sally R. Munt

NEW YORK UNIVERSITY PRESS
Washington Square, New York

HQ
75.5
.M85
1998b

First published in the U.K. by Cassell, London

First published in the U.S.A. in 1998 by

NEW YORK UNIVERSITY PRESS
Washington Square
New York, N.Y. 10003

Library of Congress Cataloguing-in-Publication Data
Munt, Sally. Heroic desire : lesbian identity and cultural space /
    Sally R. Munt.
            p.   cm.
        Includes bibliographical references and index.
        ISBN 0-8147-5606-9 (clothbound). — ISBN 0-8147-5607-7 (pbk.)
        1. Lesbians—Identity.   2. Lesbians—Intellectual life.
    3. Lesbianism—Philosophy.   I. Title.
    HQ75.5.M85 1998b
    305.48'9664—dc21   97–42268
                                                                        CIP

Title page illustration © Diane DiMassa 1993. Used with permission.

Typeset by Ben Cracknell Studios

Printed and bound in Great Britain

Contents

Acknowledgements   vi

1. The Lesbian Hero   1

2. The Lesbian Flâneur   30

3. The Butch Body   54

4. The Lesbian Outlaw   95

5. The Lesbian Nation   132

6. Lesbians and Space   162

Index   182

Acknowledgements

I would like to thank the following friends and colleagues for their kind support, encouragement and patience with me while writing this book, and for providing insightful comments on the manuscript: Rosa Ainley, Sara Bragg, Joe Bristow, Caroline Freeman, Lynda Hart, Andy Medhurst, John Rignell, Cath Sharrock, Alan Sinfield, Cherry Smyth and Bonnie Zimmerman. Roz Hopkins at Cassell gave me editorial support beyond the call of duty, and offered me humour when I most needed it. For all the women at the Lesbian Herstory Archives, Brooklyn, New York, where I stayed for six months in 1994, I am deeply grateful, most especially to Ina Rimpau and Polly Thistlethwaite. Sarah Chinn, Kris Franklyn and Sarah Kelen always gave me a loving home in New York. The Fulbright Foundation and the American Council of Learned Societies generously made me their 1994/5 Fellow in American Studies. The University of East Anglia provided me with the time to consolidate and write by appointing me Research Fellow in American Studies, 1994–7. The University of Brighton provided essential computer, software and internet support.

Copyright acknowledgements

The author wishes to thank Joan Nestle for her permission to reprint 12 lines of 'Stone Butch, Drag Butch, Baby Butch', from *A Restricted Country* (Sheba Feminist Publishers, 1988) pp. 74–7. © Joan Nestle 1988.

Earlier versions of some of the material discussed in the book have been or will be published as follows:

'In Defence of Heroes' in E. Healey and A. Mason (eds), *Stonewall 25: The Making of the Lesbian and Gay Community in Britain* (Virago, 1994), pp. 201–11. 'In Defence of Lesbian Heroes' was delivered as a paper at the University of Sussex 'QUEORY: Graduate Colloquium of Lesbian and Gay Studies', 19 November 1993; at The Multicultural Center, Department of Women's Studies, State University of New York, Oneonta, 12 October 1994; and at 'Inqueery, In Theory, In Deed', The Sixth Annual Lesbian and Gay Studies Conference, University of Iowa, 17–20 November 1994.

'The Lesbian Flâneur' in *Perversions*, **1** (1), 1994; David Bell and Gill Valentine (eds), *Mapping Desire: Geographies of Sexuality* (Routledge, London and New York, 1995); and Iain Borden, Joe Kerr, Alicia Pivaro and Jane Rendell (eds), *The Unknown City: Contesting Architecture and Social Space* (Wiley, Chichester, 1997). It was also given as a paper at

'Queer Sites: Bodies at Work, Bodies at Play', University of Toronto, 13–15 May 1993, and at the Institute of British Geographers Annual Conference, University of Nottingham, 5 January 1994.

'The Butch Body' was given as a keynote address at the 'Body and Organisations' conference, Keele University, 12–13 September 1996; a shorter version will be published as 'The Butch Body: The Regulation of Depth and Reconstruction of Surfaces', in John Hassard and Ruth Holliday (eds), *Bodies and Organization* (Sage Press, London, 1998).

'Shame, Subjection, and Subjectivity', in Sally Ledger and Stella Swain (eds), *Legal Fictions* (special issue of *New Formations*) (Lawrence and Wishart, London, 1997). It was also delivered as a plenary address at the 'Literature and Legality Conference', University of the West of England, 29–30 June 1996; at the Centre for English Studies, University of London, 14–17 June 1996; and as a paper at the 'Cultural Violence' conference, George Washington University, 7–9 March 1997.

Parts of Chapter 5 appear in 'Nationalism and Sexuality', in Rosa Ainley (ed.), *The Sexed City* (Routledge, London, 1997).

Dedication

Everyone has their own personal heroes. Mine have sustained me in so many ways over the years and in writing this book. I dedicate it to the friends who have stuck by me through thick and thin and have become my lesbian family: to Sara Bragg, Caroline Freeman, Charlie Hague, Andrea Jones, Chris Kibbey and Marion Shoebridge, with my love.

The Lesbian Hero

I like to be a hero, like to come back to my island full of girls carrying a net of words forbidden them. Poor girls, they are locked outside their words just as the words are locked into meaning. Such a lot of locking up goes on on the Mainland but here on Lesbos our doors are always open.[1]

Heroes ain't what they used to be. When I was a kid I took my Action Man everywhere. He was the deluxe talking version with 'real hair'. I spent hours building an ornate and convoluted armoury for him out of cornflake packets and toilet-paper tubes, variations on a tank theme that I'd copied from my Saturday comic. Victor for Boys *consisted of two types of cartoon strip, war stories in which the 'orrible 'Uns figured only as cowering victims to the relentless march of Our Lad Johnny, and football tales in which other foreigners, the Away Team, got righteously trounced by the local Centre Forward, fuelled only by tripe and chips. Before I was eight, I had a whole gallery of working-class heroes to deflect the shots of hostile forces.*

Whilst my family was at war over a nasty divorce and a prolonged property dispute about the house that my mother, my older brother and I lived in, I was left, by default, to my own devices. Being the only child in a big Victorian house with six lodgers meant I was often rattling around in the adult world without any guides; my Action Man and my copious tank-building gifted me with more than a few imaginative defences. A couple of years later (around the time of the Stonewall Riot), I was hiding in my attic bedroom reading A.J. Cronin's The Stars Look Down, *and having my private struggles unsealed on paper. It's a story which transforms victims into titans.*

I've always read myself out of emotional difficulty. Despite the Out and Proud dyke I've sometimes become, there is still a piquant melancholy attached to being irresolvably distanced from wherever the latest centre purports to be. Some part of me still wants to join up (but I don't think, even now, they'll have an Action Woman). As a child reading under the sheets by the light of my red plastic EverReady torch, my habit was to seek out those heroic narratives in which suffering was eventually recognized and rewarded, and I wasn't choosy whether triumph was clothed in leather-bound editions or cheap, dog-eared, dirty paperbacks.

Lesbian heroes

In the interests of defending a range of cultural strategies which evangelize a lesbian life, one particular format seems to me to stride out onto the page: the hero. Heroes offer a metaphor of the self in movement, change and process. She is a radical myth, a lesbian success story, an icon of struggle, and both we and 'mainstream' culture need her versatility. Normalization is resisted by the public discourse of lesbianism – if our lesbianism is kept secret, then our private desires become domesticated – hence the importance of images like the heroic, which exist in the popular, public realm. To live as a lesbian today, even after twenty-five years of attempted liberation, is still an heroic act. Using the lesbian heroic, then, involves the invention of a new kind of self which can decentre essential individualism in favour of a pluralistic, multivalent self. This construction allows for the expression of an authentic personal history which is understood as experience and is loyal to the lesbian's own life trajectory and her specific felt needs. However, it also provides a model of the self as a series of intersecting plates, so that the ground of the self shifts and recombines with the intervention and chafing of other selves, which sculpt a new self based on intersubjectivity.

Propounding the heroic as an instrumental model for lesbian culture runs counter to the feminist invocation of the 1970s to replace stars with 'real' women, demystifying the hierarchies implicit in the artist/audience split and encouraging anti-individualistic cultural production.[2] Joanna Russ wrote wittily on this failed 'feminine imperative' in her essay 'Power and helplessness in the women's movement'.[3] Liberal academic feminists of the 1970s, by contrast, were keen to establish a retrospective tradition of 'heroines', particularly of literature, as a feminized adjunct of, and attempt to 'balance', the heroic male canon. Because of the problematic associations attached to the status of hero*ine* – which can only ever be a heterosexist qualifier to the ordinate hero – I refuse to use this term here. Propounding the lesbian heroic also runs counter to the prevailingly parodic temperament of the queer intelligentsia. Queer activism in the postmodernist 1990s tried to deconstruct the homo/hetero binary but all too often it was assimilated by the dominant urban bourgeois discourse of the polymorphously perverse and thus failed politically. Heterosexuality has a category for queers; I suspect it is still a fairly stable one, intentionally blind to the nuances of Queer. I do not want to trivialize or dismiss the success story of Queer activism within the subcultures themselves in raising awareness about AIDS, attacking narrow definitions of sexuality and highlighting the cultural politics of representation. But I think we have been underestimating the intransigence of the opposition. Queer was right for its period, which gave up on the grand gesture. It is concerned with change on the micro-level, an appropriate response to the monolith of 1980s Thatcherism/Reaganism. Queer, as a fundamentally deconstructive and internal project, is clever but limited.[4] It is not a lifestyle, but a critique. Sometimes it slides into a Reichian belief in the power of sex to transform society; it is 1960s style without the same collectivist, revolutionary content. Queer does not deliver a vision for structural change, but continues to focus on the local where grandiose gestures are still necessary. Dominant traditions have failed to get the message of Queer diversity because at the level of daily oppression they are still maintaining the binary divide (and rule) of heterosexuality/homosexuality as fiercely separate entities.

I want to recover that sense of specialness, of distinctiveness, that formed one of the planks of Lesbian and Gay Liberation, to believe again that gay is good.[5] This is a strategic policy which recognizes that nearly thirty years later we are still plagued by the same phobic discourse which promotes a fixed binary of heterosexual/homosexual. I am not pleading for a recapitulation to essentialist 'true homosexuals' here, but I think we do need to re-evaluate Lesbian and Gay Liberation as an expedient, complex and appropriate counter-ideology for the present, one that is inflected by a more coherent and functional concept of self. My oppression as a lesbian is very specific, and my resistance has a particular subcultural history to inform it. What we are being liberated from, where liberation takes us – these things are always changing, and we require the fiction of liberatory struggle, of emancipation and progress, to steer that change. Thus, flying in the face of Queer, I am arguing for another look at identity politics. 'Lesbian', in some of the manifestations I offer here, continues to be a powerful and strategic sign, an identity – or rather a set of identities – which is responsive and resistant to the nexus of censure which reduces us to an absence. My study is immersed in the specificity of lesbian culture and experience and, as I hope to demonstrate to anti-identitarian theorists, the claim of lesbian selfhood retains a political validity.

Does it really matter whether it was a diesel dyke who threw the first punch at a police-officer outside the Stonewall Bar, way back in the dawn of Lesbian and Gay Liberation, in 1969?[6] The image is symbolic, and has an important function as a *legend*, a story or narrative which lies somewhere between myth and historical fact. Social life is full of stories, and people are located, and locate themselves, in response to a repertoire of stories. They then construct their 'experience' according to certain plot-lines, which are always contextualized through time and in space. Narrative is thus ontological: it provides us with a sense of being, and also, through shared stories, a concept of relationality. The sociologists Margaret Somers and Gloria Gibson have described how ontological narratives define who we are, which becomes a precondition for knowing what to do. They are not fixed, but at the moment of 'doing' – of interpretative experience – they produce new narratives and consequently new actions: 'the relationship between narrative and ontology is processual and mutually constitutive',[7] i.e. they make the identity and the self something which *becomes*.[8] *Heroic Desire: Lesbian Identity and Cultural Space* is concerned with some of the different modalities present in contemporary lesbian culture which explore these ontological stories, these narratives of becoming, as tactics of presence, of spatial occupation. For a lesbian to 'be' is still an insurgent statement and enactment of desire, a radical emplacement in a culture of effacement. Claiming a lesbian self remains an heroic performance for all who inhabit an intransigently homophobic culture, and the book is written out of my continuing sense of the necessity of reminding ourselves that every story is multivalenced, every self is peculiar to itself.

Somers and Gibson have also gone as far as to claim that 'narratives are *constellations of relationships*' (emphasis in original). In traditional heroic narrative the plot functions in an adversarial structure in which social life is seen as a constraint against the achievement of individualism and self-realization. Thus one of the 'metanarratives' developed was that of the heroic achieved through the dichotomous subject/object binary, in which the latter must be debased. By choosing narratives which reject this antagonism and suture the hero into multiple or intersubjectivity as a moment of closure, a different heroic is founded. I intend to explore in this chapter the subject/subject relations of the multivalent self. When people 'find' themselves in a narrative, this is a momentary identification which is perceived as instrumental: a process of recognition occurs which functions through relationality to place the subject in a web of identification with more subjects like herself. But because each person's history is different, this strategic mutuality is embraced because of common interest in a purpose or action. Thus, Patricia Hill Collins writes about the importance of dialogue for American black women in a culture which values connectedness and empathetic modes of knowledge. Despite the respect accorded individual differences in African humanism, black women make strategic alliances in an 'ethic of caring' which involves listening to and incorporating another's experience without it being at their expense:

> 'all people can learn to center in another experience, validate it, and judge it by its own standards without need of comparison or need to adopt that framework as their own'. In such dialogues, 'one has no need to "decenter" anyone in order to center someone else; one has only to constantly, appropriately, "pivot the center".'[9]

Aetiologies of place and movement are premised on the idea of a self in process. We can formulate from this an idea of the visiting self, which leans into the experience of others and listens and learns. When her story becomes (interactively) their story, identities are created. Thus identification becomes an amalgam of experience and desire, a process not of exclusion, but of 'pivoting'. This sensibility produces a sense of belonging, a sense of 'we', which is not an attempt to universalize, but rather an articulation of quite specific experiences which are highly dependent upon the use of realism as a narrative form. Hence we return to self-definition being understood as the narrative product of an heroic quest for identity, the pursuit of which is at least partially aspirational, involving processes of identification and fantasy. Each self becomes an admixture of desires drawn from dominant and subcultural imagos, amalgamating stories from a cacophony of representative forms, both local and hegemonic. Of course, this manoeuvre is never entirely voluntaristic nor conscious, and this book tries to explore how lesbians have used, and have been used by, narratives of contingency.

The book does not follow a linear argument, but like the multivalent self consists of a series of intersecting plates. A number of concepts knit the manuscript together: space, desire, the heroic, the self; these threads implicate and inform each other, and emerge unevenly, like new outcroppings in nuanced patterns, within each chapter. There is no stable ground of 'lesbian identity' that the reader can walk upon. The ideal reader will interpret the modalities I offer here – the hero, the flâneur, the butch, the outlaw, the nation – to reconceptualize that most shifting and pressing of concepts, space. (Of course, there is no ideal reader, but I write for her anyway, mirroring the utopian strain in the text.) In the final chapter, 'Lesbians and Space', I attempt to make these linkages more self-conscious, integrating the personal voice which has functioned as a counterpoint in previous sections. Ultimately, I am concerned to offer the reader the political possibilities of lesbian space, to enquire how we can embody space with our desires. I see that project as heroic. Our resistance to a homophobic culture is a relentless demand for presence, an occupation of space which we have colonized in the name of a configuration of desires we call 'lesbian'. The more reflective we can become about these tactics – including, as I will show, problematizing taxonomies of 'the lesbian' itself – the more effective becomes our rhetoric of resistance. Lesbian desire, then, is that which is productive, excessive, expansive, a pleasure-machine which can open up new spaces in which we can live. It is being and becoming.

Folk tales, myth and stereotypes

Every society needs its folk tales, the popular wisdom shared by its members and related in parables which tell us how to live. They can be described as a kind of ritualized ethics. Folk tales are non-realist and depict sets of symbolic types. The social group seen to be functioning as an interlaced, reciprocal system is intrinsic to their structure. Folk tales are a very old cultural formation, dating back to pre-industrial society, and are oral, rather than literate. They are communal texts which enjoy multiple telling. Folk tales can also be understood as operating in lesbian communities through the narrative vehicle of 'gossip', where tales of good girls and bad girls become taxonomized in a fluid framework we can call lesbian ethics. We know from various studies of reader reception that lesbians are an expertly literate 'interpretative community', which reads for affirmation and confirmation of a group identity. Books are signs of legitimate membership, and certain novels are accorded an iconic status, performing a bonding function within various lesbian communities. Lesbian culture is not homogenous but heterogeneous. However, it is possible to proffer an analysis of the prevalent structures of myth and folk tale operating at any specific historical juncture in order to understand the particular anxieties, needs and desires being expressed, and the efficacy of the identity forms emerging to cleave them.

As Vladimir Propp has shown, folk tales are strung together by a combination of types.[10] The *bête noire* of lesbian representation is a stereotype, possibly the most contested sign for any minority group. Subcultures have long recognized the damage a negative stereotype can do, but stereotypes can also hold a function of self-definition. They can short-circuit more complicated messages and are able to communicate a lot of information quickly and concisely. Much lesbian pulp fiction is concerned with the processing and redefining of the stereotypes of dominant culture, through the figure of the hero. Take the sad, sick, sinful and tragic hero of the pre-Stonewall sensationalist dime novels of the 1950s and 1960s: in contemporary lesbian novels she is transformed into a romantic hero, converted into healthy happiness. This is not just essential for the dominant culture to see, but is also the constant reassurance we need as we grapple with our own homophobia.[11] The plasticity of heroic images, as rhetorical devices, can work for us as well as against. Popular cultural critics have commented upon the pleasure of predictability in formulaic fiction; its reassuring, encouraging function has the result of reinforcing positive images of lesbianism, a pattern which lesbian readers readily recognize as a symbolic exercise. Images from the 1970s of bare-breasted beauties with bad haircuts swinging a big spanner are figures of ridicule for the postmodern punters of the 1990s. But to recall positive images with the kind of fond embarrassment we reserve for naïve versions of ourselves misreads the political power of positive images as fantasy. We underestimated the evidently pragmatic longing of readers' desire for an heroic aesthetic, one that provokes a 'pride' response in order to rebut the shame produced by homophobia.

In Orrin E. Klapp's distinction between stereotypes and social types,[12] although both types are created iconographically, social types are those expected to belong to society and stereotypes are those that are not. Social types are allowed a more flexible signification in texts, whereas stereotypes, according to Richard Dyer, are always constrained by an implicit narrative.[13] The importance of stereotypes occurs in dealing with social categories that are fluid or invisible, such as lesbianism, by enforcing visibility and boundaries around them, clearly a mixed blessing for subjugated identities. Yet gay narratives produce types too: Dyer goes on to argue in a separate essay that 'types keep the fact of a character's gayness clearly present before us throughout the text':[14]

> gay types may be both the form of desire and a defence of it; further, they may embody both what it is like to be gay and what it is gay people find attractive – gay types can embody both the subject and the object of desire.[15]

The most familiar typology of gayness, Dyer argues, is 'in-betweenism', an interspace he relates specifically to gender/sex indeterminacy, and he goes on to illustrate how these 'in-betweenies' often invert and reject the boundaries set up to restrain them. In other words, what starts as a stereotype can be read as a social type, bleeding into the boundaries of dominant heterosexuality. The heroic form appropriated by lesbian culture is able to embody and manipulate this complex function, where, as we shall see, the lesbian heroic moves between individuation and incorporation, inhabiting an 'in-between' space where these stereotype and social type categorizations become indeterminate (in the latter case because heroic narratives close with a utopian social membership). The spatial manoeuvring of the lesbian hero allows the creation of an aspirational figure who gathers the desires of the lesbian reader into an intersubjective space.

Heroes

In order to discuss the lesbian heroic we must first turn to the heritage of the notion. In the *Poetics* Aristotle classified five types of fiction according to the hero's power of action: first, the hero as god is divine; second, the romantic hero is legendary and superior in degree to his environment and other men; third, the epic or tragic hero is a leader and exemplary in his actions but subject to his environment and the forces of nature; fourth, the hero of either comic or realist fiction is 'one of us', hence his heroism is more unstable; and fifth, the ironic hero is inferior, allowing the reader to define himself against the hero's limitations. Northrop Frye compares these types with the five epochs of Western literature, which roughly corresponds to moving down the list of Aristotle's types,[16] indicating that different manifestations of the heroic have appeared at various cultural moments. The hero swings between godlike powers and human fallibility, in the midst of which the reader experiences the pleasurable exorcism of fear and pity, through catharsis. The reader being processed by the narrative swings between absorption and differentiation: s/he is appropriated by the narrative at one end of the scale and repudiates it at the other (both are forms of involvement). At the high end of the scale we can see an authoritarian narrative effect, and at the low end of the scale a reactive one. Most lesbian heroes fall into categories three, four and five, which tend to privilege a relative degree of readerly autonomy. Hence we can argue that the lesbian heroic produces a negotiation of the self in relation to society.

The heroic epic has survived as perhaps the most enduring style of story in Western culture; its founding principle of progress through agency – and through emulation – is one of the key precepts of Protestant liberal humanism. Its profoundly Christian theme, that of flaw, punishment and redemption through agency, was summed up by André Gide when he said 'without sacrifice there is no resurrection'.[17] The key text on the heroic journey as myth was written by Joseph Campbell in 1949 in *The Hero with a Thousand Faces*.[18] Campbell's study uses psychoanalytic models to interpret what he describes as transcultural myths of rites of passage, which he distils into the formula *separation–initiation–return*. As a composite adventure the stages of the heroic journey comprise *separation*: i) the Call to Adventure; ii) Refusal of the Call (the hero prevaricates or temporarily diverts); iii) Supernatural Aid (a masculine helper endows him with power); iv) the Crossing of the First Threshold (learning from the guardian of power in a test); v) The Belly of the Whale (the hero 'dies'/has a loss of self). The hero then travels through the second phase of *initiation*: vi) the Road of Trials (a succession of symbolic trials); vii) the Meeting with the Goddess (a mystical marriage with the good/bad mother which purges the infant self); viii) Woman as the Temptress (he must withhold); ix) Atonement with the

Father (the ego is shattered and rebuilt); x) Apotheosis (he renounces fear and prejudice and embraces wisdom); xi) the Ultimate Boon (he transcends human limitations); the hero must then *return*, bringing his wisdom back to his original community, for their benefit and restoration, losing his transcendental powers as a consequence. Primarily, the hero narrative provides the reader/protagonist with a new identity, but heroism involves the loss of self before another can be recovered.

The new heroic identity is not entirely predetermined, and although Campbell's model is highly heterosexualized, it has variable elements. Heroic narratives have been appropriated for many disparate purposes. Hence, they can be malleable as tactics of progress as well as reaction. Their narrative structure permeates all aspects of contemporary culture, inflected by the specificities of various ideological agendas. Heroic narratives capture and express the desires of diverse political subjects. It is this utility of heroes I wish to consider here. Because heroic narratives are so concerned with the creation of a self, mediated by the inscriptive demands of the form, they are particularly relevant to a culture required to present a self as active and visible. Twentieth-century lesbian culture has grappled constantly with this need. In a sense, every lesbian is a hero. Cast out from the bosom of 'normal' family life, we have a moment of transformation, and then spend the rest of our days fighting for a space in the world for our desire. Sometimes when I am queuing for pool in the corner of the bar I gaze around me in that sentimental glow of inclusion at least four beers brings, and I ponder the amalgam of courage which has brought each woman here, to the lesbian homeland. A ghetto, if you believe in a mainstream, but still a community of (all)sorts. Being in that bar continues to be a statement of bravery, perseverance and solidarity, and our entry ticket was expensive. Every lesbian has her heroic narrative, romantic in both senses of the word. The act of sex and/or falling in love with another woman positions lesbian identity as romantic fulfilment, but the fiction of romance also sustains us in maintaining what remains a despised identity. Claiming a lesbian identity is a utopian gesture. Desire is implicated in all aspects of living a lesbian life; it is the fuel of our existence, a movement of promise. This desire is heroic in the sense that it depends on an individual trajectory through suffering. The 'flaw' in our identity – homosexuality – is redeemed and rewarded by our fantasy of the love of women, who 'complete' our identity. The linearity of this (admittedly, rather butch) narrative, and its supposed act of appropriation, does not necessarily connote a radical process. What is interesting to me is its pervasive re-articulation in lesbian culture.

Researching the heroic in cultural texts I have found most publications reproduce a kind of unimaginative common sense of the hero-protagonist. Prior to the 1970s, the dominant interest resided in the transcendental, mythic qualities of the male protagonist and his incarnation of Manichaean struggle (good versus evil, triumph over suffering) in 'classical' literature. Due to the influence of Cultural Studies after the 1970s, critics shifted their attention to the audience and reception, typically focusing on the way heroes embody the projected desires and contradictions of specific cultural contexts. Recent mainstream work on the hero centres on popular culture and is largely characterized by work on comics and 'superheroes', or on that paradigmatic post-war hero, James Bond.[19] Only recently has lesbian theory tried to examine the heroic as a prevalent form in lesbian culture. The two main examples of this work have been produced by literary critics Bonnie Zimmerman and Marilyn Farwell, both of whom try to weave a position between lesbian feminist and postmodernist theories of the self, advocating a deconstruction and reconstruction of identity, a move I also intend to emulate.

In the literary starburst of fiction in lesbian culture since Stonewall, heroic narratives dominate. There are hundreds and hundreds of contemporary lesbian novels in print, never mind the many thousands which get rejected by publishers. The hero–protagonist on a quest for legitimation stamps the majority, and even if there are other complex narrative structures in place, the lesbian hero remains ubiquitous. In *The Safe Sea of Women* Bonnie Zimmerman writes:

> The lesbian hero, in all her various shapes, journeys through patriarchy to its point of exit, the border of an unknown territory, a 'wild zone' of the imagination.[20]

We might also say 'desire' is that wild zone, and that 'Heroic Desire' is the engine of the machine which produces imaginative lesbian identities. This is an emancipatory journey that assumes intersections between the phantasmatic and the real and that reading therefore performs a simultaneous function of escape and transformation, throwing the reader back into a perceptibly changed world on her return. Crucially this metamorphosis takes place through a process of identification and desire

– we want the hero, and we want to *be* the hero; the phallic economy of either/or is superseded. Prevailing categories of the lesbian hero, according to Zimmerman, are outlaws, witches, magicians, androgynes and artists – characters not dissimilar from Thomas Carlyle's. He published *On Heroes, Hero-Worship and the Heroic in History* in 1841, six definitive lectures on categories of the hero as divinity/prophet/poet/priest/man of letters/king. In the lesbian feminist novels Zimmerman describes, these forms have been modified over the years to fit contemporary circumstances.

Heterosexual narrative is taken to be a project intended to traverse and contain the Woman through the control of female space, which the individual hero moves through and conquers. Thus at a symbolic level the female who transgresses and exceeds the space permitted her becomes 'the lesbian', because her desire is superfluous to the (male) text. She then becomes the outlaw. The teleology of the traditional text is that a relationship of cause and effect is established through the hero's ability to reject the female and found his identity on his disavowal; thus his individualism is formed at the expense of hers.[21] But is linearity predeterminedly 'straight'? Several lesbian writers, such as Monique Wittig, Mary Fallon and Rebecca Brown, have chosen to disrupt the form of the linear narrative in order to develop a lesbian text, whose circular grammar is imagined to be resistant to the internal logic of the heterosexual text. As Marilyn Farwell has pointed out, because the male hero, even in rebellion, is a representative of dominant cultural values, repositioning the hero as a lesbian aligns the narrative differently to power because of her marginal, excessive status, opening up a lesbian narrative space:

> This interrogation happens first, when female bonding breaks up male bonding, realigning any remaining male characters; second, when the asymmetrical structural patterns of active agent and passive object are revised by the structural interjection of sameness; and finally, when these changes on a structural level affect the movement and thematics of the traditional narrative.[22]

Because the lesbian is able to occupy the in-between space which is not totally circumscribed by male heterosexuality, her position, and her movement within it, can be conceived as fluid. In reality this is not a completely free space, it is partially free, and thus amenable to manipulation and metamorphosis. Despite the associations of linearity with conservatism and lyricism with radicalism, neither are intrinsically distinct. The danger is that in reifying the lyrical text lesbian authors embrace formal complexity because of its elitist connotations, conferring the canonistic gesture 'this is Art', and forcing a false dichotomy onto lesbian readers who are performing queer readings without their guidance. One would also have to square the circle and ask in whose political interests are many postmodernist middle class male authors writing, as their formal innovation is not necessarily radical at the level of content – Brett Easton Ellis, Paul Auster and Robert Coover would all be cases in point.

Farwell argues that the struggle for control over the definition of heroism is between the lesbian image in the text and the narrative system which presents it; she resorts to the view that any lesbian hero has the potential for disruption due to her social marginality – she is un-recuperable and, unlike the male hero, her isolation is permanent. She evokes the concept of the metaphoric textual lesbian subject who is:

> always already in a narrative of liberation, a narrative that moves from the constriction of culturally defined gender boundaries and heterosexuality to a utopian space which as Ellen G. Friedman notes of some women's texts, evokes the 'unpresentable as the not yet presented'.[23]

In this context the lesbian is clearly a stereotype in the sense of Orrin E. Klapp's distinction between stereotypes and social types. What is interesting is the paradox of lesbians' clear articulation of the need for realist subjects, which, perversely, can only be represented in the 'unreal' space of the imagination. It is a dichotomy which permeates lesbian representation. Perhaps this is most clearly exemplified in the popular thirst for lesbian detective heroes: acting in a genre historically aligned with truth, rationality, masculinity and realism, lesbian detectives battle with a symbolic Law and usually win. Because detective fiction is actually highly contrived and non-realist,[24] its appearance of realism com-municates to the reader possibilities at the level of fantasy which can dialectically shift the real. 'Real' lesbians do not often triumph over the Law, hence readership of these novels constitutes a utopian gesture, not just of displacement, but of emplacement. Detective fiction is highly individualist: lesbians appropriate this individuation and commute it into the narrative discovery of an identity. Logically this should lead to lonely isolation, in that lesbian individualism is contingent on the rejection of ties to others (in every sense). But the transposed space of lesbian identity reveals that individuation is a temporary phase; the lesbian hero is almost always reinscribed into communality and her identity is customarily depicted as shared. For example, the narrative impetus of a 'coming-out story' is basically individualist, described in terms invariably realist; however, the closure is achieved when the newly converted lesbian finds her community.[25] Although she becomes at this moment a sign entered into a system, and hence risks reincorporation, there is none the less the potential for the moment of phallic closure to be exceeded.

One can find work on counter-cultural heroes in left-wing criticism, for example in Eric Hobsbawm's *Primitive Rebels* (1959), an historical study of social banditry in nineteenth- and twentieth-century Europe. Hobsbawm studies heroes in the Robin Hood tradition, local outlaws who are champions of the poor. He makes the point that these anarchistic bandits were unsuccessful in achieving structural change due to their individualistic praxis. However, as counter-cultural heroes they maintained an aura of invincibility in the eye of oppression, and were given mythic status by their home communities. Hobsbawm is one of the early theorists to remark on the power of heroic narratives for oppositional ideologies, in his case the genesis of the working-class hero. Hobsbawm's thesis is interesting in that he builds up a progression in figures of resistance from the isolated rural bandit, to the unruly city mob, to the organized labour sect. There is a parallel here with pre- and post-Stonewall forms of gay and lesbian resistance, in the way that heroic figures are brought to closure by their insertion into an heroic culture. Individual heroes of pre-Stonewall existence are often perceived as anachronistic and isolated, despite their entrenchment in 'underground' lesbian cultures; Radclyffe Hall is a case in point. The Stonewall Riots became the principal heroic symbol of the foundation of modern lesbian and gay existence, and follow Hobsbawm's next heroic figure of the city mob, which:

> may be defined as the movement of all classes of the urban poor for the achievement of economic or political changes by direct action – that is by riot or rebellion – but as a movement which was as yet inspired by no specific ideology.[26]

Crucially:

> the 'mob' was not simply a casual collection of people united for some *ad hoc* purpose, but in a recognised sense, a permanent entity, even though rarely permanently organised as such.[27]

The short-lived Stonewall Riots had a certain egalitarianism and provided the populist legitimism 'of the people' which caused a revolution in homosexual identity, based on working-class models of heroic resistance. Demonstrations tend to solidify into ritual enactments of group identity and concomitantly develop ideologies for structural change, as has happened in the post-Stonewall Pride movement. The heroic gesture of Stonewall has been crystallized in the individual gesture of 'coming out', which is also a motion of 'coming in' – to the lesbian and gay community. Thus, I explore oppositional heroic narratives in which the moment of incorporation sutures the individual protagonist into an heroic community of resistance.

Jewelle Gomez wrote a novel, *The Gilda Stories* (1991), which proffers the black lesbian hero as a vampire. She describes elsewhere her difficulty in finding black women characters of heroic dimensions, reasoning 'we have been trapped in the metaphor of slavery... [therefore] we are at a loss as to how to extrapolate an independent future'.[28] Gomez tracks the development of two literary archetypes in black fiction, explaining:

> just as *the bitch* makes her own existence the center of her life, *the hero* makes survival of the whole an extension of herself, the center of her being.[29]

Gomez's hero figure is no individualist, but a woman grounded in her community. Changes in her existence occur because of a dialectical interaction between her community and its collective imagination.[30] Catharine Stimpson calls the triumphant lesbian novel one of 'enabling escape'[31] and I think there are generic parallels between the (white) lesbian heroic novel and the black slave narrative: journeying to a freed self is the central metaphor in these texts. A community infrastructure is essential to survival in both. Texts of movement, of exile and the search for 'home' – signifying the creation of an authentic self – are common to many alienated groups. The imagery of spatial presence fuels them. Zimmerman locates this 'return to the maligned humanist self'[32] within the writing of lesbians of color, pointing out the strong tendency in their work to draw upon myth and legend. This yearning for origins represents a nostalgic desire for a process of self-through-time, which 'makes space' for a self in the present. The desire for inclusion may mean movement away from the culture of origin in order to find or found a new culture predicated on hope. These heroic journeys are iconic, they embody the desires of the reader to escape the self fractured by oppression and create a new one predicated on wholeness and inclusion. Membership of the preferred community means the protagonist metonymically stands for the communal multiple self which is commuted into the multivalent self in more structurally inventive fictions.

Realism and heroic selfhood

For me, books have been the building bricks of my butch orientation. I identified as a butch before I ever really knew one. To me, the butch *was* the lesbian hero. I know this is contentious, to conflate masculinity – even if it is camped – with agency and, logically, the heroic. But the butch temptingly promises the redeemable flaw, often the Byronic romantic melancholy, and certainly confuses and delights the reader by conflating both subject and object desiring positions. The butch is an ambiguous sign of 'in-betweenism' which opens a space into which the reader can project herself. This is a moment of ambition, but also of relinquishment: such are the erotics of reading. What the butch hero offers specifically is the magic of the cross-over figure, the stranger who mediates between the reader and the story, who is at once same and different, who seduces the reader and moves her from A to B (from Androgyny to Butch perhaps). Every lesbian has her own list of fictional role models. As with many people, Leslie Feinberg's novel *Stone Butch Blues* (1993) is near the top of mine. In its narrative structure it incorporates some of the points I have tried to introduce here. It is a novel heavily dependent on the dichotomy between heroic idealization and shameful denigration, in which the abject is explored and rejected in favour of the tragic hero's triumph over nature. I was born in the time and place of the New British Cinema of the late 1950s and early 1960s, into the culture of *A Kind of Loving, Room at the Top, A Taste of Honey*. These were tough stories about working-class heroes on a quest for legitimation, staking out the turbulence in the British class system, and prefiguring the turmoil of later decades. I was brought up in a socialist family not coy about our place in the world, and whilst there is in these fictions (and, I'm glad to say, sometimes in 'real life' too) an ethic of solidarity, there is also an ethos of estrangement. *Stone Butch Blues* is a story about a similar girl, growing up in the blue-collar city of Buffalo, in New York State. One question persecutes her childhood, 'Is that a boy or a girl?'[33] At school she is too poor to join the middle-class Jews and too white to join the working-class blacks: she is an outsider in every respect – the classic alienated hero. Its specific attraction to me is in part because of my own cultural trajectory of working-class heroes, and it was a welcome relief from the lesbian feminist novels of the 1980s, which, as Bonnie Zimmerman has pointed out, naturalized middle-class status as the heroic norm. Jess is another 'in-betweenie'; her birth evokes the myth of the changeling. When Dineh women adopt the baby, and tell her mother she 'will walk a difficult path',[34] Jess is read as a culturally unclear sign, and the narrative charts the fear and violence this indeterminacy produces. As she grows up as a butch, then as a he–she, *Stone Butch Blues* employs the rhetoric of an epic, pulling the reader into a story of heroic tragedy, of battles lost and won, of courage, vision and suffering. The narrative style appropriates realism, the mode of 'telling it like it is', but it is eclectically interspersed by dream sequences and parables, in the manner of the folk tale. Her heroic trials are numerous and border on ritualistic repetition – like folk tales retold until the reader is secured by the message. Spirit guides and moments of revelation appear after the form of the mythic.

The novel is littered with rites of passage in the style of *Bildungsroman*. It is an apprenticeship novel – Jess learns from the older butches, and from the world around her, how to comprehend and fight the enemies of homophobia and heterosexism. It is an instructional novel for the reader, not just in its delivery of lesbian history but in its insistence on the politics of coalition, and on the multivalent self. Jess's constantly invoked outsider status is in effect a plea for inclusion, concluding with a *roman-à-thèse*-like moment of political revelation, identity, a symbolic return and an appeal to utopian closure through radicalization – a public statement of the private making the personal explicable through the structural – '*Imagine a world worth living in, a world worth fighting for*' (italics in original).[35] This has an explicit pedagogic function, to instruct the reader in the complexity and contemporaneity of lesbian identity, and the plasticity of gender and the body. It is lesbian history of the 1960s,

1970s, and 1980s written with the benefit of the Queer 1990s. The novel appropriates an authoritarian literary form or structure in order to take the reader thematically into the realm of indeterminacy and difference. *Stone Butch Blues* draws on a variety of narrative resources, disguising the complicated procedures of ideological persuasion and conversion with an appearance of simplicity. It is an heroic epic in the traditional style, but it also builds on the socialist–realist appropriation of realism in the manner of its highly denotative message. The novel retains the heroic subject but manages to produce the multivalent sexual self by inserting its hero into a utopian sexual ambiguity at its moment of closure. Thus, the reader is seduced into the novel's romantically individualistic heroic journey, not only in order to bring her into a multiformed queer community, but also to give her a new kind of selfhood. S/he is not returned and absorbed by society such as in the heterosexual heroic, but returns to refound the rubrics of the self structurally.

There is a category for ideologically driven fiction called the *roman à thèse*.[36] This is a specialist type of realist fiction carrying a didactic message. Its intention is to convince the reader of the validity of a certain belief or truth. The genre is perceived as a debased form of realism – because of its association with overtly political assertion. *Romans à thèse* tend to flourish in times of cultural crisis; they are intentionally political and try to persuade the reader of the right course of action to take. Distaste for the *roman à thèse* has two origins: the devalorization of realism in general and of its supposed outmoded assumption that experience can be directly represented through language, and the idea that 'authoritarian' – instructive and rhetorical – texts are somehow innately naïve in form and content. Such novels are considered to be too close to propaganda to be artistically valid, an accusation which clearly betrays the political interests of the reader/assessor, as much as the text. The form is amenable to variable ideological projects, including bleak and even Fascistic ones. *Roman à thèse* was the genre of choice for totalitarian propaganda, and was used as a stick to beat the abstract or experimental writings of Stalinist Russia and Nazi Germany. But here I want to discuss the mutability of the *roman à thèse* for producing positive, progressive narratives.

The *roman à thèse* offers us vicarious experiences which we recognize as lessons in morality. These stories provide us with a system of values in the form of a narrative quest which the hero has to uncover in order to find selfhood. The hero passes from ignorance to knowledge, from passivity into action, guided through the maze by an ethical map. The progression is upbeat, ending in victory, and also endowing the hero with membership of a privileged (because enlightened) group. Trials undergone along the way are instituted to underline the protagonist's role of an apprentice, and to develop understanding of the character and strength of the enemy/opposition (capitalism, patriarchy, white supremacism, homophobia, etc.). A relationship of cause and effect is being established, which invigorates the reader into new perceptions of justice. The effect is also utopian, offering a vision of how the world *could* be if only we got our act together. The lesbian feminist novels of the 1970s spring to mind, in their attempts to produce 'real women' struggling for change. The same agenda persists through novels of the 1980s and 1990s. Lesbian literature is inflected so prevailingly with the *roman à thèse* because we have intelligently appropriated a model highly suitable to our ends.

The paradox of lesbians using the *roman à thèse* is that the form is father-like, often paternalistic. The authority of the text manifestly operates to eliminate ambiguity and to appeal to certainty, stability and closure. It foregrounds the production of meaning in a most unmodern way. As Susan Suleiman points out, it recalls the early form of the novel which privileged teaching and instruction, oriented as much towards the communicative function of language as towards the 'poetic' one.[37] In exchange for assuaging the fear of non-identity, it offers the reassurance of belonging. This literary endeavour is anathema to modern producers of Literature who have rejected realism and its associations with truth in favour of indeterminacy, fluidity, anti-realism, plurality and the rejection of 'self'. In gendered terms, the masculine text has been replaced by the feminine. It appears ironic, therefore, that lesbians have opted for what could be read as 'primitive' narrative forms indulging in referentiality: folk tales, stereotypes, heroic epic and the like.

But these kinds of novel establish a particularly close relationship between the text and the reader, depending on what Suleiman has identified as an illocutionary speech act, so that they demonstrate and interpolate the reader into their purpose, rather like the way rhetoric can function. She uses the model of another early form – the parable – to explain the process, which operates on three progressive levels: first, the narrative discourse tells a story; second, the interpretative level comments on it in order to establish its meaning; and third, the pragmatic discourse derives a response in the form of a rule of action, or imperative, addressed to the reader. Intrinsic to the success of this procedure is *recognition*. Now, if we pause and consider the efficacy of this formula for lesbians, reduced to near invisibility in the dominant culture, suddenly the appropriation of *roman-à-thèse*-like forms seems less naïve. These novels offer lesbians a mirror which hegemonic ideas of subjectivity lack. Recognition concerns the conferral of selfhood through desire and identification: I return to my earlier comment – we want the hero and we want to be the hero, we become both the subject and object of desire. In Richard Dyer's spatial terms, we are the 'in-betweenies', negotiating a subjectivity beyond the binary. This moment of co-option is unstable (because reading cannot be completely overdetermined). Having gained our complicit attention, the novels compensate for this insecurity and attempt a utopian shift, showing us *how it could be*, to banish loneliness in favour of membership. They give us a formula for action instead of a recipe for passivity. They give us a self, and offer us a community to share it with. Of course, this self is perceived as an 'authentic' self, which is questionable given the fact that it is, at least in part, conferred. And so we return to the nub – the origins of identity. My argument is that since we cannot avoid the prescription of identity location, lesbians choose lesbian texts which are designed to fix meaning, as a defence against invisibility and/or as a refutation of homophobic discourse (replacing negative images with positive ones). To point out that these latter are still imposed is to ignore the relative *self*-determination that lesbian texts written for lesbian readers sustain.

What I am arguing is utopian here could also be read as nostalgic. We are detecting, and introjecting, our own identities from this play of images, in the push and pull of inner imagos glistening on the walls of the psyche. Thus we are able to lean into states – maybe sites – of mind, to become tourists of reparation, travelling to appropriate selves. But the places we visit are constrained by the particularities of our psychic present and the losses that abide there. Nostalgia is commonsensically associated with a self-indulgent resistance to change, but it is more than a simple sentimental and romantic reminiscence, it is also *retrospection*, a movement towards the past from the present, and back again – another kind of return. Nostalgia is a form of mourning for the lost object of desire which also contains ambivalence for it. Thus the grief and the pleasure of nostalgia together facilitate an affective and temporal distance. Vacillation between the two states and times forms a recognition of the changes through which we have passed – in fact, Freud's reality principle intervenes, with new perspectives. As Elizabeth Wilson has argued, we 'reappropriate the present by acknowledging and understanding that past' (nostalgia), which contains an understanding of 'detachment as well as attachment'.[38] Wendy Wheeler, writing in *New Formations*, has argued that whereas much contemporary criticism avows that nostalgia is simply melancholic, she conceives of it more positively as 'a sort of half-way house between melancholia and mourning'.[39] Freud argued that repetition is a form of recollection which takes place in the realm of the symbolic, i.e. in representation. We cannot move forward until we understand the past. Nostalgia is potentially 'future-oriented' because its symptomatology is the same as grief, and its energy is directed towards reconstruction, not just remembrance. Our task, therefore, is to search for narratives that may offer us new subjectivities, not just in characterization, but also in the reading relations inscribed in the text. *Stone Butch Blues* is a utopian *and* a nostalgic text: whilst Jess mourns the self s/he has lost, s/he also revisits it in order to rebuild the present, and infuse that with hope.

Stone Butch Blues, and novels like it, are effective as political novels because they integrate the complexities of Queer without sacrificing the specificities of lesbian history, and without losing the utopian vision of liberation. I have used *Stone Butch Blues* as an example of realism and linear narrative to show how the heroic self evolves, but *Stone Butch Blues* is particularly interesting because of Jess's situation as a borderline or liminal figure who is able to shift from one kind of identity to another. To a degree, all novels contain the exemplification of an idea, and are intended to persuade the reader of something, even if it is of their own non-meaning. Whereas there may exist perfect examples of the *roman à thèse*, it is best perceived as a continuum in which chief characteristics appear. For example, Charles Grivel has defended the conviction that the novel is 'in essence an instrument of bourgeois domination',[40] but this totalistic gesture unhelpfully polarizes the attempt to identify not just specific structures but also the terms of reception. Similarly, it is most useful to think of the *roman à thèse* as a formulaic tendency which is subject to the concerns of its discursive reception. Novels contain imprints of diverse genres and generally calling a story 'science fiction' does not exclude the presence within it of adventure, fantasy and romance. And it is also important to stress that, however apparently authoritarian and dogmatic the text, the readings are always contestable. So *Stone Butch Blues* has been read variously as a lesbian novel, a butch novel, a transgendered novel and a transsexual novel, according to the projections of the reader. Despite the *roman à thèse* organizing and positioning of the reader into a series of identifications, the final movement of the novelistic structure is to place the reader according to Jess's longing for a 'home' in an identity characterized by ambiguity. Thus Jess's gender *unheimlich* produces a self which has leaned into a series of sex/gender alternatives, but only rested in an ultimate refusal of categorization. Jess, by the end of *Stone Butch Blues*, is a transperson who looks to the queer community for strategic alliance, but her ontological security occurs in her movement *between* selves, rather than in a fixed identity.[41] In *Stone Butch Blues* we see an example of the heroic individualism of classical texts being resolved in the multivalent self.

The multiple hero and the multivalent lesbian self

Aware of the contention that a call to an essentialist self can still provoke, Zimmerman poses a new concept of the 'multivalent self' that she sees being deployed by authors such as Paula Gunn Allen, Becky Birtha, Gloria Anzaldúa, and Audre Lorde, whom she quotes here:

> The self that emerges in these texts is fluid, shimmering, and mobile, because it is a self whose 'place [is] the very house of difference rather than the security of any one particular difference.'[42]

Instead of proffering a version of the self which is the defensive, hermetic, enclosed and monolithic edifice of liberal humanism, these writers adopt a view of the self which allows for interaction without the loss of power. This new self is a product of context and interpretation, constantly shifting to accommodate difference:

> Our Lesbian Nation can then expand beyond one class or race until lesbian heroes float free in imaginative space, occupying no one single position from which they always speak, but moving,

rather, among all possible positions and communicating all possible points of view.[43]

This tall order does not entail the loss of 'identity' (a fantasy anyway), but concentrates instead on the deployment of 'practices' from that identity. The shift of emphasis allows for the individual trajectory of identities to be celebrated, but not reified; the trick to keeping all these plates in the air is realizing that this project is *imaginative* and therefore consists of a constant negotiation between honesty to an authentically felt, lived self, which accumulates its own past, and the awareness that this self does not provide an exclusive truth. This is the embodiment of the 'strategic essentialism' invoked by political theorists such as Gayatri Chakravorty Spivak.[44]

Some lesbian writers cognizant of postmodern theories of the fragmented self fracture the humanist self, allowing new space for lesbian identities to open up. More commonly, writers explore the creation of an autonomous lesbian subject, who is then inserted into a lesbian community which in its diversity transposes the multiformed single subjectivity onto a multicultural community, in its idealization of difference. The lesbian community is then presented as the embodiment of the multivalenced heroic agent. Since lesbian identity is so often represented as a journey to selfhood, this heroic trajectory conventionally necessitates closure. In the traditional form the hero will succeed by repudiating and incorporating the other – Woman. In lesbian narrative the lesbian hero will still 'get' the woman, but her individualistic 'egocentrism' will be checked when incorporation becomes co-operation – she becomes an heroic fragment of the greater struggle, as in Hobsbawm's model. Heroes function as representative figures and they must contain an aspirational element in order to capture the reader's desire. Whereas the conventional hero must channel the reader back into the dominant order, the lesbian hero must take her 'elsewhere', into a world which is virtual and utopian.

The rainbow flag of lesbian utopianism seems an impossible dream, but this does not mean that it does not succeed in some displacement of the masculinist ideology of heroic infallibility. Audre Lorde's concept of the erotic illuminates this way of thinking:

the sharing of joy, whether physical, emotional, psychic, or intellectual, forms a bridge between the sharers which can be the basis for understanding much of what is not shared between them, and lessens the threat of their difference.[45]

By tempering the tendency to see difference in terms of conflict, Lorde's erotic is a longing for the other, not to colonize, but to understand. Ruth Ginsberg takes Lorde's notion of the erotic

> to be a metaphysical yearning to integrate, or to connect, that which subjectively seems separate. She applies this not only to the creation of connections between and among individuals, but also to the creation of connections between apparently different aspects of one's life and work.[46]

Thus this strongly integrationist desire does not come at the expense of heterogeneity. A homogenous identity is too often achieved at the cost of denying 'other' parts of oneself, as black lesbians and feminists have been pointing out since the 1970s. Lorde's vision powerfully enables not just social concordance but also internal rapprochement in the multivalent self. Hence the splitting mechanism intrinsic to the phallocentric self is rejected in favour of the bridging approach of the integrated self. In Audre Lorde's erotic we can read the concept of the heroic as community, but also the heroic as intersubjectivity. As Bonnie Zimmerman has observed, virtually all lesbians of color write that fragmentation is not a sign of liberation but of oppression, and express what Lorde has called 'the fever of wanting to be whole'.[47] This wholeness is temporary and contingent, a passing moment, in which we become the hero we long for.

Fictions such as *Stone Butch Blues* reinstate the past as an heroic narrative in the crucial project of understanding identities as existing in time, showing that there are unvoiced histories to oppressed identities, and reintegrating them into the present. This sense of history is used as a process of empowerment, as the heroic figure moves through suffering and isolation before becoming structured into a new self and community – she is the embodied self-through-time. As Victor Seidler has observed, the histories of oppressed groups produce identities which carry a moral weight that the postmodernist relativism of 'free-floating' identities cannot appreciate.[48] These kinds of narratives of the developmental self weave between the postmodern reinventions of the self and the modernist wish for moral and ethical frameworks into which this new self can care for itself and others. Seidler remarks on the inadequacies or 'attenuated thinness' of the postmodern self, noting that new social movements reject it as inadequate to their own needs and desires. This recovery of the – maybe 'full-bodied' – self can then take place in a matrix of social concerns which includes a creative respect for the autonomy of different people's experience, rejecting the postmodern insistence that experience is always already reducible to language. The danger in appeals to a 'full-bodied' self lies in the tendency to formulate that self around the notion of a prelinguistic 'bodily experience' that has often been marked as a stable site and located on the 'bodies' of women of color. This bridge, in other words, is too often conceptualized across the 'backs' of black women.[49]

Heroism has a deceitful clarity: it can provide an intricate statement of identity and struggle, and a fantasy of a whole, complex self. I think the concept of the heroic, multivalent self has the potential to offer the most resistance to homophobic discourse, as an external strategy to reverse the discourse of heterosexism, and as an internal strategy to combat shame and its isolationist effects. Political movements do not succeed by conspiring with their own internal destruction. We can still learn from the heroic utopianism of the 1970s as a *strategic* vision, rather than dismissing it with cynical nostalgia as being abstracted from the supposed complexity of felt needs and identities which 'suddenly' appeared with the rising star of postmodernism. We need not build a new edifice, 'The Lesbian', and thus reinvent the feminist critique of the (whose?) Women's Movement. It is possible to invent new models of lesbians which are heroic and aspirational and encapsulate desire, which honour people's sense of belonging but do not reify it. Neither should we become hostages to the false abasement of privilege arising out of a sense of fetishizing an/Other. Recovering the self can only be achieved if we have the time and space to develop an ethics which is not precluded on idealization or abjection. Lesbians have constantly reinvented themselves in relation to political and emotional circumstances and to each other. Recalling Foucault, we can call this malleability 'practices of the self', which, by inventing new ways of relating, invents new forms of subjectivity. Foucault was clear on the transgressive potential of 'becoming gay', and we need to remember that this gay or lesbian identity is constantly being remade by reverse discourse,[50] but we need to create the political space to do this, by erecting effective 'lines of force'. Again, these boundaries are not to be set, but perceived rather as nomadic emplacements, or gatherings, where like cultural terrorists we can regroup and reform at points of conflict.

Heroic narratives are productive and constitutive, operating by harnessing utopic identifications through the focusing and configuration of desires. The heroic promises the reader a self-in-process, which is also a self-in-relation, to its plane of presence. Desire provokes new relationships, attachments, connections, and propels them. Desire is profoundly spatial and produces an erotics of distance and nearness; we are moved by it, to it, from it and within it – think, for example, of the rhythms of 'attraction'. Desire pushes a space for identities to form: we want to become. These identities are not complete, but pass from here to there, in a process of reconstitution. Desire, expressed through motion, can produce a multivalent self resonant with the specificities of its past, expectant for the effects of the future and only momentarily embodied in the ephemeral, temporal, flash of the present. When desire produces spaces for identities to open up, the edges of those spaces are porous, malleable, where, in a process of listening and leaning, we expand to include the experience of others, even as, returning to our own experiences, we reinvent them. The multivalent self is a profoundly dialogic self, not just between ourselves and others, but also intersubjectively between the self, in the heteroglossic dialogue occurring between our disparate internal selves. Inventing a multivalent self involves keeping the political currency of agency resident in conceptions of identity, but alongside that building an ethics of the self which can cope with the complicated relations of reciprocity and mutuality, between and within the self. This is necessary to reconfigure strategically individual agency within the social as simultaneously multivalenced *and* powerful. Implicitly, this detachment from and refusal to be the heavily circumscribed Lesbian of heterosexism procures a new space in which connection with others is, in Lorde's terminology, an erotic desire to bridge. Heroic desire infuses the cultural environment we call the lesbian community, becoming articulated in those orienting fictions such as the flâneur, the outlaw, the butch and the Lesbian Nation, for which I offer examples below. The versatility of their production, and the shifting sands of their embodiment, is moving witness to the temporal and spatial imperative of the desire 'I want (to be) a lesbian'.

Notes

1. Jeanette Winterson, 'The poetics of sex', in Margaret Reynolds, *The Penguin Book of Lesbian Short Stories*. London: Viking Penguin, 1993, p. 418.

2. See Rosa Ainley and Sarah Cooper, 'She thinks I still care: lesbians and country music', in Diane Hamer and Belinda Budge (eds), *The Good, the Bad, and the Gorgeous: Popular Culture's Romance with Lesbianism*. London: Pandora Press, 1994, pp. 41–56.

3. Joanna Russ, 'Power and helplessness in the Women's Movement', in *Magic Mommas, Trembling Sisters, Puritans and Perverts: Feminist Essays*. Trumansburg, NY: The Crossing Press, 1985, pp. 43–54.

4. For a sustained elaboration of this argument, including the difference between 'affective' and 'reactive' political forces, see Elizabeth Grosz, 'Bodies and pleasures in Queer theory', in J. Roof and R. Weigman (eds), *Who Can Speak? Authority and Critical Identity*. Urbana and Chicago: University of Illinois Press, 1995, pp. 221–30. A longer version appeared in J. Copjec (ed.), *Supposing the Subject*. London: Verso, 1994.

5. What more radical response to AIDS could there be than *still* being glad to be gay?

6. In this chapter I refer to Stonewall as a foundational moment in the creation of the modern lesbian and gay identity, also expanding that to describe 'pre-' and 'post-' Stonewall formulations of self. This in itself is a critical shorthand and needs to be tempered with the kind of problematizing approach that recent lesbian and gay history and scholarship have taken to the issue.
Mainly I think the rhetorical move is justified by the *present* mythologization of Stonewall as a constitutive moment, although it needs also to be recognized as a cultural fiction.

7. Margaret R. Somers and Gloria D. Gibson, 'Reclaiming the epistemological 'Other': narrative and the social construction of identity', in Craig Calhoun, *Social Theory and the Politics of Identity*. Oxford: Blackwell, 1994, pp. 37–99, p. 61.

8. *Ibid*., quoting Alexander Nehamas, *Nietzsche: Life as Literature*. Cambridge, MA: Harvard University Press, 1985.

9. Quotation is from Elsa Barkely Brown, 'African–American women's quilting: a framework for conceptualizing and teaching African–American women's history', *Signs*, 14 (4): 921–9, p. 22, quoted in Patricia Hill Collins, *Black Feminist Thought*. New York: Routledge, 1991, p. 236.

10. Vladimir Propp, *Morphology of the Folktale*. Austin: University of Texas, 1968 (2nd edn).

11. Also, let us not be coy about this: lesbianism needs to be seen as desirable – positive images *do* recruit.

12. Orrin E. Klapp, *Heroes, Villains and Fools*. Englewood Cliffs, NJ: Prentice-Hall, 1962.

13. Richard Dyer, 'The role of stereotypes', in *The Matter of Images*. London: Routledge, 1993, pp. 11–18.

14. Richard Dyer, 'Seen to be believed: some problems in the representation of gay people as typical', in *The Matter of Images*, pp. 19–51, p. 23.

15. *Ibid*., p. 29.

16. Northrop Frye, *Anatomy of Criticism: Four Essays*. Princeton, NJ: Princeton University Press, 1957.

17. André Gide, *Pretexts, Reflections on Literature and Morality*. New York: Books for Libraries Press, 1959, p. 310.

18. Joseph Campbell, *The Hero with a Thousand Faces*. Bollingen Series XVII. Princeton: Princeton University Press, 1949.

19. See, for example, Tony Bennett and Janet Woollacott, *Bond and Beyond: The Political Career of a Popular Hero*. London: Macmillan, 1987.

20. Bonnie Zimmerman, *The Safe Sea of Women: Lesbian Fiction 1969–1989*. Boston: Beacon Press, 1990.

21. This is similar to the typology of the Oedipal narrative as discussed in Teresa De Lauretis, *Alice Doesn't: Feminism, Semiotics, Cinema*. Bloomington: Indiana University Press, 1984.

22. Marilyn Farwell, *Heterosexual Plots and Lesbian Narrative*. New York: New York University Press, 1996, p. 62.

23. *Ibid.*, p. 143.

24. See my earlier argument in *Murder by the Book: Feminism and the Crime Novel*. London: Routledge, 1992, where I argue that the detective genre is not realist but satiric.

25. See as a good example Katherine Forrest, *Murder at the Nightwood Bar*. London: Pandora Press, 1987.

26. Eric Hobsbawm, *Primitive Rebels: Studies in Archaic Forms of Social Movement in the 19th and 20th Centuries*. Manchester: Manchester University Press, 1959, p. 110.

27. *Ibid.*, p. 111.

28. Jewelle Gomez, 'Lye-throwers and lovely renegades: the road from bitch to hero for black women in speculative fictions', in *Forty-Three Septembers*. Ithaca, NY: Firebrand Books, 1993, pp. 109–28, p. 116.

29. *Ibid.*, p. 125.

30. In parallel to this, I wonder to what extent the restraints of our own homophobia inhibit our potential to dream, and to crystallize a common purpose.

31. Catharine Stimpson, 'Zero degree deviancy: the lesbian novel in English', in E. Abel (ed.), *Writing and Sexual Difference*. Chicago: University of Chicago Press, 1982, pp. 243–54, p. 244.

32. Zimmerman, *The Safe Sea of Women*, p. 196.

33. Leslie Feinberg, *Stone Butch Blues*. Ithaca, NY: Firebrand Books, 1993, p. 13.

34. *Ibid.*, p. 14.

35. *Ibid.*, p. 301.

36. See Susan Rubin Suleiman, *Authoritarian Fictions: The Ideological Novel as a Literary Genre*. Princeton, NJ: Princeton University Press, 1993 (2nd edn.) for the definitive description. I am indebted to her book for the material in this section.

37. See Suleiman, *Authoritarian Fictions*, Introduction, pp. 1–23.

38. Elizabeth Wilson, 'Nostalgia and the city', in Sallie Westwood and John Williams (eds), *Imagining Cities*. London: Routledge, 1996, pp. 127–39, p. 139.

39. Wendy Wheeler, 'After grief: what kinds of inhuman selves?', *New Formations*, 25, Summer 1995: 77–95, p. 82.

40. Quoted in Suleiman, *Authoritarian Fictions*, p. 240.

41. For an elaboration of Jess's transgender identity see Jay Prosser, 'No place like home: the transgendered narrative of Leslie Feinberg's *Stone Butch Blues*', in

Modern Fiction Studies, **41** (3–4), Fall–Winter 1995, pp. 483–514.

42. From Audre Lorde, *Zami: A New Spelling of My Name*. Freedom, CA: The Crossing Press, p. 226, quoted in Zimmerman, *The Safe Sea of Women*, p. 200.

43. *Ibid.*, p. 205.

44. In Gayatri Spivak, *In Other Worlds: Essays in Cultural Politics*. New York and London: Methuen, 1987.

45. From Audre Lorde, 'Uses of the erotic: the erotic as power' (1983). Quoted in Ruth Ginsberg, 'Audre Lorde's (non-essentialist) lesbian eros', in Claudia Card (ed.), *Adventures in Lesbian Philosophy*. Bloomington: Indiana University Press, 1994, pp. 81–97, p. 81.

46. *Ibid.*, p. 82.

47. From Audre Lorde, *Zami*, p. 190, quoted in Zimmerman, *The Safe Sea of Women*, p. 199.

48. Victor J. Seidler, *Recovering the Self: Morality and Social Theory*. London: Routledge, 1994, p. 176.

49. I am alluding at this point to Cherríe Moraga and Gloria Anzaldúa (eds), *This Bridge Called My Back: Writing by Radical Women of Color*. Watertown, MA: Persephone Press, 1981. Lesbian and Gay/Queer Studies have not yet arrived at a place where we have successfully constructed that embodied bridge without exploitation, exclusions and displacements.

50. For information on the operation of reverse discourses and homosexuality, see Michel Foucault, *The History of Sexuality: Volume One: An Introduction*. Trans. Robert Hurley. Harmondsworth: Penguin Books, 1976.

2

The Lesbian Flâneur

I haven't been doing much flâneuring recently. It is 1993, and six months ago I moved from the British coastal town of Brighton, where I'd lived for eight years, to the Midlands city of Nottingham, chasing a job. A four-hour drive separates the two, but in terms of my lesbian identity, I'm in another country. Geographically, Nottingham is located in the exact centre of England: the land of Robin Hood. This local hero is mythologized in the region's heritage entertainment – next to the (fake, nineteenth-century) castle, one can purchase a ticket for The Robin Hood Experience. Nottingham, formerly a hub of urban industry, is nostalgic for a time when men were men and codes of honour echoed out of hearts of oak to the hearth, to the pit. D. H. Lawrence is this city's other famous son. English national identity is thus distilled into a rugged romanticized masculinity, an essence of virile populism which is potently enhanced by its attachment to the core, the fulcrum, of England. Its interiority is endemic to the boundaries which entrap it; in its corporeality it is the heart, the breast, the bosom, and to each tourist is offered the metaphoricity of home.

Brighton is on the edge: thirty miles from France, this hotel town is proud of its decaying Regency grandeur, its camp, excessive, effeminate façades. It loves the eccentricity of Englishness, but laughs at the pomposity of England. Brighton looks to Europe for its model of Bohemia, for it is just warm enough to provide a pavement culture to sit out and watch the girls go by. Brighton, the gay capital of the South, the location of the dirty weekend, has historically embodied the genitals, rather than the heart. Its sexual ambiguity is present on the street, in its architecture, from the orbicular tits of the Prince Regent's Pavilion, to the gigantic plastic dancer's legs which extrude invitingly above the entrance to the alternative cinema, the Duke of York's. Aristocratic associations imbue the town with a former glory. Its faded past, its sexual history, is a memory cathecting contemporary erotic identifications as decadent, degenerative and whorelike. The stained window of nineteenth-century permissiveness filters my view of Brighton. Promenading on a Sunday afternoon on the pier, loitering in The Lanes, or taking a long coffee on the seafront, ostensibly reading The Observer, the gaze is gay. Brighton introduced me to the dyke stare, it gave me permission to stare. It made me feel I was worth staring at, and I learned to dress for the occasion. Brighton constructed my lesbian identity, one that was given to me by the glance of others, exchanged by the looks I gave them, passing – or not passing – in the street.

It's colder in Nottingham. There's nothing like being contained in its two large shopping malls on a Saturday morning to make one feel queer. Inside again, this pseudo-public space is sexualized as privately heterosexual. Displays of intimacy over the purchase of family-sized commodities are exchanges of gazes calculated to exclude. When the gaze turns, its intent is hostile: visual and verbal harassment make me avert my eyes. I don't loiter, ever, the surveillance is turned upon myself, as the panopticon imposes self-vigilance. One night last week, I asked two straight women to walk me from the cinema to my car. The humiliation comes in acknowledging that my butch drag is not leather enough to hide my fear.

As I become a victim to, rather than a possessor of, the gaze, my fantasies of lesbian mobility/eroticism return to haunt me. As 'home' recedes, taking my butch sexual confidence with it, my exiled wanderings in bed at night have become literary expeditions. As I pursue myself through novels, the figure of the flâneur has imaginatively refigured the mobility of my desire. These fictional voyagers offer me a dream-like spectacle which returns as a memory I have in fact never lived. Strolling has never been so easy, as a new spatial zone, the lesbian city, opens to me.

The flâneur and modernism

The flâneur is a hero of Modernity. He appeared in mid-nineteenth-century France and is primarily associated with the writing of the

Romantic poet Charles Baudelaire; he appeared subsequently in the criticism of the German Marxist and founder of the Frankfurt School, Walter Benjamin, in the 1930s. The economic conditions of rising capitalism that stimulated his appearance had resulted in the boulevards, cafés and arcades that were new spaces for his consumption of the city-spectacle. Neither completely public nor completely private, these voyeuristic zones were home to the flâneur, engaged in his detached, ironic and somewhat melancholic gazing. He was also a sometime journalist, his writings on the city being commodified as short tableaux in the new markets for leisure reading. His origin, in Paris, that most sexualized of cities, traditionally genders his objectification as masculine, his canvas, or ground, as feminine.

The prototype flâneur was the dandy, the well-dressed man-about-town from the first years of the nineteenth century. Feminist critic Ellen Moers traced dandyism back even further, at least to the 1770s, in the plebeian ditty of the American colonies 'Yankee Doodle Dandy'. The oldest stanza goes as follows:

> Yankee Doodle came to town,
> Riding on a pony,
> Stuck a feather in his hat
> And called it Macaroni![1]

The joking insult is played against the badly dressed common American soldiers, since the Macaroni was a cosmopolitan London club founded in 1764, reputedly the haunt of fashionable gentlemen. Interestingly, the evolution of the dandy emerges between the cracks of class formulations; Moers interprets the development of dandyism as an aesthetic ridicule of aristocratic pretensions, being a product of the revolutionary upheavals of the late eighteenth century when social stratifications were being upset. Pretenders to gentility could dress up and affect, through costume, their aspirations. The dandy's labour was simply to appear: he was perhaps an early commodity fetish, a consumable spectacle, a paradox of capitalism, for his function was to have no function, except to exist in his symbolic ostentation. Here was a solipsistic hero:

> a Hero so evidently at the centre of the stage that he need to nothing to prove his heroism – need never, in fact, do anything at all.[2]

The dandy was a paradoxical figure, a man who claimed the status of a gentleman through arrogant superiority, whilst simultaneously managing an independent, isolated and subversive disregard for social protocol. The dandy temperament is to 'attain perfection in all the accessories of life',[3] maintaining his chimera by wit and verbal flourish. He exhibits hypersensitive refinement. One apocryphal tale concerning George Bryan ('Beau') Brummell (1778–1840), the first great dandy, illustrates this delicate disposition: a hostess, on enquiring whether he ever ate vegetables, received the sneering response, 'Madam, I once ate a pea'.[4] Moers describes in detail the obsessional performance of Brummell's two-hour daily ritual of dressing observing 'the ideal of the dandy is cut in cloth'.[5] Brummell was from the upper servant class, hence his self-conscious exaggeration of gentlemanly temperament is an unstable parody, effectively both satirizing social snobbery whilst remaining complicit with its reproduction. His death in poverty is a testament to the fragility of his artifice.

Rather coyly, Moers asks if there was something 'sexually uncommon' about Brummell – 'How affected was he?', she ponders:

> The question bemused Brummell's contemporaries and returned to plague the *fin de siècle* when it became clear what company dandyism was keeping.[6]

Commenting that Brummell had no known liaisons with women, she concludes the section with a biographer's quote that 'Brummell had too much self-love ever to be really in love'.[7] This proto-gay narcissist prefigures in literary history that colossus of the queer cloth and the definitive dandy, Oscar Wilde. Wilde, like Brummell, was an outsider to London high society, coming from a family of eccentric Irish intellectuals. This 'Professor of Aesthetics' became known for his decadence and dandyism as much as for his writing. Take these two innuendoes from Moers on Wilde's dress:

> [His clothes] were an expression of his willingness to sell his privacy . . .
>
> [Lord Alfred] Douglas wrote 'I doubt whether I would have "swallowed" the aesthetic Oscar'.[8]

Wilde's dandyism cannot be extricated from his homosexuality for the two are now synonymous, and inevitably it is that to which Moers homophobically alludes when she refers to 'the tedious nastiness of the Wilde story'.[9] Wilde's sexual wanderings, amongst the aristocracy, the working class and as a Westerner in the 'Orient', can be read, imaginatively, as urban *ur*-flâneuring. Elements of his sexual journeying recall the flâneur's, and the modern flâneur is indissoluble from Wildean wit.

Fin de siècle decadence was marked by a blurring of gender distinctions: the 1890s saw the advancement of the New Woman at the same time as it witnessed the effeminacy of the dandy. Androgyny was mooted as a new aesthetic, and marriage roles became depolarized: Moers reports the New Woman heroine being given the benefit of a new masculine foil – the decadent dandy; she describes them in the novels she discusses as 'unsavoury' 'kept men'.[10] Elaine Showalter analyses the coupling of the dandy with the New Woman, describing how both figures celebrated the added transgression of class taboos within sexual associations. 'Decadence', she writes, 'was also a *fin de siècle* euphemism for homosexuality'.[11] In that contemporary moment, as Showalter describes, the discourses of gender blurring and homosexuality emerged at the same time, making a number of political cross-identifications possible.[12]

However, nineteenth-century anti-naturalism also enhanced a misogynistic worship of narcissistic masculinity, a reaction against women encapsulated by this quotation from the archdandy, Baudelaire:

> Woman is the opposite of the dandy. Therefore she inspires horror. Woman is hungry so she must eat; thirsty so she must drink. She is in heat, so she must be fucked. How admirable! Woman is natural, which is to say abominable.[13]

Charles Baudelaire was the creator of the flâneur, his best-known depiction of him being in the essay 'The Painter of Modern Life' (1863). The movement of Baudelaire's writing can be characterized as literary flâneuring on the streets of Paris, his poetry an attempt to depict the trajectory of the modern hero, the flâneur. This urban epistemologist accumulates his identity in part by the appropriation of the prostitutes who shower his texts. The flâneur is the dandy on the move, applying his dry observations to the passing tableau of the city. He is the active agent, and the city is a sexualized woman – a prostitute – to be consumed.

Elizabeth Wilson[14] has taken issue with the predominant feminist opinion that the flâneur is essentially male. She writes in the presence of women as subjects in this urban narrative. She also directs us to acknowledge the figure's insecurity, marginality, and ambiguity, rejecting the preferred version of the flâneur's voyeuristic mastery:

> Benjamin's critique identifies the 'phantasmagoria', the dream world of the urban spectacle, as the false consciousness generated by capitalism. We may look but not touch, yet this tantalising falsity – and even the very visible misery of tramps and prostitutes – is aestheticised, 'cathected' (in Freudian terms), until we are overcome as by a narcotic dream. Benjamin thus expresses a utopian longing for something *other than* this urban labyrinth. This utopianism is a key theme of nineteenth- and twentieth-century writings about 'modern life'. In Max Weber, in Marxist discourse, in the writings of postmodernism, the same theme is found: the melancholy, the longing for 'the world we have lost' – although precisely what we have lost is no longer clear, and curiously, the urban scene comes to represent utopia and dystopia *simultaneously.*[15]

The flâneur is fascinated, transfixed, and thus trapped into representing wishes, without fulfilment:

> The flâneur represented not the triumph of masculine power, but its attenuation... In the labyrinth, the flâneur effaces himself, becomes passive, feminine. In the writing of fragmentary pieces, he makes of himself a blank page upon which the city writes itself. It is a feminine, placatory gesture...[16]

Is the flâneur someone to be appropriated for our *post*modern times? I do not wish to rehearse the arguments concerning whether the flâneur is a good or bad figure, partly because they tend to be articulated within a heterosexual paradigm, reliant upon heterosexual discourses of the city. I am interested in this observer as a metaphor, who offers at once a symbolic hero and anti-hero, a borderline personality in a parable of urban uncertainty, of angst and anomie. Within the labyrinth, the process of making up meaning in movement becomes the point, and perversely too the pleasure, as we become lost among the flowing images.

Queering the flâneur

Wilde himself commented on late nineteenth-century London society as 'entirely made up of dowdies and dandies... The men are all dowdies and the women are all dandies.'[17] This act of performative interpretation is crystallized in another early urban tale of lesbian cross-dressing:

> So I had made for myself a *redingote-guérite* in heavy gray cloth, pants and vest to match. With a gray hat and large woollen cravat, I was a perfect first-year student. I can't express the pleasure my boots gave me: I would gladly have slept with them...[18]

What happens if the flâneur is cross-dressed not just in actuality, here as George Sand vogueing in her butch drag dandy suit, but symbolically too? Writing in 1831, she claimed 'my clothes feared nothing'.[19] When she is dressed as a boy, she is all-image, a spectacle of auto-eroticism, desired only by herself – 'No one knew me, no one looked at me, no one found fault with me...'.[20] As such she is a simulacrum, if, as Wilson continues on to argue 'the flâneur himself never really existed',[21] for then there is no material ground of maleness or femaleness to be invoked. Is the flâneur a transvestite? Can s/he be a cross-dressed lesbian? It is possible that the flâneur is a borderline case, an example of a roving signifier, a transient wild card of potential, indeterminate sexuality, trapped in transliteration, caught in desire.

One crucial problem with the conventionally romantic line on the flâneur is the idea that he roams the streets *untouched*. As pure male essence his visual trajectory is read as uncorrupted – he sees windows, not mirrors. But, to stretch the analogy, even the most clear window will frame the picture and reflect back the tiniest reflection of self. I am simplifying, condensing, extracting and probably bowdlerizing the flâneur here, as a vessel to be filled by the lesbian narrative, so that I can contribute to the unfixing of the supremacy of the heterosexual male gaze in urban spatial theory. Secondly, the figure of the prostitute is problematic in the conventional flâneur narrative – prostitutes, more than most women, have mobility on the streets, and furthermore have a certain power of the gaze themselves, if only to procure business. As Wilson asks, provocatively, 'Could not the prostitutes themselves be seen, ultimately, as the flâneuses of the nineteenth-century city?'[22] To construct prostitutes simply as passive objects is a masculinist act of interpretation, ignoring the divergent class dynamics of city life. Although bourgeois women were to some extent 'trapped in the home', working-class women had much more mobility on the streets, even then, whether they were selling on stalls, or themselves, or merely getting to and from employment in service.

Preliminary female writers to procure the form included Renée Vivien and Djuna Barnes. The poet and traveller Renée Vivien imagined a visionary lesbian city, Mytilène, as an escape from early-twentieth-century Paris. The lesbian voyager's imagination is freed from cultural constraints to wander at will, for in this Sapphic paradise all temporal and spatial barriers are excised. The fantasized map of Lesbos has no restrictions, but critic Elyse Blankley has noted how the real island of Lesbos turned out to be Erewhon: Vivien, on her frequent visits, refused to leave her villa, finding the native women 'unattractive and disappointing'.[23]

Djuna Barnes's descriptions of the 1920s Paris salon culture in her publication of the *Ladies Almanac* (1928) and in the black-clad absinthe drinker Dr O'Connor of *Nightwood* (1936) both retain elements of the Modernist flâneur.[24] Flâneuring is also evident in her journalistic sketches collected together in *Djuna Barnes in New York* (1990), which combine to form a panorama of city life from 1913 to 1919. Barnes is remembered predominantly as an expatriate in Paris, thus a traveller and an outsider ideally located to comment on an alien, European culture. Her positioning in the New York text as an exile is particularly revealing; she returns to the city not as a native, but retains the inside/outside dichotomy of the alienated raconteuse, rendering snapshots of a foreign territory. She is the first to export the flâneur, taking a European-derived model and appropriating it for US culture. The flâneur reappears in twentieth-century US culture principally since individualism, the city and a historical preoccupation with space became prime signifiers in the culture of the New World. The flexibility of this romantic hero means s/he can be adopted as a cipher for desires despite variable historical and geographical circumstances.

During the 1920s, homosexuality was located in New York in two identifiable spaces, Greenwich Village and Harlem. Homosexuality was made permissible by journeying to a time zone happening; one *experienced* a present event, rather than took one's preformed sexual identity, intact and inviolate, to the party. Social mobility was a prerequisite for sexual experimentation – the bourgeois white flâneurs who went 'slumming' in Harlem[25] paid to see, in the exoticized black drag acts and strip shows, a voyeuristic legitimation of their own forbidden fantasies. Flâneuring involves seeing the turf of the city as an exotic landscape, revelling in the emporium of the spectacle, and thus discursively it is an activity developed out of the nineteenth-century colonialist project of conquest and control; it is at least notionally an imperialist gaze. Is this flâneur thus structurally white?

Arguably, no: Isaac Julien rewrites the flâneur as a black gay man in his film *Looking for Langston* (1989). Margins and centres shift, with subjectivities constantly in motion. At the beginning of the twentieth century there was a massive migration of black people from the South to the North of the USA, and many of them came to New York, specifically to Harlem,[26] to make a home. Writer James Weldon Johnson dated the beginning of black Harlem to 1900, calling it 'the greatest Negro city in the world... located in the heart of Manhattan'.[27] A character in a story, 'The City of Refuge', printed in *Atlantic Monthly* in February 1925, exclaims 'In Harlem, black was white.'[28] This was (and is) black space, not white space.[29] Art and literature have mythologized the migrant's arrival in Harlem into the making of a new black identity, stimulating the emergence of a new consciousness. It is a continuous happening, endlessly repeated with the arrival of each new traveller from the South, emerging from the subway station. Can we read Ralph Ellison's *Invisible Man* (1952) as another alienated and invisible – and black – flâneur?

> This really was Harlem, and now all the stories which I had heard of the city-within-a-city leaped alive in my mind... For me this was not a city of realities, but of dreams... I moved wide-eyed, trying to take in the bombardment of impressions.[30]

The utopian/dystopian paradox of hope for the city is that more pleasure is taken in the journeying towards it, as a process of desire and transformation, than in the (deferred) arrival. Models of the labyrinth, in which the journey is represented as circular, make this explicit. The boundaries of physical geographies are rebuilt in mental images. 'Harlem' operates as a symbol of black consciousness rather as Africa does – as 'a self-created ontology of blackness',[31] a myth of 'home' that makes home bearable.[32] The flâneur, as a stranger, simultaneously inhabits the geography of exclusion at the same time as his cultural capital facilitates his mobility.

Here is epitomized a crucial structuring principle of the flâneur: at the same time as he is the master of his own agency, his symbiosis with the city is such that his individualism is constantly threatening to implode, as he himself becomes commodified, collapsed into the spectacle. His objective mastery bequeaths him form and presence, but, correspondingly, his malaise is that of the emasculated, alienated outsider. The figure of the flâneur encapsulates a poignant ambiguity; Walter Benjamin wrote of his fundamental plasticity.[33] I am interested in the appropriation of the flâneur by marginalized identities. What can we learn of spatial relations from the deployment of the flâneur by marginalized identities (in my particular example, lesbians)? How do we read the ambivalence and contradictions expressed in those appropriations? One way of exploiting the metaphor of the flâneur is to examine how it is possible to deconstruct the gender polarity active/masculine, passive/feminine through its installation in lesbian cultural history. Secondly, we are able to see how the flâneur, like the dandy, is not only gender-flexible, but also conveniently expropriatable to class formulations. Wilson argues that the flâneur is 'subtly déclassé'.[34] 'Racing' the flâneur is not so easy: his home in white European culture means he was exportable to the colonies, and therefore assimilable to other local narratives, but work has yet to be done on discovering an indigenous equivalent.

The most visible gay culture of the early twentieth-century USA was largely male, working-class and assembled around the immigrant neighbourhoods of New York City. George Chauncey's fifty-year history of gay New York[35] makes the point that gay sexuality was very much in and of the streets, in part, like working-class culture in general, due to the economic and spatial limitations of the tenements. Enclaves of lesbians interacted with their gay male counterparts, congregating in the speakeasies, tearooms and drag balls of Harlem and Greenwich Village during the 1920s. These were different worlds of homosexual identification, divided by race and class. Greenwich Village bohemian life tolerated a degree of sexual experimentation which conferred upon the area an embryonic stature as erotica unbound (a construction much enhanced during the 1950s and 1960s with the Beat homosexuals, Allen Ginsberg and William Burroughs). Lesbian and gay clubs in the Village were founded on the 'Personality Clubs' of the bohemian intelligentsia.

Chauncey describes the sexual 'free zone' of this apparently utopian space:

> The gay history of Greenwich Village suggests the extent to which the Village in the teens and twenties came to represent to the rest of the city what New York as a whole represented to the rest of the nation: a peculiar social territory in which the normal social constraints on behaviour seemed to be suspended.[36]

As Harlem had functioned as the Mecca for black people, now Greenwich Village became the Promised Land for (mainly) white homosexuals. Chauncey too makes this point: 'In the 1920s Harlem became to black America what Greenwich Village became to bohemian white America: the symbolic – and in many respects, practical centre of a vast social experiment.'[37] These new gay and lesbian identities were predominantly urban, emanating from the social geographies of the streets, built out of this moment of mutable space. In Harlem black lesbian culture centred around the clubs, chiefly those starring the powerful Blues singers such as Ma Rainey, Bessie Smith and Gladys Bentley. Harlem represented the potential dissolution of a strictly regulated ideal of chaste black bourgeois female sexuality, imported from the South, to working-class lesbians. Many of these African–American women[38] had friendship networks which held house parties where guests would pay a small entrance fee for food. But during the 1920s and 1930s some working-class black and white lesbians would come together and meet in the clubs. Both Greenwich Village and Harlem had their own specific internal social fracturings around class, gender and race.

World War II created unprecedented mobility for lesbians and gay men,[39] who moved to military centres in cities in their tens of thousands. Men and women of the 1950s resisted the small-town conformity that was to arise in post-war US surburbia; they were drawn, or driven, to cities as places to express their 'deviant' sexuality.[40] The anonymity of the city made a gay life realizable in a repressive era. This odyssey is well represented in the lesbian novels of the period.[41] Nightclubs were a visible site for women interested in 'seeing' other women, and it is in this literature of the 1950s and 1960s that the bar becomes consolidated as the symbol of home.[42] Lesbian/whore became a compacted image of sexual consumption in the dime novel of the period, read by straight men and lesbians alike. The lesbian adventurer inhabited a twilight world where sexual encounters were acts of romanticized outlawry initiated in some backstreet bar and consummated in the narrative penetration of the depths of maze-like apartment buildings. She is the carnival queen of the city: 'Dominating men, she ground them beneath her skyscraper heels',[43] a public/private figure whose excess sensuality wistfully transcends spatial and bodily enclosures. This Modernist nightmare of urban sexual degeneracy is crystallized in the identification of the city with homosexuality. Lesbian-authored fictions of the period set in the Village, like Ann Bannon's *Beebo Brinker* series (1957–62), are less-sensationalist syntheses of the available discursive constructions of 'lesbian',[44] but still depend on that myth of the eroticized urban explorer. Transmuted in more liberal times into the lesbian sexual adventurer, this figure can be recognized in such diverse texts as Rita Mae Brown's post-Sexual Revolution *Rubyfruit Jungle* (1973)[45] and the San Franciscan postmodernist porn parody *Bizarro in Love* (1989).[46]

In this brief outline of the flâneur I have tried to gesture to both the textual history of the form and its echo in the narratives of lived identities. As a cultural form its status as 'myth' as opposed to 'lived experience' is irreducible. The flâneur is an incongruent and complex figure suggesting a number of antitheses: motion/stasis, mastery/fragility, desire/abstinence, complacency/alienation, presence/intangibility. Singularly, perhaps, the flâneur is a symbol of urbanity. When Walter Benjamin described *flânerie* as going 'botanizing on the asphalt'[47] his turn of phrase hinted at a gender ambiguity facilitating this poet to be read as less – or more – than male. The lesbian flâneur is one step from here.

The lesbian flâneur in New York

The lesbian flâneur appears as a shadow character or a minor theme in a number of recent novels, and I want briefly to offer examples of her appearance as a structuring principle in four New York fictions: a stanza of a poem by Joan Nestle, a short story, 'The Swashbuckler' by Lee Lynch (1985), *Don Juan in the Village* by Jane de Lynn (1990) and *Girls, Visions and Everything* by Sarah Schulman (1986). Within contemporary lesbian writing we encounter a specific, even nostalgic, image of the stroller as a self-conscious lesbian voyeur. The years of feminist debate engrossed with the political acceptability of looking are the background to these lesbian vindications of the right to cruise:

New words swirl around us
and still I see you in the street
loafers, chinos, shades.
You dare to look too long
and I return your gaze,
feel the pull of old worlds
and then like a femme
drop my eyes.
But behind my broken look
you live
and walk deeper into me
as the distance grows between us.

Joan Nestle's first stanza from 'Stone Butch, Drag Butch, Baby Butch'[48] ends with the comment 'Shame is the first betrayer.' The extract epitomizes the mechanisms of a necessarily coded visual exchange in a potentially violent, dangerous and sexualized arena, the street. The pun of the title of the anthology is *A Restricted Country* and the spatial penetration of the poem recalls this analogy between the streets and the lesbian body. Inside/outside dichotomies break down, both becoming colonized. A subculture made invisible by its parent culture logically resorts to space-making in its collective imagination. Mobility within that space is essential, because motion continually stamps new ground with a symbol of ownership.

Is the butch dandy strolling through the doors of the bar just a romanticized inversion of heterosexual occupation? The flâneur may not have to be biologically male for the gaze to enact masculine visual privilege. The politics of butch/femme and their relation to dominant systems of organizing gender relations have been bloodily fought over,[49] and whilst I am sympathetic to claims that butch/femme constitute new gender configurations which must be understood within their own terms, they are not intrinsically radical forms springing perfect from the homosexual body. Nor are they naïve forms in the sense that they express a naturally good, pure and primitive desire. Nestle's poem is interesting in that it represents the push/pull, utopian/dystopian contrariety of the ambivalent flâneur, balancing the temptation and lust for the city (embodied as a woman) with the fear of connection and belonging. Note that the narrator of the poem initiates the glance, then returns the gaze and then becomes the owner of a 'broken look' (line 9). The butch penetrates with her gaze ('walk deeper into me' (line 11)) an assumed femme who is only 'like a femme' (line 7). Evading categorization, this 'almost femme' narrator is the one whose closing comment of the stanza rebukes invisibility and averted eyes. Who is claiming the gaze here? All we can assume is that it is a woman.

The poem describes movement: both characters are in motion on the street, and the looks that they exchange have their own dynamic rotation. Images of mobility are particularly important to lesbians *as women* inhabiting the urban environment. Feminist struggles to occupy spheres traditionally antipathetic to women go back to the imposition of post-Industrial Revolution bourgeois family divisions into male public/female private spaces, an ideological construction disguising the fact that the domestic space, the 'home', as Mark Wigley has written, is also built for the man, to house his woman:

> The woman on the outside is implicitly sexually mobile. Her sexuality is no longer controlled by the house. In Greek thought women lack the internal self-control credited to men as the very mark of masculinity. The self-control is no more than the maintenance of secure boundaries. These internal boundaries, or rather boundaries that define the interior of the person, the identity of the self, cannot be maintained by a woman because her fluid sexuality endlessly overflows and disrupts them. And more than this, she endlessly disrupts the boundaries of others, that is, men, disturbing their identity, if not calling it into question.[50]

The familiar construction of woman as excess has radical potential when appropriated by the lesbian flâneur. The image of the sexualized woman is double-edged, a recoupable fantasy. Swaggering down the street in her butch drag, casting her roving eye left and right, the lesbian flâneur signifies a mobilized female sexuality *in control,* not out of control.[51] As a fantasy she transcends the limitations of the reader's personal circumstances. In her urban circumlocutions, her affections, her connections, she breaks down the boundary between Self and Other. She collapses the inviolate distinction between masculinity and femininity. Her threat to heteropatriarchal definitions is recognized by hegemonic voices, hence the jeering shout, 'Is it a man or is it a woman?', is a cry of anxiety, as much as of aggression. The answer is neither and both: as a

Not-Woman, she slips between, beyond and around the linear landscape. The physiology of this flâneur's city is a woman's body constantly in motion, her lips in conversation.[52]

Like Nestle's protagonists in the poem, Lee Lynch proffers another working-class hero:

> Frenchy, jaw thrust forward, legs pumping to the beat of the rock-and-roll song in her head, shoulders dipping left and right with every step, emerged from the subway at 14th Street and disappeared into a cigar store. Moments later, flicking a speck of nothing from the shoulder of her black denim jacket, then rolling its collar up behind her neck, she set out through the blueness and bustle of a New York Saturday night.[53]

Perhaps the name 'Frenchy' gives it away – this short passage previews a parodic portrait of the bulldagger as Parisian flâneur, complete with portable Freudian phallus (the cigar), given a sexualized ('blue') city to penetrate. The fetishized butch drag, the black denims, blue button-down shirt, sharply pointed black boots, garrison belt buckle and jet-black hair slicked back into a blade like a DA,[54] constitute the image of the perfect dag. The text foregrounds the plasticity of the role by camping up Frenchy's casanova, gay-dog, libertine, diddy-bopping cruising. The sex scene takes place next to some deserted train tracks, a symbol of transience, travelling and the moment. This generic butch then catches the subway home.

On the journey towards home this flâneur undresses. In a classic scene of transformation she then makes herself 'old maidish, like a girl who'd never had a date and went to church regularly to pray for one'.[55] In a classic conclusive twist the short story ends with a revelation – she goes home to mother. Fearful of her mother's detecting the sex smell still on her, Frenchy slips quickly into 'the little girl's room'[56] to sluice away her adult self. In the metaphors of change which structure this story, both the closet and the street are zones of masquerade.

The lesbian flâneur appears in a more extended narrative as the main protagonist in Jane De Lynn's episodic novel *Don Juan in the Village*. Thirteen short scenes of conquest and submission structure this narrator's sexual odyssey. Kathy Acker has called the book 'a powerful metaphor of our intense alienation from society and each other. An intriguing portrayal of that strange and trance-like locus where lust and disgust become indistinguishable',[57] a comment which both recalls the flâneur's anomie and highlights the way in which her space is so sexualized. As in 'The Swashbuckler', this novel problematizes the predatory erotics of the stroller by using irony, encouraging a feminist critique of the excessively cold and exploitative sexual consumption of women by the conventional flâneur. In *Don Juan in the Village,* although the protagonist is ostensibly writing from Iowa, Ibiza, Padova, Puerto Rico, or wherever, her actual location is immaterial. The text employs the American literary convention of the traveller in search of (her)self. Delivered with irony, she is a manifest tourist whose every foreign nook temporarily begets a colony of New York City, specifically a Greenwich Village bar, the topos of urbane lesbian identity, the flâneur's café. Her butch diffidence and boredom unsuccessfully screen a deluded, tragi-comic, self-conscious sexual desperation. Her targets invariably fail to be compliant, and each escapade is a testimonial to her perpetual frustration. This is one moment of supposed sexual triumph:

> As I slid down the bed I saw the World Trade Center out the window, winking at me with its red light. I was Gatsby, Eugène Rastignac, Norman Mailer, Donald Trump... anyone who had ever conquered a city with the sheer force of longing and desire.[58]

She is going down on that most evasive of spectacles, the gay Hollywood film star. The star, very politely, but very succinctly, fucks her and dumps her. *Don Juan in the Village* is the solitary flâneur stalking the city with the torment of Tantalus in her cunt. Although the narrator confers upon herself the gaze, she is unable to see it through, or through it. De Lynn's flâneur wears the melancholy of the disappointed desire, searching the labyrinthine city for a vast, unfulfilled promise.

Finally, Sarah Schulman's second novel, *Girls, Visions and Everything* (1986), recalls the quest of the American hero/traveller Sal Paradise in *On the Road* (Jack Kerouac, 1957):

> Somewhere along the line I knew there'd be girls, visions, everything; somewhere along the line the pearl would be handed to me.[59]

The pearl, a symbol of female sexuality, is something the active masculine narrator seeks to own. This predatory macho role is located historically in the flâneur, it is the story of an alienated, solitary sexuality voyeuristically consuming the female body as a right/rite of passage. Modelling herself as *On The Road* with Kerouac, protagonist Lila Futuransky's adventure is similarly self-exploratory, but based on the *female* experiences urban travel offers. Her comparison with Jack is the dream of being an outlaw, reconstructed by a feminist consciousness. Lila's trip is a constant circling between compatriots. Living in the Lower East Side of New York, she walks the streets, marking out the geography of an urban landscape punctuated by a city mapped out with emotional happenings. Locations are symbols of connection, and constant references to criss-crossing streets remind the reader of the systematic patterns of neighbourhood, in antithesis to the standard early Modernist images of alienation. *Girls, Visions and Everything* is about Lila Futuransky's New York, 'the most beautiful woman she had ever known'.[60]

A sardonic wit suffuses *Girls, Visions, and Everything*, but there is also melancholic sadness; a sense of decaying nostalgia for a mythical 'home', for streets filled with sisters and brothers sitting languid on the stoop, swopping stories and cementing *communitas*. This is the feminization of the street, the underworld with a human face, with its own moral and family code. It is rich kids who beat the gays and harass the poor, the prostitutes and the pushers. The lesbians are on the streets, working the burger bar, cruising the ice-cream parlour and clubbing it at the Kitsch-Inn, currently showing a lesbian version of *A Streetcar Named Desire*. Lila meets Emily here, performing as Stella Kowalski. The romance between Lila and Emily is the main plot development in the novel, structuring its five parts. The final chapter sees Lila torn between the 'masculine' desire trajectory of *On The Road* individualism and the 'feminine' circularity and disruption of affective liaisons. Her friend Isobel urges Lila not to pause:

> you can't stop walking the streets and trying to get under the city's skin because if you settle in your own little hole, she'll change so fast that by the time you wake up, she won't be yours anymore... Don't do it buddy.[61]

The text's constant engagement/disengagement with change and transformation is signified by the urban landscape, which is out of control. Even the protective zones are folding, and yet there are pockets of resistance which pierce the city's metaphoric paralysis with parody:

Gay Pride is one such representation, fifty thousand homosexuals parading through the city streets, of every type, presenting the Other of heterosexuality, from Gay Bankers to the Gay Men's Chorus singing 'It's Raining Men', a carnival image of space being permeated by its antithesis. The text tries to juxtapose a jumble of readerly responses, almost jerking the reader into some consciousness of its activity of forming new imaginative space. Lila reinvents New York from her position of other as a heterotopia of cultural intertextuality; she *is* Jack Kerouac, the character not the author, claiming, even as a Jewish lesbian, that:

> the road is the only image of freedom that an American can understand.[62]

The street is an image of freedom and paradoxically of violence. The female flâneur is vulnerable – Lila walks unmolested until the final part of the book whence she is sexually harassed by 'Hispanic' men, and saved from serious injury from potential queerbashers by the black and sick drug dealer Ray. Lila's zone is breaking down:

> People's minds were splitting open right there on the sidewalk.[63]

The fictional worlds start clashing together: Blanche DuBois appears to Emily aged eighty-five and begging for a dollar. Lila resorts to Emily with a resignation that can only be anti-romance, knowing it is the wrong decision, and nostalgically lamenting the end of the road of selfhood:

> *I don't know who I am right now*, she thought. *I want to go back to the old way.*[italics in original][64]

This whimsical nostalgia also highlights some disillusionment with the postmodernist models of space, wherein the public and private are collapsed onto the street, and the same space is being used by different people in different ways. Hierarchies still exist. Being part of a bigger spectacle, being visible as one subculture among many, may not necessarily create empowerment, only more competition over a diminishing resource. To the postmodernist flâneur freedom in this space is a relative concept; the flâneur is a victim to as well as an agent of it: abstraction has its costs. His/her freedom is to be suspended in perpetual motion, disconnected from effective social activity, in a state of melancholic play.

Four flâneurs: Joan Nestle's butch, Frenchy, Don Juan and Lila Futuransky. Each is a descendant of eager European voyagers who migrated with their ticket to Utopia; each with their separate, feminized, vulnerabilities; each a sexualized itinerant travelling through urban time and space towards a mythical selfhood, trying heroically to construct intelligibility from their experience, to collect an identity. None has the sex/gender/class privileges (fixities) of the Modernist flâneur, but they all retain his romanticism. Capitalism, despite itself, has produced the lesbian/flâneur: although the floppy, wandering body of the flâneur is the antithesis of the modern, mechanized, automated body, both are inscribed within capitalism's (over)production. Each flâneur here has a central ambivalence infusing her sexual wanderings, being pulled between detachment from and insertion into city regimes. Temporary, simultaneous, multiple identifications mapped out in moments, in the margins, masquerading as the male, make these flâneurs engage with the politics of *dis*location. Baudrillard's extended road-poem *America* (1988) speaks that masculine fragmentation:

> And the crucial moment is that brutal instant which reveals that the journey has no end, that there is no longer any reason for it to come to an end. Beyond a certain point, it is movement itself that changes. Movement which moves through space of its own volition changes into an absorption by space itself – end of resistance, end of the scene of the journey as such...[65]

His narrative of dystopian exhaustion is from the point of view of something being lost – significantly he, like Kerouac, is driving and not walking through America. But spatial reconstruction occurs in the moment of presence, however brief. The vacuum sucks us further in, but we need our fictions of consciousness or we will disappear. The tantalizing fantasy of Benjamin's 'phantasmagoria' is here present for the lesbian in the urban scene, embodying melancholia and desire simultaneously. Hence the grief of alienation is only partial; the apparitional flâneur lost in the streets also stumbles toward hope, and embodiment.

Lesbian identity is constructed in the temporal and linguistic mobilization of space, and as we move *through* space we imprint utopian and dystopian moments upon urban life. Our bodies are vital signs of this temporality and intersubjective location. In an instant, a freeze-frame, a lesbian is occupying space as it occupies her. Space teems with 'possibilities, positions, intersections, passages, detours, u-turns, dead-ends, [and] one-way streets';[66] it is never still. Another philosopher, Michel de Certeau, offers us the urban *mise en scène* as productive: in *The Practice of Everyday Life* Certeau writes about New York as a city of regeneration. Standing on the 110th floor of the World Trade Center he looks down upon Manhattan, drawing on Foucault's model of the panopticon. As his 'view' travels down to the streets he sees a city constantly reinventing itself, and his scopic, gnostic drive falters. Taking up the position of the walker he discovers another, more anarchic spatiality: the city as concepts exceeded by the many pluralities which are generated in, of and between it – it cannot be fully regulated; the city is a machine which produces an excess, a proliferation of illegitimacy, which discursive practices cannot contain. Pedestrian life has a singularity which escapes the cartological discipline of the architect's plans:

> The long poem of walking manipulates spatial organizations, so no matter how panoptic they may be: it is neither foreign to them (it can take place only within them) nor in conformity with them (it does not receive its identity from them). It creates shadows and ambiguities within them. It inserts its multitudinous references and citations into them... These diverse aspects provide the basis of a rhetoric.[67]

Certeau sees walking as a space of enunciation and the pedestrian's journey, like the speech act, has an unlimited diversity; within the city-as-text there is an anti-text:

> Things *extra* and *other* ... insert themselves into the accepted framework, the imposed order. One thus has the very relationship between spatial practices and the constructed order. The surface of this order is everywhere punched and torn open by ellipses, drifts, and leaks of meaning: it is a sieve-order.[68]

The perambulations of the lesbian flâneur on the streets of the city marks out a territorial discourse – to extend the spatial analogy – one of heroic proportions. Her journey from 'here' to 'there' invokes an active 'I', a phatic statement of subjectivity and location which refuses verbal and spatial effacement. Her desire is the machine of her incarnation. *Briefly returning to Brighton for the Summer, my eye follows a woman wearing a wide-shouldered linen suit. Down the street, she starts to decelerate. I zip up my jacket, put my best boot forward and tell myself that 'home' is just around the corner.*

Notes

1. Quoted in Ellen Moers, *The Dandy: Brummell to Beerbohm.* Lincoln and London: University of Nebraska Press, 1972, p. 11. I am grateful to Roger Sayles for this reference.
2. *Ibid.*, p. 13.
3. *Ibid.*, p. 18.
4. *Ibid.*, p. 21. Note this aversion to fresh vegetables has been reversed in present mythologies of class.
5. *Ibid.*, p. 21.
6. *Ibid.*, p. 36.
7. *Ibid.*, p. 37.
8. *Ibid.*, p. 298.
9. *Ibid.*, p. 307.
10. *Ibid.*, p. 313.
11. Elaine Showalter, *Sexual Anarchy: Gender and Culture at the Fin de Siècle.* London: Virago Press, 1990, p. 171.
12. Wilde's flirtation with socialism illustrated that the new gender fluidities of the New Woman and homosexual were ideologically connected (also taken up by the reformers Edward Carpenter, John Addington Symonds and E. M. Forster). The dandy's motility as a symbol of class can be evidenced by the fact that the upper-class dandy had become a working-class figure by the end of the century and continues to be read as such even today. Similarly, the appropriation of the dandy sensibility is seen blazing brightly in that working-class hero, the drag queen. Susan Sontag in her famous 1964 essay on camp makes the connection between homosexuality and dandyism clearer. There are differences between British and US manifestations though; as Sarah Chinn has pointed out, in US culture dressing up in women's clothes is much more burlesque, and much less seamless, for example in Milton Berle or Flip Wilson, whose drag is purposely incomplete.
13. Quoted in Showalter, *Sexual Anarchy*, p. 170.
14. Elizabeth Wilson, 'The invisible flâneur', *New Left Review*, 195, Sept–Oct 1992: 90–110.
15. *Ibid.*, p. 108.
16. *Ibid.*, p. 110.
17. Moers, *The Dandy*, p. 314.
18. Quoted in Ellen Moers, *Literary Women: The Great Writers.* New York: Doubleday Anchor Press, 1977, p. 12.
19. *Ibid.*
20. *Ibid.*
21. Wilson, 'The invisible flâneur', p. 109.
22. *Ibid.*, p. 111.
23. See Elyse Blankley, 'Return to Mytilène: Renée Vivien and the City of Women', in Susan Merrill Squier, *Women Writers and the City.* Knoxville: University of Tennessee Press, 1984, pp. 45–70, p. 59.
24. See Deborah Tyler Bennett, *Djuna Barnes.* Unpublished doctoral dissertation, University of Loughborough, 1993.
25. See Lillian Faderman, *Odd Girls and Twilight Lovers: A History of Lesbian Life in Twentieth-Century America.* New York/London: Viking Penguin, 1992, Chapter 3, pp. 62–92; George Chauncey, *Gay New York, Gender, Urban Culture and the Making of the Gay Male*

World 1890–1940. New York: Basic Books/Harper Collins, 1994.

26. See Christopher Mulvey, 'The black capital of the world', in Christopher Mulvey and John Simons (eds), *New York: City as Text*. London: Macmillan, 1990, pp. 147–65. Only one of the twelve chapters of this book is written by a woman. Perhaps the urban gaze is male after all.

27. James Weldon Johnson, 'Harlem: the culture capital', in Alain Locke (ed.), *The New Negro*. New York: Atheneum, 1975, p. 301.

28. Rudolph Fisher, 'The city of refuge', in A. Locke, *The New Negro*, p. 57.

29. Although clearly these terms were still in contestation, and inscribed within existing racialized power relations: for example, many of the Harlem clubs employed black performers for shows that were open to white audiences only, most notoriously The Cotton Club.

30. Ralph Ellison, *The Invisible Man*. Harmondsworth: Penguin Books, 1982, p. 132.

31. James L. De Jongh, 'The image of black Harlem in literature', in C. Mulvey and J. Simons (eds), *New York*, pp. 131–46, p. 145.

32. In Leslie Feinberg's *Stone Butch Blues* (Ithaca, NY: Firebrand Books, 1993) the Jewish protagonist Jess Goldberg is a he/she, a passing woman, who journeys to New York City to consolidate and make safe her emerging identity. Significantly, as her train travels through the outer urban detritus of NYC, it is seeing Harlem which symbolizes her arrival.

33. See Walter Benjamin, *Charles Baudelaire: A Lyric Poet in the Era of High Capitalism*, trans. H. Zohn. London: New Left Books, 1973, p. 26.

34. Wilson, 'The invisible flâneur', p. 105.

35. Chauncey, *Gay New York*.

36. *Ibid.*, p. 244.

37. *Ibid.*, pp. 245–6.

38. As also reported by Elizabeth Lapovsky Kennedy and Madeline D. Davis in their wonderful history of Buffalo, *Boots of Leather, Slippers of Gold: The History of a Lesbian Community*. New York: Routledge, 1993.

39. There is insufficient space to develop this here; please refer to Allan Bérubé's excellent *Coming Out under Fire: The History of Gay Men and Women in World War Two*. New York: Plume Books, 1990.

40. Various work has charted this migration; see for example Peter Jackson, *Maps of Meaning*. London: Routledge, 1992, pp. 120–30.

41. A thorough study of these texts is offered in Angela Weir and Elizabeth Wilson, 'The Greyhound bus station in the evolution of lesbian popular culture', in Sally R. Munt (ed.), *New Lesbian Criticism: Literary and Cultural Readings*. New York: Columbia University Press, 1992, pp. 51–74.

42. See Katie King, 'Audre Lorde's lacquered layerings: the lesbian bar as a site of literary production', in Sally R. Munt, *New Lesbian Criticism*, pp. 51–74. The lesbian bar was not necessarily a home for African–American lesbians who often, because of the racism of white women's bars, and lacking the same (limited) access to capital that running a bar themselves would require, preferred the forum of the house party. See Rochella Thorpe, '"A house where queers go": African–American lesbian night-life in Detroit, 1940–1975', in Ellen Lewin, *Inventing Lesbian Cultures*

in America. Boston: Beacon Press, 1996, pp. 40–61.

43. Nan Keene, *Twice as Gay*. New York: After Hours Book No. 109, 1964, back cover.

44. See Diane Hamer, '"I Am a Woman": Ann Bannon and the writing of lesbian identity in the 1950's', in Mark Lilly (ed.), *Lesbian and Gay Writing*. London: Macmillan Press, 1990, pp. 47–75.

45. Rita Mae Brown, *Rubyfruit Jungle*. New York: Bantam Books, 1977.

46. Jan Stafford, *Bizarro in Love*. San Francisco: A Cheap Shots Publication, 1986.

47. Walter Benjamin, *Charles Baudelaire: A Lyric Poet in the Era of High Capitalism*, trans. H. Zohn. London: New Left Books, 1973, p. 26.

48. Joan Nestle, *A Restricted Country*. London: Sheba Feminist Publishers, 1988, pp. 74–7.

49. See for example Amber Hollibaugh and Cherríe Moraga, 'What we're rollin' around in bed with: sexual silences in feminism: a conversation towards ending them' (1981). Reprinted in Joan Nestle (ed.), *The Persistent Desire*. Boston: Alyson Publications, 1992, pp. 243–53.

50. See Mark Wigley, 'Untitled: the housing of gender', in Beatriz Colomina (ed.), *Sexuality and Space*. New York: Princeton Architectural Press, 1992, pp. 326–89, p. 335. See also L. Knopp, 'Sexuality and the spatial dynamics of capitalism', *Environment and Planning D: Society and Space*, 10, 1992: 651–69.

51. Although I do admit that there is an assumption here – a masculinist one – that being in control equals power and is preferable, more safe, than being out of control.

52. Luce Irigaray, *This Sex Which Is Not One* ['*Ce sexe qui n'en pas un*'].

Ithaca, NY: Cornell University Press, 1985 (1977).

53. Lee Lynch, 'The Swashbuckler', in Joan Nestle and Naomi Holoch (eds), *Women on Women: An Anthology of American Lesbian Short Fiction*. New York and London: Plume/Penguin Books, 1990 (1985), pp. 241–62, p. 241.

54. 'The DA – the letters stand for duck's ass – was a popular hairdo for working-class men and butches during the 1950s. All side hair was combed back and joined the back hair in a manner resembling the layered feathers of a duck's tail, hence the name. Pomade was used to hold the hair in place and give a sleek appearance' – Elizabeth Lapovsky Kennedy and Madeline Davis, '"They was no-one to mess with": the construction of the butch role in the lesbian community of the 1940's and 1950's', in Joan Nestle (ed.), *The Persistent Desire*, pp. 62–79, p. 78.

55. Lynch, 'The Swashbuckler', p. 260.

56 *Ibid.*, p. 261.

57. Jane De Lynn, *Don Juan in the Village*. New York: Pantheon Books, 1990, back cover.

58. *Ibid.*, p. 186.

59. Jack Kerouac, *On the Road*. Harmondsworth: Penguin Books, 1972, p. 14.

60. Sarah Schulman, *Girls, Visions and Everything*. Seattle: The Seal Press, 1986, p. 177. I am aware that I am in danger of entrenching the discourse of 'American exceptionalism': concentrating my examples in New York encourages the view that it is a 'special' place. It is and it is not: the myth of New York has a political and cultural specificity in world culture and I am curious about that manifestation. For lesbian and gay people it has a particular set of meanings and

associations and to resist mythologizing New York is difficult.

61. *Ibid.*, p. 178.
62. *Ibid.*, p. 164.
63. *Ibid.*, p. 14.
64. *Ibid.*, p. 178.
65. Jean Baudrillard, *America*. London: Verso Press, 1988, p. 10.
66. Susan Sontag, 'Introduction', in Walter Benjamin, *One-Way Street and Other Writings*. London: New Left Books, 1979, pp. 7–28, p. 13.
67. Michel de Certeau, *The Practice of Everyday Life*, trans. Steven Rendall. Berkeley: University of California Press, 1984, p. 101.
68. *Ibid.*, p. 107.

3

The Butch Body

Butch is *the* recognizable public form of lesbianism; despite the media hype of chic femme in the early 1990s, it communicates a singular verity, to dykes and homophobes alike. Butch – despite the evidence of butch heterosexual women and the passion of femmes for women – is the gospel of lesbianism, inevitably interpreted as the true revelation of female homosexuality. Butch is the signifying space of lesbianism; when a butch walks into a room, that space becomes queer. Explicitly and implicitly the butch stands for the lesbian in the Lesbian Imaginary; this not entirely unproblematic as much of the power and entitlement of masculinity which has been appropriated is not wholly other to straight masculinity, however 'heroically' it is claimed.

In this chapter I intend to explore gender as the primary frame into which butch meanings are absorbed, and then examine how those signals have been ascribed onto the butch body, historically through pathologization, and more recently in a reverse discourse of elevation, circumscribed by the pride/shame dichotomy I will elaborate in Chapter 4. Butch pride is invested in the butch's generation of a lesbian presence and her making of actual and symbolic space is predicated on her own apparent hermeticism. For the butch to shift space, her own boundaries must be secured; her apotheosis is in the stone butch's untouchability.[1] Crucial to the butch performance is a sense of autonomous embodiment, an imperviousness which constructs the butch body as a sexual agent, something that *does* rather than *is*. Butch phallicism, I shall argue, becomes spread across the surfaces of the body, which are eroticized because of the paradox of inside/outside extant in the enigma of the masculine woman.

Katie King identified the butch as lesbianism's magical sign.[2] Judy Grahn, in her hugely popular mythological etymology of gay history, *Another Mother Tongue* (1984), claims:

the butch is, ceremoniously speaking, Puck. Cross-dressing is a magical function, and the butch is the equivalent of the traditional cross-dresser who may also become a magical/shaman of the tribe.[3]

As an outlaw figure the butch has been highly romanticized by lesbians; the butch carries the shame of social ostracism and turns it inside out as heroic pride. Signs have histories, some of which are allocated retrospectively.[4] In the 1990s, from the perspective of the present, butch is a sign which continues to carry disparate, reusable meanings to lesbians through differing generations. Key contemporary icons of butchness include Boadicea, Joan of Arc, Anne Lister, Gertrude Stein, Radclyffe (John) Hall, Rosa Bonheur, Marlene Dietrich, Mabel Hampton, Lee Lynch, Pat Califia, Leslie Feinberg, Cherríe Moraga, Kitty Tsui, Martina Navratilova and k.d. lang. The diversity of this list suggests the mobility of the designation, butch. Critics have evaded a binding definition; here I intend to perpetrate that evasion by illuminating some of my own multivalent uses of 'butch', rather than delineating the term as a fixed concept. As I will go on to show, even the most seemingly banal term, 'the masculine woman', has its problems.

I have not examined the uses of femme with the same energy. Undoubtedly this lays me open to the accusation that I have perpetuated the straight discourse of femme invisibility. Although I think this could be true, first, I do not think that butch and femme are interdependent categories but have separable histories; second, excellent writing by femmes about femmes exists;[5] third, at risk of perpetuating the butch chauvinism 'Femmes – who can understand them?', I confess I cannot attempt an intellectual authority on femmes in the same way that I can with butches. Although identities are relational entities, and certainly 'femme' has historically enjoyed a cogent influence on 'butch', to treat the terms as coterminous would be to reproduce the polarized heterosexist retrenchment I am committed to undoing. The idea that lovers must always be complementary – even that butch 'tops' need butch 'bottoms', a displacement of the same system – is a conservative one. Nevertheless, to ignore 'femme' would be capricious, so I refer to it parenthetically only as a qualifier of 'butch' identity. Butch becomes effectively recentred as an identity here, one regretted effect of which is that other identities become marginalized; indeed, all identity formations work this way. In the poor economy of representation featuring butches and femmes, the keen desire for coverage demands higher stakes, and I understand there will be those who perceive my analysis to be incomplete.

Gender 'roles'

I am attending a Butch/Femme Workshop in Brighton. In a room of twenty lesbians, only two self-identify as such in the introductory session. I grow increasingly uncomfortable as the group proceeds to list enthusiastically on a flow chart their definition of femme qualities, and then butch. These characteristics are predictable, hypostasized versions of Barbie and Ken (or more probably, Clint). The group, initially awkward, quickly coheres into a consensus, eager for the task to be completed unanimously. After multiple traits have been transcribed before us, there seems to be a gradual quietening in the room, not I feel because we had exhausted the lists, but that the lists themselves were beginning to look increasingly extravagant. The polarized contradistinction between butch and femme emerging doesn't resemble us or anyone we know. Having exorcised this butch and femme – a travesty we had conspired to reproduce – hesitatingly we begin to offer the sub-vocal experiences of our more secluded discourse.

Butch, in common use, is a term as unstable as the gender configurations of masculinity and femininity. Indeed, butch and femme are often sympathetically interpreted as lesbianism's corresponding gender roles. Gayle Rubin describes butch as the 'lesbian vernacular', defining it so: 'Butch is most usefully understood as a category of lesbian gender that is constituted through the deployment and manipulation of masculine gender codes and symbols.'[6] In lesbian culture, butch and femme, like masculinity and femininity, are generally frequently constructed as attributes layered onto discrete male or female bodies. The application of a bipolar androgyny model is similar to the way heterosexuality operates in maintaining gender ideals, on a scale with a 'perfectly masculine man' at one end and a 'perfectly feminine woman' at the other. Androgyny is contained within this system because it delivers the perfectly balanced centre. Recognizing that people occupy disjunctive gender positions ('plenty of men cry'), heterosexuality promotes the add-up method of understanding gender: thus a man may be awarded 8/10 marks for masculinity and 2/10 for femininity, on the gender continuum.[7] Similarly, in a recent British television programme on butch/femme, participants were asked to hold up numbered cards to show how much they considered themselves femme, and how much butch.[8] This idea originated in Jo Ann Loulan's earlier text *The Lesbian Erotic Dance* (1990). She analysed 589 questionnaires, employing the Sandra Bem Sex Role Inventory (BSRI) of the 1970s. Loulan reports remarkably few deviations from traditional sex role stereotyping (femme/femininity, butch/masculinity) when respondents were asked to define the categories in principle:

> The butches were given the 'male' characteristics (including 'dominant', 'aggressive', etc.) that are seen as less acceptable in the lesbian community. They only moved out of the traditional 'male' roles when given 'moody' or 'jealous' from supposedly androgynous characteristics and 'loyal' from the supposedly feminine characteristics.
>
> The femmes were never assigned anything but female characteristics, which is remarkable. Here you have it, femmes are like heterosexual women and butches are like men. Once again the androgynous women are the good people.[9]

But Loulan observed that respondents describing themselves on the BSRI system consistently defied predictable associations, using many terms across gender-aligned identifications. Butches asked to name words to describe the kind of women they found erotic chose 'soft, gentle, sensual, sexual/sexy, beautiful, and "the way they dress"'; femmes chose 'strong, confident, assertive, muscles, independent, tough'.[10] Strikingly, 'When butches describe butches, femmes describe femmes, androgynous women describe androgynous women, they do so with exactly the same words that outside groups use to describe them'.[11] Cultural theorists are often dismissive of such surveys, drawing attention to the many variables which exist, the often contrived parameters of the survey and the questionable status of the 'truths' submitted. But even in this self-selecting sample of predominantly Caucasian (85 per cent), middle-class (45 per cent),[12] Protestant (75 per cent), thirty-somethings (50 per cent) from the West coast of the USA, there is a glaring inconsistency – all respondents offered a consistently hegemonic formulation of butch/femme, which corresponded to heterosexist norms. Their diagnosis of themselves, however, was noticeably dysphoric.

There are two levels at which we operate the butch/femme system in lesbian culture. Neither is ultimately separable. In the first we believe, in Loulan's words, 'that lesbians are an ersatz version of the heterosexual model'.[13] Here we conspire to use shame and blame to marshall all those we perceive as too outlaw in their 'inappropriate' gender display. The nuances of butch and femme identities escape this homophobic gaze. A gaze, often enough, turned inward to police ourselves. De-butching, in order to pre-empt a stranger's negative response, is complicit with the self-hatred that also turns on another with whom we feel too embarrassed to walk down the street. Butches who are used to this resign themselves to the drip, drip of acid onto their self-esteem. We learn to practise an involuntary anthropological gaze gauging the level of acquiescence available in every straight space to the open display of our lesbian self. This lesbian vigilante stalks our self-regard. The rule is portable: we take it into ostensibly lesbian spaces and repeat the pattern, stretching its subliminal parameters. We become adept at stage-dressing our lesbian identity by degree. The taboo skulking in the twilight is the FTM – the female to male transsexual. S/he is the spectre the hyper-butch invokes, the fear that at some indeterminate point we stop being a woman and start to become a man:

> When a woman's body begins to change into a male body, the transposition of male to female signals that constitutes 'butch' begin to disintegrate. A cross-dressing, dildo-packing, body building butch may use a male name and masculine pronouns, yet still have soft skin, no facial hair, the visible swell of breasts or hips under male clothing, small hands and feet, or some other detectable sign of femaleness... [but] when he begins to read like a man, many lesbians no longer find him attractive and some want to banish him from their social universe... A sex change is a transition...[14]

And therefore a very threatening state of indeterminacy. Some FTMs choose to resolve this by naturalizing the gender transition ('I was a man all along'), thus seeking some recuperation. Some butches similarly profess a gender essentialism which attributes their sexual prowess to the conviction that they are a Real Woman underneath. Whereas butches suffer this hyper-visibility, femmes endure invisibility by the bouncer telling them: 'Sorry girls, it's gay night'.[15] The general principle – the censure of too much butch in straight contexts, too much femme in dyke contexts – promotes a boundary across which no lesbian should slip. To neologize Eve Sedgwick: this is a form of *heterosexual panic*, a kind of paranoia whose manifestation is a covert acknowledgement that the thin line between homosexuality and heterosexuality *is* indicated in butch/femme behaviour. Conversely, the absence of certain signs can also be read as material evidence of sexual practice too – the missing second earring, or handbag – apocryphally alerts to the presence of lesbianism. Perhaps there is an equally subversive message being conveyed: the lack of accessories signifying a lack of heterosexuality. The principle that heterosexuality itself as an add-on is being evoked; for some, lesbianism is the substrate onto which heterosexuality must be grafted.

On the second level we protect a secret eroticism from the prurient gaze of heterosexism by making it signify an intimate theatre for the subculture alone. Butch and femme are rituals for which there are acknowledged rites of passage. For butches, 'my first tie/dildo/Doc Martens' are symbols marking moments of transgression into a lesbian self. The mechanics of recognition are integral to all subcultures, and within butch culture the smallest sign – for example, short, clean fingernails – can connote intense meanings. Eroticism is stimulated by the apparent secrecy of these exchanges: I brush my fingers across my face, you swallow and look at them. Sexuality is charged by this highly coded intimate reciprocity. Hegemonic lesbian invisibility has forced the invention of subtlety in courtship rituals. Born of necessity, these nuances are developed to the point of a skilled romanticism, encapsulated in such texts as Joan Nestle's pioneering *A Restricted Country* (1988), and documented in recent oral history projects. Gayle Rubin draws attention to the plasticity of masculinity, commenting how there are many ways to be butch:

> There are as least as many ways to be butch as there are ways for men to be masculine; actually there are more ways to be butch, because when women appropriate masculine styles the element of travesty produces new significance and meaning. Butches adopt and transmute the many available codes of masculinity.[16]

The interdeterminacy of signs conveys different messages: a potential lover will respond to the ubiquitous silk tie by telling me how elegant/pressed/soft it is. A different, more derisory comment accuses me of trying to look like a man, or be a man. Historically, as a self-evident human truth, gender is soldered to the body. Actually, in their own ways, both are true: in the latter I *am* trying to look like a man, to be his corollary, because of what 'looking like a [certain type of] man' conveys: neatness, unbroken lines, smoothness, protectiveness, solidity, assertion, consistency, controlled eroticism, patience... *et cetera*. I may even want to be a man, and in rare circumstances this insult may become a compliment, because of what 'man' can signify. How does this differ from the implication of Judith Butler's argument[17] that men are also performing their masculinity? The 'man' I have conveyed here is closer to the romantic fiction produced by women for women in Western culture. Perhaps the coded eroticism is in the open secret, in the shared awareness that I am simultaneously reifying and disavowing maleness. Crucially I am a lesbian woman performing masculinity, and it is this paradox, this 'travesty', the riddle, which is so erotically charged. I am (not) what I am.

Sexology

I visit the doctor's surgery. There is a replacement locum GP on duty (another male, etc.). His manner becomes hostile as soon as I enter the office. I ask him for a repeat monthly prescription for magnesium injections. He refuses, on the grounds that the medication is not proven safe. I ask him why, when my own doctor, who is a senior partner in the practice, has previously approved of it. He blusters. He is obviously ignorant of the treatment but doesn't want to appear so. Instead of deferring, I argue with him. He claims the dosage details are not even in my notes. I reach across the desk and grab my medical file, asserting it is in there; I pull out the sheet. The doctor is affronted, and begrudgingly fills in the prescription. I am still considering the brief memo I glanced at in my file, from my GP to a hospital consultant, dated a couple of years before:

Please investigate this patient for a suspected anal fissure. She is a practising homosexual.

At the hospital the recipient of the letter (male, etc., consultant)
greases the colonoscope to insert into my rectum. No nurse is
present. Being an 'anal virgin' I am especially apprehensive, and
tell the doctor I am nervous. He tells me not to be so stupid and,
suddenly, deliberately rams the long tube into my arse. The tear
splits, and pain rips into my body.

Butchness is associated with biological discourse in the emerging
nineteenth-century science of sexology. We cannot seriously apply the
category butch more retrospectively than this, as it functions as a form
of homosexual identity – not possible therefore before the campaigner
Karl Maria Kertbeny employed the term 'homosexual' in Prussia in 1869.
Karl Heinrich Ulrichs was a pioneer sexologist, lawyer and homosexual,
born in Hannover, Germany, in 1825. He was the first to formulate a
scientific theory of homosexuality, published in five episodes between
1864 and 1865. Ulrichs used the existing idea of hermaphrodism to
propose his own formulation, the 'urning', which he saw as part of
nature. The female version, the 'urningin', was a sexual invert, her same-
sex desires not corresponding to her female body. The urningin not only
had (what we would call) lesbian desires, she also had a masculinized
psyche. S/he was a man trapped in a female body, a metaphor taken up
literally by many subsequent apologists. Ulrichs was one of the earliest
to believe that there was a separate identity for homosexuality that was
inborn, innate and constituted an essence; his 'third sex' was a product
of biological inheritance, and against his own emancipatory aims,
ironically, these ideas were to reinforce subsequent sexologists' view of
homosexuality as a degenerate sickness, or 'contrary sexual feeling' as
defined by Karl Westphal in 1869.[18]

The major inheritor and protagonist of the sickness model was the
German–Austrian sexologist Richard von Krafft-Ebing (born 1840),
who was professor of psychiatry at the University of Vienna. He
adopted Ulrichs' congenital rationale for forms of homosexuality, but
rejected hermaphrodism as causal. Both, though, understood
homosexuality to be an inversion founded on the attraction of
opposites, essentially reinforcing the only conceivable structure of
desire – heterosexuality.[19] Krafft-Ebing in his *Psychopathia Sexualis*
(first volume 1886) identified causes for female homosexuality as
hypersexuality and automasturbation, attendant most frequently

'among the ladies in large cities', prostitutes, servants and teachers, opera singers and actresses. Also:

> Uranism may nearly always be suspected in females wearing their hair short, or who dress in the fashion of men, or pursue the sports and pastimes of their male acquaintances.[20]

This 'masculine soul heaving in the female bosom':

> may chiefly be found in the haunts of boys. She is the rival in their play, preferring the rocking-horse, playing at soldiers, to dolls and other girlish occupations. The toilet is neglected, and rough boyish manners are affected... At times smoking and drinking are cultivated even with passion.

But Krafft-Ebing, in the same essay, argued that 'Hermaphrodism represents the extreme grade of degenerative homosexuality', in his definition ascertained by the fact that the nugatory femininity in the subject was restricted to the genitalia. Although a minority of these strongly sensual individuals would 'resort to cunnilingus or mutual masturbation', most of these women would restrict sexual behaviour to kissing and embracing. He ends with the idea that the most severe grades may even desire the use of 'the priapus', and that in sexually neurasthenic females, ejaculation occurs.

Fascination with the butch body can be best illustrated by quoting at length from one of Krafft-Ebing's case-studies, 'S':

> She was 153 centimetres tall, of delicate build, thin, but remarkably muscular on the breast and thighs. Her gait in female attire was awkward. Her movements were powerful, not unpleasing, though they were somewhat masculine and lacking in grace. She greeted one with a firm pressure of the hand. Her whole carriage was decided, firm and somewhat self-conscious. Her glance was intelligent, mien somewhat diffident...

He proceeds to offer an extremely detailed set of measurements of her body:

> Extensor surfaces of the extremities remarkably well covered in hair... hips did not correspond in any way with those of a female ...upper jaw strikingly projecting... voice rough and deep... Mons

veneris covered with thick, dark hair. Genitals completely feminine, without trace of hermaphroditic appearance, but *at the stage of development of a ten-year-old girl.* The labia majora touching each other almost completely; labia minora having a *cock's-comb-like form,* and projecting under the labia majora. Clitoris small and very sensitive... Vagina so narrow that the insertion of an erect male member would be impossible; also very sensitive; certain coitus had not taken place. Uterus felt, through the rectum, to be about the size of a walnut. [my italics]

I have selected here; Krafft-Ebing concludes his description that in his opinion:

in S. there was a congenitally abnormal inversion of the sexual instinct, which, indeed, expressed itself, anthropologically, in anomalies of development of the body, depending upon great hereditary taint; further, that the criminal acts of S. had their foundation in her abnormal and irresistible sexuality.[21]

Her female sexuality had withered to be replaced by an inferior cock-like substitute. She was linked to criminality and hysteria. The most striking aspect of this case-study, the style in which it is written, contrasts a subjective, adjectival sketch with an extended scientific effusion of empirical measurements. I cannot read it without thinking of this woman's humiliation and pain as the good doctor rummages around in her 'very sensitive' genitalia. Presumably she had not been penetrated *until then.* Construction of the masculinized lesbian body by the institutions of medical and legal discourse is rife in this literature: the obsessive prurience with which reports are compiled indicate the barely concealed desire to touch, measure, tabulate and control through the glance of power. Despite the fact that Krafft-Ebing's empiricism was typical of his era, and that his criminality/homosexuality conjunction arises partly from his choice of case-studies (mostly asylum patients), and the fact that he became less stigmatizing and more liberal towards the end of his career, the discursive associations he made were to become highly influential in the creation of a twentieth-century lesbian sensibility.

Magnus Hirschfeld (born Kolberg, Germany, in 1868), a political reformist writing later than Krafft-Ebing in historically different circumstances, proffered the idea of a third sex which relied on the positioning of the naturally occurring intermediate body (mirroring the gender scale which centres androgyny). Hirschfeld argued that everyone is naturally psychically hermaphroditic, and that some people exhibit characteristics of the opposite sex. Nevertheless, he put female homosexuality down to an atrophied clitoris. Hirschfeld also compared homosexuality to defective physiological development, although he managed to maintain that this did not result in mental aberration or weakness. Hirschfeld, according to Charlotte Wolff, was the first to link lesbianism with the Women's Movement, referring admiringly to 'those courageous manly women of high intelligence'.[22] He thought of mainstream lesbians as masculinized women, suspecting that the feminine lesbian was either physically infantile or neurotic, unlike the former, whom he admired.

The British sexologist Havelock Ellis embraced the structure of congenital sexual inversion in his *Studies in the Psychology of Sex* (1897), which was indebted to John Addington Symonds. Like Hirschfeld he was a sex reformer, but more cautious. Adopting prevailing myths of womanhood he seemed to think that the defining gesture of lesbian sexual behaviour was 'lying spoons',[23] although he also seemed to accept lesbians deploying dildos with equanimity. Ellis continued to view lesbians in more conventional ways; despite his seeing male homosexuals as able to break out of the (feminine) gender positions ascribed to them in science, he insisted that 'true' female inverts always betrayed distinct traces of masculinity. Ellis held contradictory views during his career: he jettisoned the association of lesbianism with degeneracy, argued for the hereditary nature of inversion and was reluctantly persuaded by Radclyffe Hall and Una Troubridge to write a short prefatory statement to *The Well of Loneliness* (1928). Stephen Gordon's archetypally butch body (the muscular, angled frame, the narrow hips and wide shoulders, etc.) was a fictional amalgamation of Havelock Ellis's case-studies presented in *Sexual Inversion,* the first of the *Studies in the Psychology of Sex.*

Words like degenerate, abnormality, contrary, disease, disturbed, deformity, overstimulated, reversion, weakness, tendencies and susceptibility are spattered throughout nineteenth- and twentieth-century sexological texts. These terms alert the lesbian reader to their attempts to pathologize same-sex desire by using medical language. The predominant tone of this work betrays the attempt to explain female homosexuality by using the body as an originating force. Isolating individual sexologists' work – however influential – does not convey how saturated the field still is with feverish interest in the homosexual body (as opposed to acts, or practices). These specialists in sexual pathology are fascinated by the homosexual body as colonized object; endless scrutinization of the homosexual body sets it up as the sphinx of sexual identity. It becomes, like all desired and feared marginalized entities, magnetically powerful, and a repository for the uncomfortable taboos of the colonizing gaze.[24] There have been contemporary efforts to refute the view of sexology as deterministically oppressive, arguing that it had liberatory effects for homosexual men and women (indeed, many were eager volunteers for case-studies and treatment, and perceived that it opened up discussion of their desires for the first time).[25] My focus in this section is not directly on the reverse discourse that has evolved specifically in relation to sexology, but to re-emphasize its deleterious consequences for the pathologized butch body.

Research which focuses on the body is highly problematic. In reading nineteenth-century case-studies it is disturbing to recognize how the form they take is indistinguishable from similar endeavours to analyse the criminal, the Jew, the prostitute and the black, and to ascribe to them a speciology distinct from the centred norm.[26] Eugenics discourse circulating at the time was all too zealously using evidence of 'deviation' as vindication enough to institute social controls. It was precisely this ideology which became assimilable into Nazism, seen resurfacing today in the visualization of the AIDS body as degenerative and morally diseased. The butch body in sexology continues to represent a deviant sign. Many sexologists attempted to differentiate between *inborn* and *acquired* homosexuality, which were split, in today's parlance, into *butch* and *femme*. After disinterestedly dispensing with the contextual variety (feminine – or femme – women are only temporary homosexuals), they concentrated their investigations on the masculine lesbian body as the incarnation of the true homosexual.

European sexology largely developed under the shade of nineteenth-century reformism; in the USA twentieth-century sexology was driven by an ideology of 'civilized morality' which resulted in an intransigent prudery in American public discourse still visible today. A fairly representative popular sexology book from the 1950s is Frank Caprio's *Female Homosexuality* which asserts that 'Lesbianism is capable of influencing the stability of the our social structure'.[27] Compiling his study,

Caprio 'circled the globe',[28] to interview lesbians, in a gesture evoking the imperialist travelogues of the nineteenth century. Indeed, the contents page promises such exotic journeying as 'Lesbianism in the Orient, Lesbianism in the Tropics, Art Erotica... Lesbian Practices among Prostitutes in Various Parts of the World'. Caprio travels the lesbian body in similar colonizing vein:

> The lesbian in resorting to different methods of sexual gratification is able to satisfy various unconscious psychological cravings. When she lies on top of her partner and achieves an orgasm via friction of the clitoris (tribadism), she gratifies her *masculine component* – identification with the male sex (penis). In sucking the breast of another woman she is able to assume the role of the *child* suckling the mother's breast. Reversing the role in giving her breast to her partner she gratifies her *maternal instinct* – that of protecting and nourishing her loved one.
>
> Cunnilingus, active or passive, of course is the equivalent of breast sucking (return to infancy). Lesbians are unable to appreciate the unconscious psychology behind these various roles which they assume in an attempt to gratify each other.[29] [my italics]

Thus Caprio incorporates any materially active *lesbian* desire into the heterosexual model.

Sensationalist narratives saturate the book. Anecdotal evidence is frequently configured as empirical knowledge in the socio-psychological genre of case-studies – take this gem on a lesbian 'with cannibalistic tendencies':

> Her life history revealed an Electra complex (a strong attachment to her father) and an identification with an older brother. She had been a tomboy as a child and throughout her life displayed a masculine type of aggressiveness. Whenever she was in a fight with a boy in the neighbourhood, she would bite him on the arm and face. Following her first attempt at cunnilingus she developed the habit of eating hair. The hair swallowing represents a desire to devour the genitals of her sexual partner. She had had sexual relations with a young man but discontinued because on one occasion while performing fellatio she feared she might bite his penis (desire to castrate him – oral sadism); eating toothpicks and

pencils represents the desire to devour the penis (phallic symbolism).

She also discovered that she became sexually excited by biting her roommate on the neck and shoulders during mutual masturbation. She liked to bite and suck the flesh until she was able to produce a red spot on her partner's body (ecchymosis). On one occasion her girlfriend cut herself while opening a can of vegetables. She went over and sucked the blood from the bleeding finger telling her friend that her saliva was antiseptic and would heal the wound. The evidence tends to support the existence of sexual excitement associated with this peculiar deviation known as 'Vampirism' (blood sucking). She reports that she felt a sensation in her vagina as she tasted the blood of her friend's finger...[30]

An interesting cauldron of associations gets brewed here – the eroticism of the finger, which is also clearly a parallel castration fantasy; the elevation of giving a love bite into a pathological injury; the equivalence of lesbianism with female vampirism – another metaphorical castration as she 'sucks the life blood' out of her victim; she desires to 'devour the genitals' of her partner (beware of using toothpicks when out to dinner with a potential date). Behind this lesbian is the spectre of the woman who gains the phallus by devouring it, a motion for which she is doomed to suffer. Throughout the text, the author's increasingly baroque – even poetically perverse – explanations of derangement are clearly intended to dissuade any wavering woman from straying from the straight and definitely narrow path of heterosexuality. However, the many vivid narratives of sexual encounters would stimulate any reader – male or female – to include these figures in their sexual imagination. The style of this study, in spite of (because of) its framing with medical expertise on 'Mental Hygiene', is characteristically pornographic. *Female Homosexuality* is a classic example of the pseudo-scientific uses to which sexology may be put: it positions the masculine lesbian as preternaturally strange, whilst providing reassurance and prurient titillation.

The symptoms of homosexuality have been ascribed to enlarged female genitalia (the clitoris masquerading as a small penis),[31] abnormal chromosomes or glands, lack of secondary female characteristics (e.g. enlarged breasts), hirsuteness, a deep voice, pronounced intellect or excessive ability at sports (dissolving fat and substituting muscle), body-carrying angle, skeletal formation, sterility and more. US sexological research continued to foreground these iconic marks of lesbianism :

> Muriel Wilson Perkins studied 241 lesbian women and found that the members of her sample had narrower hips, increased arm and leg girths, less subcutaneous fat, and more muscle than a sample of 1,260 adult women measured between 1960 and 1968. She divided her sample into groups by the women's dominance in the sex act and noted that the dominant group was significantly taller than other lesbian women.[32]

A culturally based approach might just have pointed out that any sample of publicly identifiable US lesbians from the period 1960–68 would probably have been corralled from the local softball team, which would account for all that athletic muscle and butch sexual assertiveness. Liberal socio-biologists do no better: Edward O. Wilson in the 1970s hypothesized that the 'gene of altruism' caused homosexuality, i.e. for the good of the species this meant more adults in the family were available for non-parental functions 'to serve as aunt, uncle, shaman, or medicine man'.[33] Our adjunctive roles, as satellite family members, were envisioned as having purpose only to the extent that we resourced the (primary) function of the robust reproduction of siblings. Endocrinology resurfaced in gay culture in the 1990s with Simon LeVay's research on the male homosexual's hypothalmus (the control tower of the brain which regulates hormones). We can deduce from his research that size *does* matter. Previous endocrinological hypotheses had proposed that androgen turned girls into tomboys[34] and certain masculinizing (e.g. testosterone) and other defeminizing agents in the brain created passive lesbians.[35] There is a wealth of this kind of medical and quasi-empirical research available to the curious reader, another whole book's worth. Universal to these 'ologies is the unstinting equation of female masculinity with the lesbian body – the butch body.

Freud

When changing doctors during my frequent moves, there is always an obligatory inquisition about 'birth control'. To state one doesn't need it is never enough, these agents insist on an explicit confession

> *of homosexuality. I have said repeatedly I do not want this added*
> *to my medical notes. In my most recent relocation I see a female*
> *physician. I go through the familiar process, to the point where I*
> *reiterate clearly: my lesbian identity is not to be written down.*
> *'What do you mean?' she responds. 'It's all over your notes, here,*
> *and here and here… I can't change it anyway, it's against the law'.*
> *It is written: 'homosexual', 'confirmed homosexual', 'practising*
> *homosexual', going back through all the years.*

Freud in his 1920 paper 'The Psychogenesis of a Case of Homosexuality in a Woman' disagreed with gender and sexual polarization, maintaining that homosexual orientation was a blend of physiological and psychical aspects which could not be analytically separated or conflated with gender dysphoria. He observed the following:

> The removal of genital inversion or homosexuality is in my
> experience never an easy matter… in general, to undertake to
> convert a fully developed homosexual into a heterosexual is not
> much more promising than to do the reverse, only that for good
> practical reasons the latter is never attempted.[36]

Freud refused to engage with the biological imperative of much sexology, asserting instead 'It is not for psychoanalysis to solve the problem of homosexuality'.[37] Famously, Freud advocated the view of a fundamental human bisexuality, debunking the idea of the third sex popular with his predecessors: 'in both sexes the degree of physical hermaphroditism is to a great extent independent of the psychical hermaphroditism'.[38] Still, in masculine women, Freud continued to anticipate latent lesbianism. He tended to contradict himself, and even at the end of this same article, when he is commenting on and discouraging the difficult treatment for female homosexuality, he makes an aside regarding the removal of her 'probably hermaphroditic' ovaries, betraying his ambivalence.

Freud's work is renownedly ambiguous and contradictory, not least because he changed his theories over time. Defenders of Freud argue that rather than being prescriptive he was merely offering a prescient theory of the social formation of sexual identity. Whereas the majority of sexologists argued for homosexuals as a distinct physiological species, Freud, generally, tended to ascribe to the subject a process of *homosexual development*. But Freud is notorious for the two founding scenarios of female homosexuality: arrested development/narcissism and penis envy. These prevail in popular conceptions of causes of homosexuality, behind which lurks the butch lesbian. First, the idea of arrested development is read as a formula to explain the 'tomboyish excesses' of the adult, a patronizing assumption that women naturally mature into a demure femininity on becoming sexually active. Narcissism is implicated when the woman puts her own (lesbian) desires before the needs of society's (normative heterosexual reproduction). Penis envy can apply to any lesbian when taken literally: anyone can strap on. But the metaphorical weight is strapped to the butch lesbian – it is she who visibly usurps the patriarchal prerogative by appropriating masculinity, and attracts the hostility that this transgendering produces.

Cross-dressing?

Prior to 1970s feminism many butches adopted the sexologists' view of themselves, that they were a third sex, enacting Foucault's 'reverse discourse' theory[39] and taking the identity of a sex-variant species. This was a credible response to the hegemonic view of homosexuality, which hoped to capitalize on liberal tolerance for a 'natural deviation'. Many lesbians still do take scientific research on the body as proof enough of the natural origins of homosexuality (despite the fact that this work has virtually exclusively concerned gay men). With the accession of the feminist theory of the 1970s that gender was an entirely superficial political accoutrement added to the transcendent ground of the naked body, the perception of butchness changed. Lesbians wondered whether it was politically pragmatic to engage with the presupposition that there is a homosexual body, even with an audience interested in liberating it from oppression. The predominant ideology characterizing the decade after 1968 was the liberatory idea of 'throwing off' the chains of oppression to let the 'real' self escape. Feminists wanted to shake off femininity and unshackle the authentic female body underneath. Displaying the real (naked) Woman became de rigeur at feminist events, which were usually sited in places of natural beauty (wimmin's land) that provided an ideological backdrop to this new naturalism. The unadorned female body was an icon of lesbian feminism, unspoilt by Man. This pastoral utopianism was generally diffused within 1970s counter-culture.

Lesbian feminists forced a radical challenge to the suburban domestication of women during the 1950s, and another contestation over what was considered naturally female.

Butch has been read by lesbians influenced by feminism since the 1970s as being a supplementary identity, one that is 'dressed'. The idea of butch as clothing resonates with the symbolic items of butch identity: ties, shiny belt buckle, black lace-ups, rolled-up sleeves on a blue cotton Oxford shirt, man's analogue watch, argyle socks, boxer shorts, skinny vest, sharp, waxed haircut, dark tailored suits. This is not unlike the maligned 'Saturday Night Butch' of the 1950s and 1960s, who was not considered to be a real butch by the predominantly working-class butches who, at least since the postwar period, refused to 'pass' as heterosexual during the working week. There appears to be a class distinction operating here, one which is underpinned by the pervading class dualism of working-class/butch, middle-class/femme, evidenced most visibly in the way that lesbian chic in the 1990s was so clearly marked as middle-class/bourgeois femme. Ironically, the prevalently middle-class movement of lesbian feminism designated a uniform of working-class butch 'day wear' for the duration of the 1970s: denim, checked shirts, work boots, donkey jackets – these were the symbols for the new agency of female sexual desire. Although adopting 'male-identified' behaviour was anathema to these lesbians, eroticizing cross-class, cross-gender style was not. Idolizing young, working-class white masculinity in butch culture has its history in the leather-clad biker gangs of the 1950s, as Gayle Rubin points out.[40] This glamorous outlaw figure eroticizes rebellion, but also carries the political danger of legitimating a violent hypermasculinity. One might also ask to what extent the remaking of the butch as worker in the 1960s was a reaction against the upper-class butch dandy of the 1920s and 1930s, with its taint of pre-war Fascism.

The new butch body?

The body-as-ground/gender-as-dressing idea predominated for twenty years until the advent of postmodernism and queer theory, which challenged the idea that gender was 'extra' to the body. Butch bodies themselves became stylistically fashioned. The ur-model here was Martina Navratilova; media coverage of her body-building into the 1980s synchronized the desires of a new generation of lesbians nurtured by ideologies of personal achievement, individualism and commodity fetishism. This new butch body was a very American phenomenon: think, for example, of the dumping of Czech Martina for the re-built, honed and blonde Martina; the vitality and fitness of the American body was being idealized. The new 'body culture' of the 1980s drew dykes to the gym in droves. Butch aesthetics became muscle-bound, nouveau macho replacing the finesse of 1950s romanticism. The ethic of chivalry which had enveloped sexual liaisons in previous decades became satirized. In the new performativity an adjectival hardness became intrinsic to the reconstruction of butch. Softness became alluded to with irony, vulnerability being a quality that deflected rather than enforced the designation. One has to ask why butch appeared to homogenize into a brutal, fantasy, hyper-masculinity during the 1980s: did it coincide with a metadiscursive individualistic capitalism into which all women were implicated? Did we have to earn the right to become butch? To what extent did this new butch body belong to the old butch body of sexology?

A crucial modern reinterpretation of butchness developed from the postmodernist emphasis on play. Playfulness with sexual identity coalesced by the end of the decade into the new Queer identity(ies) of the 1990s. Many lesbians felt safer with an idea of butch that they felt they could transcend, taking it on and off at will. The androgyny model occurs when a lesbian maintains she can 'put on' butch or femme, depending on how she feels on the gender scale, at a particular moment. Gender voluntarism underpins the assertion that visible lesbians can always choose to avoid prejudice by dressing up as women. Implicit in this view is a homophobic attempt to diminish the intrinsicality of the butch persona, to imply that, unlike 'sex' markings, it is a temporary and superficial identity. Whereas this may be true for some, for many women their butch identity is felt to be their core identity (or one of their core identities), experienced as a deep self which is there to be expressed. Whilst the 1980s emphasis on fractured and flexible identities enabled many women to explore and experiment with desire in a radical way, lived identities are ontological practices which eventually become formative and constitutive over time. Do they, though, mark the body in any conclusive sense? Perhaps we might ask why the body is elected by many to be the final determinator in any search for an essential identity. Locating the truth of identity *in* the body does have an opprobrious past; likewise searching for signs of truth *on* the body has also resulted in grossly oppressive customs. But, in negotiating the complexity of social belonging, searching for the stable kernel of purpose quietly germinating in the body has an understandable appeal.

Although I have offered a model of historical progression so far, it is important to stress that many groups are not conveniently coherent and do run counter to prevailing discursive changes. There were 'old-time' butches in the bars of the 1970s, 1980s and 1990s, running concurrent with rampant feminist constructionism. The 'old-gay' insistence on their inborn, predestined natures can be judged neither as entirely hegemonic nor as clearly counter-cultural. Setting up the traditional dichotomy between hegemony and resistance does not service the indeterminacy of many practices and identities – acts/states which cannot be fixed, which remain ambiguous. Our deepest sense of ourselves can simultaneously be a commodity to be desired and consumed. But this is not to endorse a conception that appropriation is a simple process, on the contrary, for example, unconscious and obscure psychic structures are fundamental to the mechanisms of identification. Whereas these structures have been used historically to incorporate butchness into sexual pathology, this need not necessarily be the case. The premises of psychoanalysis, that there is a sex/gender system reproduced by unconscious desires, is largely a narrative description of what *is* rather than what could be. Desire is premised on the eroticism of difference through power relations, but this is not a natural law. However seemingly intransigent, however poignantly experienced, lived identities are complicated fictions essential to our social function. Pragmatically speaking, this means that an equivocal response to identity is required: that we tender our theoretical scepticism with an unaffected respect for the way individuals have negotiated their own desire through the swamp of sexual possibilities.

The stone butch

In the interests of problematizing rather than solving the enigma of butchness, I want to focus on its paradigmatic icon: the stone butch. A consideration of stone butchness distils a range of more dispersed reactions, as it is taken to embody both the ideal and the abjected essence of butchness. The stone butch is more than an anthropological type, s/he[41] is an icon, hence s/he incarnates in symbolism a range of desires and taboos. The stone butch belongs to the caste of the untouchables.

The borders of untouchability vary – some butches refuse to be stimulated genitally but will accept stroking of breasts, some permit clitoral contact, others disallow even nakedness in bed. Some will not orgasm, considering that the loss of control in coming instigates a loss of bodily integrity. Crucial to the butch's identity is the setting of some boundary over which a lover may not step. This frontier is set on the physical and the psychic body. Body image has a definitive space, which is not to be transversed. The maintenance of lines of demarcation are inherent to the stone butch persona. S/he creates those barriers in a Foucauldian sense, as lines of power, lines of force.

However fiercely protected, these lines of force are imaginary and can be violated. Indeed, homophobic discourse sets up an imperative that they *must* be, sensing that which will incur a fracturing of selfhood. Institutional harassment of stone butches need not extend to actual rape – being forced to strip for a visual examination can be enough to shatter the bodily imago. Medical and legal state apparatuses enacting their scopophilic desires also succeed in reducing the butch's ontological presence to what they wish to see – a latent womanhood, a vestige of female corporeality. The stripping down, the skinning of a stone butch, is to render the stone butch as an emasculated Woman. This symbolic castration does its violence intrapsychically. The stone butch is forced to 'see' 'her'self in the 'truth' of the body. For example, in *Stone Butch Blues*, young Jess is stripped and locked into a coal bunker by a gang of boys who insist s/he shows them 'how you tinkle'.[42] As Jay Prosser has commented, incidents of sexual violence like this: 'centralize and subjugate Jess's body, serving to exacerbate her shame over its abjection and her identificatory distance from it'.[43] The shame is spread across her whole body, and its effect is clearly to separate, and smash, the self.

The metaphor of penetration surrounds the stone butch. The eroticism of butch identity is located in the desire to unwrap her, that s/he holds a forbidden secret: a woman's body. Uncovering this body, penetrating the butch's defences, is sometimes the goal of successful sex, as though the admission of vulnerability, in intimacy, is the *sine qua non* of sex. Is it 'real' sex unless the butch has been penetrated? Some would say this is the defining moment, when that secret has been given up, the truth has been breached. There is more than a little sadism involved here, reminiscent of the heterosexual woman who retains power over her man by being the sole repository of his vulnerability. This seems to me to be one of the cruelties of love, emanating from the power struggle peculiar to desire. By extension, one has to wonder what desire drives homophobia to exact the same punishment, where penetration is an intention to break, to destroy, the seamless form of stone identity. One is reminded of the fate of Brandon Teena, the young stone Nebraskan who passed as a man, who was raped and murdered as a result of police provocation and collusion. An interview with contemporary stone butch Kris Kovic in *Girlfriends* magazine counters the hostility of homophobia with this explanation:

> Being stone is just a limiter... Heterosexuality draws limits all the time: 'I don't do those things. I don't take it up the butt. Only a woman sucks my dick,' or whatever. They are stone about their preferences and that's fine. But whatever people say about homosexuality is pathologized.[44]

The butch/femme system circulates around conceptions of womanhood. In an opposition consisting of the failed Woman and the idealized Woman, the stone butch goes one further, as s/he is the abnegation of Woman. The stone butch is lesbianism's martyr; s/he carries a Christ-like burden of being at once the most perfect embodiment and the most reviled sacrifice. The stone butch's renunciation of womanhood is both sacred and profane. The archetype in twentieth-century lesbian culture is Stephen Gordon in *The Well of Loneliness*, a novel rife with Christian imagery:

> They were calling her by name saying 'Stephen, Stephen!' The quick, the dead and the yet unborn... '... speak with your God and ask Him why He had left us forsaken!' ... They possessed her. Her barren womb became fruitful – it ached with its fearful and sterile burden. It ached with the fierce yet helpless children who would clamour in vain for their right to salvation... They would cry out accusing: 'We have asked for bread; will you give us a *stone*'.[45] [my italics]

The elevatory power of her final soliloquy is a fine piece of melodramatic rhetoric, calculated to endow Stephen with the stigmata of a divine victim: heady symbolism indeed. Stephen sacrifices her desire for her lover Mary's, as she sees it. The structure – that the actively (phallic) desiring woman refuses her own desire in order that the Woman's desire may be centred replays a warped feminist dynamic intended to release Women's desire. However, Stephen's sacrifice is predicated on a fundamental misreading of Mary – she reads Mary as a Woman, the idealized category, rather than as a woman and a femme. Stephen is blind to Mary's femme desire for her. Like the conventional male, she does not see or trust that Mary's desire is active and autonomous. Confusing the idea of Woman and women's desire is still a weakness of butch behaviour; taking on the active phallic and masculine desiring position does not prevent butches from colluding with the elision of feminine desire.

Central to the stone butch identity is an abjection, a suffusion of shame, which is internalized. Peeling off the protective layers of a stone butch, one will eventually uncover the evidence of her body, which in a reproduction of sexological discourse reduces her to a damaged or incomplete femaleness. A reoccurring trope of the butch body is that she is a failed Woman. The core conception at work here is of the Woman as 'O'. If Woman is a hole, a blank space, a receptacle, waiting to be filled, to be inscribed, then a stone butch who renounces penetration throws that desire back onto itself; s/he is a solipsism, s/he closes the circle. The stone butch is a strongly bounded identity. The stone butch resists the permeability of the conventional Woman; rape is her inimitable humiliation.[46] S/he erects a psychic shield between the body and the world, and is read symbolically as a warrior or an outlaw. Crucially, s/he has individuated the self, s/he has 'exited the patriarchy', s/he exists in a separable sphere.

The bathroom

I am visiting Warwick Castle, a popular tourist attraction in central England. I enter the toilet facility labelled 'Ladies'. On the way in I pass two people who exclaim indignantly 'That's not a woman!'. I ignore them and lock myself in a cubicle. Seconds later there is a loud banging on the door and shouts of 'Open up!'. I reclothe myself and open the closet door to face a confrontation with the attendant, who has apparently been told there is a man in the toilet. Firstly she demands that I leave immediately: I refuse. Doubt enters, she surveys my body and asks aggressively and repeatedly 'Well – are you a man or a woman?'. The attendant is an immigrant doing a shit job, and I don't know whether she's been ordered to do this by the well turned-out white women who complained, or whether her hostility is masking defensiveness. I don't know whether to act aggrieved, or appease. Finally, as the many other occasions of toilet harassment queue up in my consciousness, I tell her 'What do you think?', shut the door, and get on with it.

In the USA toilets are called bathrooms, even when there are no washing facilities in evidence. I was amused to find that in sites of particular transience, such as the highway or the beach, the toilet was euphemized more quixotically as the 'comfort station'.[47] This 'nice-nellyism' smacks of sexual services, an irony not lost on a European. In Britain the public bathroom is more prosaically English; the public toilet is more specifically gendered and class-specific. The intention is that females attend the 'Ladies' and males the 'Gents'. For me, it is the discomfort station. Recently, after enduring years of harassment when trying to avail myself of facilities offered in the 'Ladies' I've started to use the third alternative: the disabled toilet. In Britain the disabled toilet, like the third sex, is placed between the Ladies and the Gents. It is generally more roomy, you can turn around in it, and carry in with you all the baggage you desire. Used by variously sexed individuals, the disabled toilet, with its generous full-length mirror, offers a space for reflection. In there I can strip off my gender-dysphoric regalia, lengthily scrutinize every extra roll of fat in the fluorescent light (there is never a queue), and yield to a vulnerability I would not contemplate in the Ladies next door. For me, it is a stress-free location, a queer space in which I can momentarily procure an interval from the gendered public environment, and psychically replenish.

Conversely, the disabled toilet is also a room set aside for the disjunctive, ungendered and strange. The disabled toilet provides isolated privacy and secrecy for the marked body. In the intimacy of bathroom culture, the bodily differentiated are required to use this separated sphere. Entering and leaving the door branded 'disabled', I anxiously scan the floor, rather than acknowledge I have been seen. Using this toilet is inflected by shame. I am treading on another borderline, not 'worthily' disabled, but certainly afflicted. It is at once a perfect and a false designation, the same positioning simultaneously dis- and en-abling.

The uncomfortable feeling that a butch in the Ladies' toilet provokes is an open recognition of Sexuality, and hence the homophobic cries of

'Is that a man or a woman?' are Althusserian interpellations and calculated, knowing attempts to deny the sexual presence. This butch stands for sexual *knowledge*, both within lesbian culture and in Woman's culture. Motorway service stations are by butch consensus the worst places for this kind of abuse. They are so bad precisely because they are anxious places of transition, hence known boundaries must be even more vigorously enforced, and unsettling eruptions of desire denied.[48] The public toilet is a breach-zone between public and private, between gender and the body. The butch belies the myth of gender separatism, heterosexual binarism. She instigates female homosexual panic amongst the women, a violent reaction which betrays the disturbing belief that sexuality is the solvent of stable identities.[49] Leo Bersani has identified one rationale for homophobia as a reaction against the fear of recruitment; homophobia produces the 'fearful excitement at the prospect of becoming what one already is'.[50] Although the butch can signal the 'gay presence', she also metonymically signifies the 'gay absence', in the sense that the butch nudges the straight's paranoia that we are indeed everywhere, and often deceptively disguised as the same. Take this passage from Bersani:

> [Judith] Butler emphasises the dangers for the social system of 'permeable bodily boundaries'. Homosexual sex – especially sex between men – is a threatening 'boundary-trespass', a site of danger and pollution for the social system represented synecdochically by the body.[51]
>
> Any activity or condition that exposes the permeability of bodily boundaries will simultaneously expose the factious nature of sexual differences as they are postulated within the heterosexual matrix.[52]

In a complex fermentation of associations, bodily discharge/inside-out, shit/homosexual, butch masculinity/'female' body, nakedness/sex, a number of boundaries tremble. Toilets are liminal spaces; the butch is a liminal identity. The butch in the toilet is like a science-fictional trope, when the 'real' breaks down and becomes the 'possible'.

The closet is *the* signatory metaphor of modern gay identity.[53] Going into the Ladies produces an inverse dynamic: she leaves the anonymity of the public space – which in this scenario functions as the closet – in order to claim (female) body essentialism, in the Ladies. The restroom hopes to provide relief from the labour of concealment. But the butch in the toilet is already ill at ease with the movement of entering the 'Ladies' space, as she is so often 'outed' as not-Woman. Her anxiety can be cruelly exploited. In the toilet she locks the door, and 'ins' (her)self. On re-emerging into the semi-public space she is shamed by rebuke and revulsion, producing a tormenting confirmation of her outlaw status. Conversely, on leaving altogether, she can sometimes return to the safety of passing on the street.

The public toilet is a place of exposure as much as concealment, predeterminedly eroticized with Western codes of sexual excitement. A Freudian would see the shame co-existent with physical excreta metonymically writing itself over the entire body – witness the ritualistic shame behaviours evident in any visit to the 'Ladies' (avoidance of direct eye or physical contact, assiduous hand-washing). Notice also the titillation which brushes it. Toilets produce moisture and warmth. Toilets have not received the same kind of fetishized attention in lesbian culture that they have had in gay men's. The eroticism of sodomy and the concomitant scatological fantasies of gay male literature are not generally mirrored in lesbian porn, except in occasional s/m leather writing. But Joan Nestle's 'The Bathroom Line' plays on the more specifically lesbian ambivalence towards toilets in bars, in a short piece defining the parameters of the lesbian underworld during the 1950s:

> But the most searing reminder of our colonised world was the bathroom line. Now I know it stands for all the pain and glory of my time, and I carry that line and the women who endured it deep within me. Because we were labelled deviants, our bathroom habits had to be watched. Only one woman at a time was allowed into the toilet because we could not be trusted. Thus the toilet line was born, a twisting horizon of Lesbian women waiting for permission to urinate, to shit.
>
> The line flowed past the far wall, past the bar, the front room tables, and reached into the back room. Guarding the entrance to the toilet was a short square, handsome butch woman, the same every night, whose job it was to twist around her hand our allotted amount of toilet paper. She was [to] us, a man's obscenity, doing the man's tricks so we could breathe. The line awaited all of us every night, and we developed a line act. We joked, we cruised, we

commented on the length of time one of us took, we made special pleas to allow hot and heavy lovers in together, knowing full well that our lady would not permit it. I stood, a femme, loving the women on either side of me, loving my comrades for their style, the power of their stance, the hair hitting the collar, the thrown-out hip, the hand encircling the beer can. Our eyes played the line, subtle touches, gentle shyness weaved under the blaring jokes, the music, the surveillance. We lived on that line: restricted and judged, we took deep breaths and played.

But buried deep in our endurance was our fury. That line was practice and theory seared into one. We wove our freedoms, our culture, around the obstacles of hatred, but we also paid our price. Every time I took the fistful of toilet paper, I swore eventual liberation. It would be, however, liberation with a memory.[54]

For the femme, the co-existence of masculinity with the female body in the butch incarnates a particular lesbian eroticism. This narrative emanation of the contradictions of the toilet space manages to display the heroics of the abjected (both butch and femme): the trick is to play on, despite the derision. The spatial metaphor of the bathroom line carousing through the bar adeptly illustrates the discursive limits of both parties. The frisson occurs in the juxtaposition between shame and pleasure; pushing the edges of the forbidden produces a highly erotic anger.

Butch as fetish/the lesbian phallus

The butch, as the masculine woman, is perceived as actively desiring; she is the *subject* of desire. In Freudian terms, she has the power of desire and carries the symbol: the phallus. For feminism, this is inevitably problematic, collapsing, as it does, active sexual desire with a masculine – or effectively male – position. Hence the denial that butches 'suffer' from penis envy – we do not want to be seen as failed, castrated males, and yet that is the logic of heterosexism. In psychoanalytic terms, butches manifest the 'masculinity complex', a kind of psychic disturbance which originated in a futile attempt to identify with and impress a real or symbolic father figure – a mission we are bound to fail in, pathologically shamed as we are by the lack of a 'real' organ. Within the heterosexual economy of desire, the foundational structure of difference – man/woman, active/passive – is intrinsic and essential to heterosexuality's reproduction. Within heterosexuality, difference and antagonism are eroticized. Difference produces desire, and so the heterosexual woman has a nugatory, displaced desire – she desires to desire. Her desire is enabled by her proximity to a phallus. Thus, as de Lauretis quips: 'Put in a nutshell: All women equally have penis envy, but lesbians have it more'.[55]

The most fundamental trope of desire in contemporary thought is the idea of a split construction between self and other. Bersani argues that this organization is so naturalized that we fail to see it as it is – the result of a trauma (the little boy's 'flight to the father following a horrified retreat from women').[56] Bersani, Andrew Sullivan[57] and Monique Wittig[58] appear to be arguing for a new, less aggressive erotics based on sameness, something Sheila Jeffreys has also argued for in her rhetorical polemic *The Lesbian Heresy*.[59] Sameness, in traditional psychoanalytic discourse, produces identification. Eroticism based on sameness has generally been scoffed at by lesbians who do not subscribe to lesbian feminism, predicated as it is on producing empathy and identification between women as notional equals. It is tempting to proscribe sameness as a radical restructuring of desire. Certainly the intention would be to level the hierarchic jealousy underpinning self/other. Potentially, the idea is a truly revolutionary one. But the present mundane, nascent, re-enactments of the erotics of sameness, in butch/butch and femme/femme scenarios, have yet to convince me, each set tending to define itself against a despised and repudiated other – the former against a caricatured 'Barbified' femininity, the latter against the masculinized Lesbian of popular (homophobic) consensus. The erotics of sameness often mobilize against a repudiated other; the organizing structure of difference is more intransigent than we had hoped. In Sheila Jeffreys's work, for instance, as in much historical lesbian feminism, any form of masculine identification is an anathema. I speculate whether the (jealous?) rage that counterposes some of the homilitic excesses of woman-identified feminism can be flipped into a destructive desire for dominance. For all desire, whether it is based on identification or disidentification, contains within it, at the very least, an element of aggressivity.[60]

My own experience of a butch/butch relationship quintessentialized the familiar dilemma – did I want her or want to be her? The concomitant battle for dominance was perpetual, exhilarating and annihilative (someone kept having to lose) and, unfortunately, absolutely erotic. The butch embodies a potent fusion of female desire; as de Lauretis has said, she is both desiring subject and desiring object.[61] The butch, as a highly coded romantic figure of lesbianism, is the object of an active, omni-gendered female desire. In the extract from *A Restricted Country* quoted above ('the power of their stance, the hair hitting the collar, the thrown-out hip, the hand encircling the beer can') it is the butch body which is eroticized. The butch compounds this dichotomy of the self and other; she is both. And more – the butch is an excess: de Lauretis again:

> the butch-femme role-playing is exciting not because it represents heterosexual desire but because it doesn't; that is to say, in mimicking it, it shows the uncanny distance, like an effect of ghosting, between desire (heterosexually represented as it is) and the representation; and because the representation doesn't fit the actors who perform it, it only points to their investment in a fantasy – a fantasy that can never fully represent them or their desire, for the latter remains in excess of its setting, the fantasy that grounds it, and that continues to ground it even as it is deconstructed and destabilized by the mis-en-scène [*sic*] of lesbian camp.[62]

Here is the nitty-gritty of butch/femme, the idea that like all genders it is performative.[63] Butch/femme, as the playful representation of masculinity and femininity, enacts a fantasy of deferred pleasure, one in which the apotheosis of masculinity and femininity is never reached. Like all desire, it is both beyond and more, an impossibility, simultaneously found and lost.

The corollary here is in the concept of the phallus, such a powerful focus for desire, and yet utterly unobtainable. Playing with accoutrements like the dildo crystallizes this perfectly. Fitting the plastic penis onto the female body simultaneously yearns for and derides phallic power; the masquerade is both homage and burlesque. The dildo metonymically represents the phallic woman – reinserting femaleness and lack as it also extrapolates the fantasy of forceful desire. The butch wielding a dildo is an auto-erotic spectacle. This fantasy imago is the corrective corollary to the shamed castrated butch of homophobic fable. We encounter the pairing of pride and shame, ideal and scorned. The butch is either the magical sign of lesbianism or a failed, emasculated and abjected man, either supra-active or semi-passive. The 'gender dysphoric' (the effeminate male homosexual, MTF or FTM) is the butch's closest relative. Positing the role as performative is not the same as saying it is a voluntaristic one – the lived experience of butchness lies somewhere between the two.

Judith Butler in 'The Lesbian Phallus and the Morphological Imaginary'[64] rereads Lacan's distinction between the phallus and the penis *back* through the mirror stage, arguing that this reading reveals that despite Lacan's proclamations to the contrary, there remains an ontological connection (albeit negatively) between the phallus and the penis. Teresa de Lauretis, on the other hand, takes issue with Butler's framework of the lesbian phallus and argues to circumvent this seemingly inevitable connection through the discourse of the fetish, which 'serves as the sign or signifier of prohibition, difference and desire, without which the lesbian lovers would be simply, so to speak, two women in the same bed'.[65] The author becomes more precise:

> in a cultural tradition pervasively homophobic masculinity alone carries a strong connotation of sexual desire for the female body. *That* is the lure of the mannish lesbian – a lure for her and for her lover. The fetish of masculinity is what both lures and signifies her desire for the female body, and what in her lures her lover, what her lover desires in her *and with her*.[66] [original emphasis]

The fetish always stands for the lost object of the female body. What a lesbian wants is not identification, but for the M(Other) to desire her. It is tempting to relate this loss ('my mother never loved me') to the often melancholic, wounded quality of lesbian love. Being wounded is pandemic to literary butches (Stephen Gordon, Jess Goldberg). Whether the wound is caused by i) being a 'Woman'; ii) being 'castrated'; iii) losing the Mother; or iv) homophobia is unascertainable, but in this purview it appears to be 'The Lesbian Condition'. Lesbian self-mutilation has been read as the mark of the castrated subject, a morbid association which the contemporary fashion for piercing, cutting, scarring and tattooing has not totally dispelled. Marking – puncturing – the lesbian body has a contentious history. Still within subject/object relations, the fetish seems to be desire for the whole and healed female body, the one in the mirror so much more perfect and bounded than our own. Can the butch be reduced to repetitively, neurotically, regrouping the desired and lost object, the fantasy whole female body? To problematize further, is the butch's desire for the whole body really for the body of the other, or an introjected fantasy of/for her own?

What use are these formulations to the way we think about the butch body? Circulating images of castration, the phallus-as-power, the lost M(Other) – these ideas are projects embedded within psychoanalysis, a concept of limited use in explaining lesbian desire, as Elizabeth Grosz has pointed out in her review of de Lauretis' book.[67] Eroticizing masculinity is not estranged from heteropatriarchy, rather it is endemic to it. The fusion of masculinity with femaleness becomes the amalgam that is the butch body, which is the taboo. The reviling of the butch in culture is contaminated with desire and fascination, and as the trope of lesbianism she carries the symbolic load of oppositional appetites. Butch makes masculinity strange, defamiliarizing. A consequence of idealizing phallic butchness is that femininity can be degraded, seen as swampy ground to be resisted and transcended; or the femme, by constrast, is perceived as 'fortunately' gender-congruent, and hence *complicit* with heterosexuality. Perhaps the femme has the really perverse desire as the actively desiring hyperfeminine woman.

Synthesis: is there such a thing as a butch body?

Nineteenth- and early-twentieth-century sexologists were complicit in using the colonial discourse of raced and 'hysterical' bodies. Sustaining the classificatory project of imperialism (to *know* and implicitly to own the other), they tried to identify, by scientific analysis, the lesbian body. Notions of the invert tried to fix the 'real' lesbian in a body quintessentially represented by narrow hips, broad shoulders and surly bearing – a butch body. An enlarged clitoris or labia also came to stand for lesbianism, in a discourse which collapsed 'nymphomania' and 'prostitution' into a morally determined morass of sexual 'deviation'.[68] Recent biologistic bids to legitimize homosexuality with reference to the hypothalmus or claims of a gay gene, in order to naturalize liberal discourse of 'different but equal', have been open to co-optation by the political right as reasons to promote eugenic imperatives. (You can have your homosexual baby aborted.) It is an area of research fraught with reactionary consequences. Whilst aware of these dangers, I still maintain that the attempts by lesbians themselves to locate their desire in a unique corporeality must be respected as explorations in making material the invisible, and of speaking and claiming something which has historically been either silenced or sensationalized. The politics of articulation are highly contested, here, and imply many risks.

Centrally, the argument rests on whether the evidence of a metaphorical trope of the lesbian body image has material effects in the creation of a manifested, organic lesbian body. I suggest that at certain moments and in certain contexts there is, but this is not to argue that there is an original body out of which lesbianism can be expressed as symptomatic. Lesbian sexual behaviour is mapped on to a body which is always in a state of flux, changing in relation to the inscribing effects of social power surrounding it.[69] The dualism apparent between social constructionism and essentialism in academic feminist criticism is slowly being deconstructed.[70] Whereas in the 1970s and 1980s the predominant focus for feminist theory was on the purely ideological construction of gender, in the 1990s there has been a growing interest in the way sexed bodies become affects, products, of social discourse (Grosz, 1994). If the 'new' sexual difference (male/female bodies) is perceived as partly or wholly a result of ideology (and certainly the *organization* of this dualism seems to result from a heterosexist prerogative (Butler, 1990)), then the split idea of the body as ground and ideology as lawn-dressing can no longer be sustained.

The designation 'butch' as an erotic identification in lesbian culture is an association of the body with a set of meanings and signs specific to a particular cultural and historical context. Certainly eroticism has been ascribed to the lesbian since social and fictional writings began. This eroticism shifts and alters according to time and according to the subject position of the speaker. Lesbianism is about sex, which is at the same time in and of the body, as well as in the mind. In this chapter I have explored the idea that there may be such a thing as the lesbian and, specifically, the butch body (or bodies). How might this body express/contain/manifest/'embody' lesbian desire(s)? Is it possible, in a particular time/space, to name? Is it expedient, given the repressive apparatuses' attempts to control and police difference, to claim this endeavour?

85

Images of permeability structure both dominant and subcultural versions of butchness. The butch body is constituted as corporeal fastness, fixity, but also as containing boundaries being breached through vulnerability. The fascination with breaching those boundaries present in intimate relations – the idea that the butch's surface constitutes an implicit challenge to *penetrate* – implies a sacrifice of self not similarly gestured in femme-sex. To puncture the unwilling butch is to perform a symbolic castration. Images of penetration, therefore, surround/enclose/suffuse the (butch) lesbian aesthetic. What does this sacrifice (with all that word's connotations) imply? Are the mechanisms of desire designed to destroy the butch's inscrutability in the same way whether perpetrated by a sexologist or a lover? Butch-baiting persists within the lesbian community, where butch as a sign continues to carry the despised weight of lesbianism. This relates too to femme-phobia, in that mistaken belief that femmes can never be true lesbians.

Butches are frequently marked by the suspicion of a hidden trauma, an internally damaged psyche. Butches are bestowed an inner wound, a symbolic castration sublimely evoking Womanhood. The causes are differentiated, but the infantilization of the butch persists: i) the myth of the butch's emotional immaturity, the association with childlikeness, in sexological literature or in lesbian narratives which, for example, depict her crying like a baby after the (infrequent) act of coming; ii) the idea of butch narcissism (the gaze the butch directs at herself), the 'obsessional' checking of appearance, the parting of the hair in the mirror, the measuring against other butches, recalling the Freudian construction of arrested development on the universal path to heterosexuality. Does the shame of being around an idealized heterosexual masculinity make us internalize a conviction that we cannot 'make it' without an organic dick? Why is the ethos of competition, the teasing for being a failed butch between butches so prevalent; why do we tolerate the anxiety that we will never 'measure up'? The stake in masculinity is necessarily insecure as butches know and have appropriated its ambiguous functionality. The butch evokes the parameters of an idealized Womanhood and an idealized Manhood, and simultaneously deconstructs those paradigms signalling the fuzzy continuum Woman>Man.

Dualisms of outside and inside rule the butch existence. Butch is a liminal state, which the concomitant obsession with boundaries exposes. The conventional association of lesbianism with outlawry, and the butch's distillation of social ostracism, pre-empts (her) vacillation between outside and inside constructions of social space. She is predeterminedly outside. But the butch also peculiarly embodies corporeal metaphors of space, in the embattled space she occupies, the boundaries of selfhood are heroically defended. But osmosis as a process of disruption is an effect of desire: in sex the boundaries of the body melt and merge. Within that tenderness is a sometimes violent and destructive assault on the subject's autonomy. Catherine Waldby, writing on the heterosexual male body, contends:

> Erotic pleasure arguably requires a kind of momentary annihilation or suspension of what normally counts as 'identity', the conscious, masterful, self-identical self, lost in the 'little death' of orgasm. These momentary suspensions, when linked together in the context of a particular relationship, work toward a more profound kind of ego destruction... each lover is refigured by the other, made to bear the mark of the other upon the self. But all such transformation involves the breaking down of resistance, of violence to an existing order of the ego.[71]

Men cannot tolerate the infringement on their selfhood by another, seeking instead to be the destroyer of women's egos, reformulating and dissipating them – she conforms to, accommodates, his ego. Waldby, addressing the 'homosexual panic' defence used in queerbashing cases, points out how any form of penetration is read as an absolute violation by the heterosexual male. She qualifies this by reminding us of the gendering of certain acts: 'Anal eroticism carries disturbingly feminizing connotations'.[72] (This reminds me of the historical association of lesbianism with sodomy.)[73] Waldby's article describes the 'monotonous imagos' of a moribund heterosexuality. Butch sexuality procures aspects of this masculine mechanism and perverts them: whereas in heterosexual masculinity 'the rest of the body is drained of erotic potential in favour of its localisation in the penis',[74] in butch sexuality all surfaces carry erotic signification, distributing the fixed phallus of heterosexual masculinity across the body. In butch sexuality, though, the instability of the subjectivity of the butch – in the sometimes shamed perception that there is a 'woman' underneath – means that that penetration of her boundaries is to be feared. Shame produces a shattering of the self. Shame is also a Woman. It is this conjunction which makes the butch's fantasy of impermeability simultaneously sad and brave. The butch knows full well the momentary annihilation of sex. The toil and exertion expended in the maintenance of her boundaries of selfhood in a hostile world can be temporarily relaxed. Her vulnerability is fetishized in lesbian culture because it is her pleasure and pain which mark the preservation and continuance of a lesbian identity. For the butch, sex is profoundly important because it can be the one place she is allowed to refigure the self without shame. Hence the romantic bathos of butch identity, in the crippling grief of a ruined love affair her sense of self is demolished, lost and she is reduced once again to an open wound.

Or – we can look at butch in another way: in Elizabeth Grosz's essay on 'Refiguring Lesbian Desire'[75] she produces a critique of the idea of wanting to be a lesbian or to command a lesbian identity, which she reads as a mistaken (though understandable) ontological effort. Presumably, Grosz would see 'butch' as a comparable trap. Dumping the Lacanian lack model of desire,[76] she traces Spinoza through critical theorists such as Deleuze, Guattari and Lingis, expanding their work to suggest a new conception of the lesbian body as surface, and sexual desire as positively productive, intense, momentary, connective, 'aim[ing] at nothing in particular, above and beyond its own self-expansion, its own proliferation'.[77] Desire is not fixed in any irretrievable phallic imago, but just an instant in the combustion of nerves, a spurt of energy, a momentary pullulation – a real event – 'surface effects between one thing and another';[78] moreover:

> The sites most intensely invested always occur at a conjunction, an interruption, a point of machinic connection; they are always surface effects between one thing and another – between a hand and a breast, a tongue and a cunt, a mouth and food, a nose and a rose. In order to understand this notion, we have to abandon our habitual understanding of entities as the integrated totality of parts, and instead we must focus on the elements, the parts... the coming together of two surfaces produces a tracing that imbues both of them with eros or libido.[79]

This is joy-full desire, the excess, the ecstasy, indeed the *ek-stasis* of sex, taking us out of ourselves. I propose that the butch is the ur-model of this new lesbian body, for butch sexuality does foreground the eroticism of surfaces, prioritizing touch over depth. She is Grosz's new kind of 'lesbian-machine'.[80] She is constituted by the reciprocity of touch, by the abrasion of surfaces, hence the hands as the primary agent of touch are a privileged sign in butch/femme writing. This touch does not even have to be physical; for example Minnie Bruce Pratt, on first seeing her butch lover *S/HE*, writes:

> Twice, three times, without moving in any other way, she let her eyes drift toward me, an almost invisible movement, delicate as breath exhaled on my cheek by a stranger leaning across me on a crowded dance floor. As her cool gaze touched my hot one, I tremored between my legs.[81]

Judith Halberstam's essay on transsexuals, 'F2M: The Making of Female Masculinity',[82] denaturalizes the gendered body by making the surface area of (trans)sex organic or plastic:

> we all derive a different degree of pleasure – sexual or otherwise – from our costumes. It is just that for some of us our costumes are made of fabric or material, while for others they are made of skin; for some an outfit can be changed; for others skin must be resewn.[83]

Skin, here, is a costume, but not one that contains an essential corporeality, a fixed being, layers of ontology, inside it:

> The cross-dressing sexuality is worn outside the body like another skin, it replaces anatomy in the chain of signifiers that eventually stabilizes into something like a sexual identity: sexual identity in this model is a surface that hides and is hidden, an outfit that covers and lays bare. ... There is, in fact, nothing naked about nakedness; it is simply another costume, a skin costume that may or may not fit.[84]

Minnie Bruce Pratt illustrates the analogy in *S/HE* when she eroticizes her approach in a familiar butch tableau: 'I am the woman who touches the shirt, startled to be so translated to a place I think I've never been.'[85] Romantic, to be sure, but to foreground the erotic energy of contiguity, to privilege the interactivity of sex, to incite pleasure in another for its own sake through the contact of surfaces, this is the remarkable eroticism of 'butch magic', as it is colloquially called. An insubstantial, moving surface in its conjunction with another momentarily creates sex; sex is *made* by this friction. Morbidifying the butch who always wears a T-shirt in bed is to misread the signals: the clothes carry all the erotic significance of skin, as does the silicon dildo, or the leather which hangs it.

It is futile to search for a deep meaning resident within the interiority of the butch body, but butch does function as a multivalent sign. Critic Johanna Blakeley offers a short comment on Julia Kristeva's treatment of 'abjection' in *Powers of Horror*: 'Kristeva proposes abjection as the experience of disrupted "identity, system, order" which occurs when "borders, positions, rules" are made ambiguous' (p. 4).[86] Referring in passing to abjection's close relation to *jouissance*, this strikes me as a dualism coming perilously close to the butch's charge as a liminal figure. Judith Butler has written[87] on the way the role of the abjected is to occupy 'unliveable' and 'uninhabitable' zones outside the bounds of the subject, the subject whose domain is circumscribed by this repudiation. In a way, the abjected is dematerialized into excess, but she is also accorded a paradoxical freedom with which to *dis*identify, thus mobilizing desire rather than subjectivity. The disidentification is forced by the shaming of the butch, who is disconnected from social belonging. The butch's reconstruction of the self is a reaction against the self-shattering violence of homophobia. In the crafting of a new and bounded self, the butch displaces homophobia by erecting lines of force, which are simultaneously constituted by and a refusal of shame. Here, she consciously attracts and rebuts homophobia. This bounded identity is a result of specific social and psychic histories, not least of which is a repudiation of the femininity which is read as representing a loss of self, or a dangerous intersubjectivity, in counterpoint to the butch's refounding of a fantasized hermetic self. But the butch continues to mourn the self which was lost, because the logic of her existence is desire, and lack is intrinsic to the formation of a self. The butch, in honour of and in spite of herself, brushes across, against, these boundaries, disturbs them and commutes them into a place of melancholy or a place of joy.

> *My butchness is consolidated by touch: the touch of a plain white T-shirt against my breasts, the touch of my hand-tailored Yorkshire worsted jacket, the touch of a woman on my jacket. My butchness is a series of layers which shield me and pleasure me. My clothes are a metonym for the sexual self I have built. A lover understands that to peel these away will not take her deeper. A lover tells me I am beautiful: I say no, but I can live with handsome. Handsome is as handsome does.*

Notes

1. On this point see Ann Cvetkovich, 'Untouchability and vulnerability: stone butchness as emotional style', in Sally R. Munt (ed.), *Butch/Femme: Inside Lesbian Gender*. London: Cassell, 1997, pp. 159–69. Untouchability, however, is not the sole preserve of butches. Stone *femmes* also refuse the permeability of bodily boundaries. The relationship between stone femmes and gender configurations of masculinity and femininity has yet to be explored.

2. Katie King, 'Audre Lorde's lacquered layerings', in S. R. Munt, *New Lesbian Criticism*. Hemel Hempstead/New York: Harvester Wheatsheaf/Columbia University Press, 1992, pp. 51–74.

3. Judy Grahn, *Another Mother Tongue*. Boston: Beacon Press, 1984, p. 158.

4. And by transporting meaning from appropriated cultures; c.f. 'shaman' above.

5. See Joan Nestle, *A Restricted Country*. London: Sheba Feminist Press, 1988; Joan Nestle (ed.), *The Persistent Desire*. Boston: Alyson Publications, 1992, including articles by Dorothy Allison, Madeline Davis and Amber Hollibaugh; Lisa Duggan and Katie Kent, *A Femme Manifesto* (forthcoming); see also various chapters in Munt, *Butch/Femme: Inside Lesbian Gender*.

6. Gayle Rubin, 'Of catamites and kings: reflections on butch, gender, and boundaries', in Joan Nestle (ed.), *The Persistent Desire*. Boston: Alyson Publications, 1992, pp. 466–82, p. 467.

7. A similarly crude and common-sense scale is applied to heterosexuality/homosexuality, with bisexuality somehow perfectly balanced in the middle.

8. *Butch/Femme*. Channel Four, 16 September 1995. Dir. Emma Hindley, London: Polari Productions, 1995.

9. Jo Ann Loulan, *The Lesbian Erotic Dance*. San Francisco: Spinsters Book Co., 1990, p. 219.

10. *Ibid.*, p. 222.

11. *Ibid.*, p. 216.

12. The question asks the respondent to state in which class they were *raised*. Therefore arguably this proportion could be higher, given that most questionnaires were obtained from conferences, requiring money and mobility to attend.

13. *Ibid.*, p. 48.

14. Rubin, 'Of catamites and kings', p. 475.

15. I've done this myself: enough said.

16. Rubin, 'Of catamites and kings', p. 469.

17. Judith Butler, *Gender Trouble: Feminism and the Subversion of Identity*. New York: Routledge, 1990.

18. Karl Westphal, 'The contrary sexual feeling: symptom of a neuropathic (psychopathic) condition' ['Die conträre Sexualempfindung. Symptom eines neuropathischen (psychopathischen) Zustandes'], *Archiv für Psychiatrie und Nervenkrankheiten*, 2 (1), 1869: 73–108.

19. See Jonathan Ned Katz, *The Invention of Heterosexuality*. New York: Plume/Penguin Books, 1996.

20. Richard von Krafft-Ebing, 'Congenital sexual inversion in woman', in 'General Pathology', *Psychopathia Sexualis, with Especial Reference to the Antipathetic Sexual Instinct: A Medico-Forensic Study*. Trans. from the 12th German edn by

Franklin S. Klaf. New York: Stein and Day, 1965, pp. 262–72, p. 263.

21. *Ibid.*, pp. 290–1.

22. Charlotte Wolff, *Magnus Hirschfeld: A Portrait of a Pioneer in Sexology.* London: Quartet Books, 1986, p. 37. Others have argued that it was more likely to have been Edward Carpenter or Havelock Ellis. My thanks to Laura Doan for this observation.

23. Quoted in Vern Bullough, *Science in the Bedroom: A History of Sex Research.* New York: Basic Books, p. 82.

24. This prurience is displaced upon the 'other other' too – when lesbians 'gender-congruent' with their womanhood wish to police their boundary by excluding lesbians who before sex-reassignment surgery were male. There is a thin line between the intrigue evident in our response to passing women and stone butches and the horror we rally when those individuals cross over into male identity. The porous walls of lesbian identity are impossible to patrol.

25. See, for example, Harry Oosterhuis, 'Richard von Krafft-Ebing's "Step-children of nature": psychiatry and the making of homosexual identity', in Vernon Rosario (ed.), *Science and Homosexualities.* New York: Routledge, 1996, pp. 89–107.

26. See Sander Gilman, *Difference and Pathology: Stereotypes of Sexuality, Race, and Madness.* Ithaca, NY: Cornell University Press, 1985.

27. Frank S. Caprio, *Female Homosexuality: A Psychodynamic Study of Lesbianism.* New York: The Citadel Press, 1954, Preface, p. viii.

28. *Ibid.*, p. ix.

29. *Ibid.*, p. 22.

30. *Ibid.*, p. 178.

31. For a fascinating analysis on the symbolism of the clitoris in sexology, see Margaret Gibson, 'Clitoral corruption: body metaphors and American doctors' construction of female homosexuality 1870–1900', in V. Rosario, *Science and Homosexualities*, pp. 108–32.

32. Muriel Wilson Perkins, 'Female homosexuality and body build', *Archives of Sexual Behaviour*, 10 (1981): 337–45, quoted in V. Bullough, *Science in the Bedroom*, p. 230.

33. Bullough, *Science in the Bedroom*, p. 231.

34. Anke A. Ehrhardt and Heino F. L. Meyer-Bahlburg, 'Effects of pre-natal hormones on gender related behaviour', *Science*, 211 (March 1981): 1278–84.

35. Assorted references in Bullough, *Science in the Bedroom*, p. 229.

36. Sigmund Freud, 'The psychogenesis of a case of homosexuality in a woman', in *Collected Papers*, Vol. 2 (1920). Translated James Strachey. London: Hogarth Press, 1948, pp. 206–7.

37. *Ibid.*, p. 230.

38. *Ibid.*, p. 210.

39. See Michel Foucault, *A History of Sexuality: Volume One.* Harmondsworth: Penguin Books, 1984.

40. Rubin, 'Catamites and kings', p. 469.

41. I use the split gender form of s/he in this section to disconcert the notion that there is a clear-cut (excuse the pun) 'she' underneath the masculinity of the stone butch. I wish also to respect the wishes of some stone butches not to have the feminine gender designation 'she' imposed upon them.

42. Leslie Feinberg, *Stone Butch Blues.* Ithaca, NY: Firebrand Books, 1993, p. 18.

43. Jay Prosser, 'No place like home: the transgendered narrative of Leslie

Feinberg's *Stone Butch Blues*',
Modern Fiction Studies, **41** (3–4),
Fall–Winter 1995: 483–514, p. 493.

44. Heather Findlay, 'What is stone
    butch – now?', *Girlfriends*,
    March–April 1995, pp. 20–2, 44–5.

45. Radclyffe Hall, *The Well of
    Loneliness*. London: Corgi Books,
    1968, pp. 509–10. The pun on stone
    would be available to the readers of
    this edition, whether or not it was
    intended in the original.

46. I do not wish to imply here that the
    rape of the stone butch is in any way
    worse than the rape of non-butch
    women. The multiple connections
    between butchness and masculinity
    also intersect with straight men's
    homophobic resistance to
    penetration. In the cultural
    imagination, anal rape of men is
    figured as worse (more painful, more
    traumatic) than the rape of women. I
    am addressing the particular psychic
    configurations of butchness which
    makes the act of rape specifically
    symbolic, but this should not imply
    a hierarchy of suffering.

47. Although it comes close to the OED
    definition from 1662 of 'water
    closet' as 'closet of ease'.

48. See Lacan's discussion of the image
    of the twin (toilet) doors
    symbolizing 'through the solitary
    confinement offered Western Man
    for the satisfaction of his natural
    needs away from home, ... by which
    his public life is subjected to the laws
    of urinary segregation'. J. Lacan,
    'The agency of the letter in the
    unconscious or reason since Freud',
    in *Ecrits*. New York: Norton, 1977,
    pp. 146–78, p. 151.

49. I am paraphrasing from Eve
    Kosofsky Sedgwick, *The
    Epistemology of the Closet*. Hemel
    Hempstead: Harvester Wheatsheaf,
    1991, p. 85.

50. Leo Bersani, *Homos*. Harvard
    University Press, 1995, p. 28.

51. Reference in the original Judith
    Butler, *Bodies That Matter: On the
    Discursive Limits of 'Sex'*. New
    York: Routledge, 1993, p. 137.

52. Bersani, *Homos*, pp. 46–7.

53. See Eve Kosofsky Sedgwick, *The
    Epistemology of the Closet*.

54. Joan Nestle, *A Restricted Country*.
    London: Sheba Feminist Press, 1988,
    pp. 37–9.

55. Teresa de Lauretis, *The Practice of
    Love: Lesbian Sexuality and
    Perverse Desire*. Bloomington:
    Indiana University Press, 1994,
    p. 56.

56. Bersani, *Homos*, p. 39.

57. Andrew Sullivan, *Virtually Normal*.
    London: Picador Books, Macmillan,
    1995.

58. See Monique Wittig, *The Straight
    Mind and Other Essays*. Boston:
    Beacon Press, 1992.

59. Sheila Jeffreys, *The Lesbian Heresy*.
    London: The Women's Press, 1994.

60. See J. Lacan, 'Aggressivity in
    psychoanalysis', in *Ecrits*, pp. 8–29.
    For an extension of this discussion
    see Leo Bersani, *The Freudian Body:
    Psychoanalysis and Art*. New York:
    Columbia University Press, 1986.

61. De Lauretis, *The Practice of Love*,
    p. 156.

62. *Ibid.*, pp. 109–10.

63. I am, of course, referring to the
    work of Judith Butler; see *Gender
    Trouble: Feminism and the
    Subversion of Identity*. New York:
    Routledge, 1990.

64. Judith Butler, 'The lesbian phallus
    and the morphological imaginary',
    in *Bodies That Matter*, pp. 57–92.

65. *Ibid.*, p. 232.

66. *Ibid.*, p. 243. We might ask here – so
    what is the lure of the femme?

67. Elizabeth Grosz, 'The labors of love.
    Analyzing perverse desire: an
    interrogation of Teresa de Lauretis's

The Practice of Love', *Differences: A Journal of Feminist Cultural Studies*, 6 (2+3), Summer/Fall 1994: 276–95. Possibly psychoanalysis is of even less use in explaining heterosexual women's desire, as Jacqueline Rose took up, following Freud, in (with Juliet Mitchell), *Feminine Sexuality: Jacques Lacan and the Ecole Freudienne*. Basingstoke: Macmillan, 1982; and *Sexuality in the Field of Vision*. London: Verso, 1985.

68. A colonialist discourse also raced this configuration as Other, hence in discourse there is often a conflation between markers of racial and markers of sexual difference – in the linked association with hypersexuality, for example.

69. For a sustained and sophisticated treatise on bodily inscriptions see Elizabeth Grosz, *Volatile Bodies: Toward a Corporeal Feminism*. Bloomington: Indiana University Press, 1994.

70. See Diana Fuss, *Essentially Speaking*. New York: Routledge, 1991; Gayatri Spivak, *In Other Worlds: Essays in Cultural Politics*. New York and London: Methuen, 1987.

71. Catherine Waldby, 'Destruction: boundary erotics and refigurations of the heterosexual male body', in Elizabeth Grosz and Elspeth Probyn (eds), *Sexy Bodies: The Strange Carnalities of Feminism*. London: Routledge, 1995, pp. 266–77.

72. *Ibid.*, p. 272.

73. See both Barbara Creed, 'Tribades, tomboys, and tarts', in Grosz and Probyn, *Sexy Bodies*, pp. 86–103; and Emma Donoghue, *Passions Between Women: British Lesbian Culture 1668–1801*. London: Scarlet Press, 1993.

74. Waldby, *op. cit.*, p. 271.

75. Elizabeth Grosz, 'Refiguring lesbian desire', in Laura Doan (ed.), *The Lesbian Postmodern*. New York: Columbia University Press, 1994, pp. 67–84.

76. Elizabeth Grosz, *Jacques Lacan: A Feminist Introduction*. London and New York: Routledge, 1990.

77. *Ibid.*, p. 76.

78. *Ibid.*, p. 78.

79. *Ibid.*, p. 78.

80. *Ibid.*, p. 81.

81. *Ibid.*, p. 67.

82. Doan, *The Lesbian Postmodern*, pp. 210–28.

83. *Ibid.*, p. 212.

84. *Ibid.*, pp. 222 and 224.

85. Minnie Bruce Pratt, *S/HE*. Ithaca, NY: Firebrand Books, 1995, p. 65.

86. Johanna Blakeley, 'Abrotica in Anaïs Nin's *House of Incest*', in Karla Jay (ed.), *Lesbian Erotics*. New York University Press, 1995, pp. 227–40, p. 228.

87. Judith Butler, *Bodies That Matter*, p. 4.

4

The Lesbian Outlaw

> the exclusive choice between being law-abiding and
> being criminal, between being within (and under, subject
> to) the law and being an 'outlaw', is not logically given but is
> socially structured by the current regime of power/knowledge.
> In this regime, breaking the law 'makes' one into something –
> a 'criminal', an 'outlaw' – that then, for many, becomes a
> badge of pride. (Shane Phelan[1])

Lesbians break the law but not usually in the name of lesbianism. In the UK lesbians were not explicitly mentioned in British law until 1988, in Section 28 of the Local Government Act.[2] Historically lesbianism has been outside the law, but lesbian acts have been prosecuted under various other laws designed to punish sexual or gender deviance. From the religious laws proscribing heresy, to 'hygiene' laws controlling prostitution, lesbians have been penalized. Some lesbians are more equal than others, however, prescribed laws have been applied disproportionately over a matrix of class and racial subjects, relatively ignoring the nineteenth-century 'passionate friends', but arresting a servant for lewd behaviour, and examining her clitoris for 'oriental' size. In the USA about half the jurisdictions criminalize lesbian behaviour and in many states lesbians have been imprisoned for having sex in private. Legal theorist Ruthann Robson makes the point that 'the violence of the lesbian sex statutes is the violence of propaganda, the propaganda of nonlesbianism'.[3] She makes the argument that the recent low implementation of these laws in the USA sends a paradoxical message: that lesbianism is not worthy of the law's attention, except to criminalize it, re-enforcing the feeling that many of us have that our sexuality is wrong. Robson argues that the effect of the rule of law is to domesticate us. In that she retains the wish for a lesbian space outside the law. At the end of her excellent book on US legal theory and lesbianism, she exhorts lesbians to resist law in the name of desire: 'A desire that is not singular;

desires that are not defined by places we put our fingers, our tongues, our possessions. Desires that mark us as our own (out)laws.'[4] It is this heroic desire I investigate here.

Figuratively, the lesbian is beyond, out there, exterior, peripheral, foreign and different. She has exited the heteropatriarchy. In lesbian outlawry, she occupies – colonizes – a deregulated space unconstrained by the norms and common sense of mainstream culture. In this utopic space she can operate with self-determination. If Homi Bhabha is right, 'from Foucault's *Discipline and Punish* we have learned that the most individuated are those subjects who are placed on the margins of the social',[5] she ceases to be subjected, and becomes an autonomous signifier of rebellion. Allegedly, she is a revolutionary. Her home is in transgression and subversion. I want to think about the benefits of conceptualizing this romanticized outlawry, how this vanguardism has a specific function, or effect, on material lesbian existence. Recent critical texts[6] have encouraged us to think about the structural relationship between the lesbian and a centred culture, and whether the lesbian is outside, or Other. What are the implications of such a modernist binary structure, especially if we also want to claim truth in the – perhaps postmodernist – graffito: 'lesbians are everywhere'? Can the space of the closeted Other be like Dr Who's Tardis, a gateway to exponential worlds? Is the idea of a symbolic void necessary to lesbian incarnation?

Lesbians have appropriated the outlaw position to explore their own identities, something which I have described at length in my previous work on lesbian detective novels.[7] In this chapter I intend to describe the historical placing of lesbians as outlaws, by lesbians themselves, a position focused figuratively in recent years in the heroic icons of amazon and avenger. I argue that outlawry creates a sense of belonging, an affiliation, and that these figures have helped to coalesce cultural movements of lesbian feminists in the 1970s and queer lesbian activists in the 1990s. The lesbian outlaw structure is further characterized by an *affect* – the binary opposition of pride/shame. Outlaw status entails an elevated sense of self and a denigrated sense of self, to which mechanisms of identification and separation are intrinsic. Within the models of lesbian identity I discuss lies a series of antitheses condensed into the two contrapositions: heroic idealization/abject denigration. The pride/shame dichotomy, which frames the chapter, represents the two sides of being an outlaw.

Pride is dependent on shame; pride is predicated on the – sometimes conscious – denial of its own ostracized other. This explains the hegemony of pride in the post-Stonewall era, as a strategic deployment against the pathological homo. Cognizant of our outlaw status we impose a heterodoxical sense of pride. Its counterpoint of shame is no more (or less) real – it is not a deeper truth – but equally a consequence of social locution. I do not want to reinscribe a 'cultural probity' of homosexual shame in this chapter, reinventing the iconography of victimization and playing into the hands of homophobia. Pride remains strategically essential, but shame and its effects are powerful historical players, and cannot be rhetorically subsumed. Even in the nineteenth century shame can be traced as standing for homosexuality itself: Alfred Douglas's poem 'In Praise of Shame' (1894) was read for its implications to the Oscar Wilde trials, since shame, in common historical parlance, was understood as a synonym for homosexuality.[8]

Out(law)ing 'the lesbian'

Within the Foucauldian analysis put forward by materialist feminists and historians of male homosexuality, the defining moment for the categorization of lesbians is proposed as coterminous with the advent of sexology at the end of the nineteenth century. The newly classified 'invert' was associated with pre-existing typifications of otherness; female homosexuality was seen as a predominantly non-white and lower-class phenomenon. This was sympathetic to the Victorian task of purifying Woman – separating Her from any class, racial and sexual markers. In *Fatal Women: Lesbian Sexuality and the Mark of Aggression* Lynda Hart points out that at the juncture of 'lesbian' being spoken, the term was simultaneously silenced, secret(ed) by its distancing from white bourgeois sexual practices. The speech act of naming is an attempt to locate, possess, control and then shift; lesbianism became defined by an edict of exclusion which set it apart. By contrast Woman is always already constructed as white and heterosexual, her function is the reproduction of white men; she symbolizes white men's desire for themselves. Lynda Hart has demonstrated how the white middle-class lesbian desire has managed to be excised – one may say excused – and how the 'real' of female homosexuality has been displaced onto women of color and working-class women,[9] constellating configurations of lesbianism and conflating them as 'butch' (desire, as a masculine trait, could not come from a real woman). The semantic weight of lesbianism is predeterminedly to be cast out; its outlawry is hysterically underscored by class antagonism and racism. As Anna Marie Smith puts it, 'It is simply not true that all lesbians are equally "invisible"':

> The relative invisibility of lesbian desire in the white middle-class English lesbian is therefore the product of a complex intersection of gender, race, class, and sexual differences. Wherever she actually benefits from her relative invisibility, she does so only within a structure which penalizes her working-class, black, and criminal counterparts all the more severely. For every privileged woman with lesbian desires who disappears in a visual sense back into heterosexuality with relative ease, there is always some 'other' woman who is subjected to increased surveillance.[10]

Recently, more historical work has been published that argues for a pre-sexological construction of female homosexuality, one that favours the recognition of practices rather than identities. Discursively, lesbianism was effectively, but not ever explicitly, on the wrong side of the law. Historically the law has prosecuted women for lewd behaviour, fraud and for witchcraft, crimes frequently enforced by evidential suspicions of same-sex practices. In Europe the appellation 'sodomite' was used to accuse someone guilty of a range of unorthodox sexual conducts, although it was not until the late nineteenth century that it was directly related to (male) homosexuality. The female sodomite was assumed to penetrate another woman, vaginally or anally, with her clitoris or with an inorganic object. She could also be construed as a tribade – and both these designations could result in her mutilation or execution. The crime was interpreted as being one against gender, as the impersonation of a male. Similarly hermaphrodism was used as an anatomical justification to explain sex between women as occurring between 'freaks of nature'. A full treatment of these historical transgressions is given by Emma Donoghue in *Passions Between Women: British Lesbian Culture 1668–1801*; my one example from the book illustrates the legal repercussions for working-class lesbians for practising same-sex. Donoghue quotes from Robert James' *Medical Dictionary* (1745):

'Henrica Schuria' is described as a rebellious woman 'of a masculine Turn of Mind' who becomes 'weary of her Sex', crossdresses and enlists as a soldier. On her return home she lets her disguise slip and her relationships with a number of women, including a widow, cause her to be 'accus'd of uncommon and preternatural Lust'. On examination, she is reported to have a large clitoris ('half a Finger long') with which she has been pleasuring the Widow, 'of whom she was excessively fond, so well, that, if the Laws of the Land had permitted, [the widow] would have married her'. They are both whipped, James records with satisfaction, and Henrica (presumably as the masculine, sexually 'active' and so guiltier party) is banished.[11]

Donoghue notes in her historical study how 'lesbian culture seems to have been understood [by participants and by legal discourse] as a matter of relationships and habitual practices rather than self-identifications'.[12] 'Lesbian' desire was regulated unspecifically by the ideological prescription against active female desire, and enforced with the general legal sanctions against 'unnatural' *acts*. But the prevalence of social commentary appearing in diverse medical, religious and pornographic forms of literature circulating throughout Europe, which described and attempted to explain same-sex liaisons, can be interpreted as Foucault's first phase of the formation of objects in discourse, the 'surface of emergence'. It was not until the late nineteenth century that the second phase began, when the 'authorities of delimitation' – principally through sexology – began to define the lesbian as a specific object. From then on the lesbian began to be classified and placed within the systems of dominant discourse, or 'grids of specification' as Foucault puts it.[13] But for the purposes of my argument, it is clear that despite proscription, forms of autonomous female desire, or subjugated knowledges, infused seventeenth- and eighteenth-century society.

'Inning' the lesbian

Emerging archival records contained in manuscripts like *The Diaries of Ann Lister* proffer a narrative of relatively uninhibited 'lesbian' customs and pleasure. Significantly, Ann Lister (1791–1840) came from a family of British landed gentry so that her social status rendered her behaviour permissible because 'invisible' and 'unspeakable' in law. (A lower-class woman enjoying such sex might have had her behaviour spoken of as lewd behaviour, or prostitution, in a court of law, and been punished accordingly.) Lister, as Terry Castle has pointed out,[14] like the tribades, tommys and 'hermaphrodites', adopted a masculine identification to pursue sexual fruition. Like a regular butch she had her prized dildo and a rakish affectation borrowed from that romantic rebel, Lord Byron. Lister's appropriation of Byron is another example of an enabling icon, a mainstream rebellious masculine sexuality, but also a figure that can be queered, an appropriation understandable if one reads Byronic romanticism as contested and unstable. The extra-discursive freedom allowed in the nineteenth century begat the institution of passionate friends – a socially condoned fashion for training adolescents to become brides. The liberty offered enabled sexual relations between upper- and middle-class women,[15] often giving them the emotional outlets necessary for survival in an enforced marriage. Before the morbidification of female friendship by the sexologists, these erotic fervours were subtly condoned, servicing marriage whilst quietly and paradoxically subverting the myth of the 'sexless' white bourgeois Woman.

Although all these societies reified marriage, there seemed also to be a tacit recognition that pleasure was often external, or supplementary, to it. Despite inexplicit censure against homosexuality, same-sex desire between women percolated through into the public consciousness and was manifest throughout sundry classes, with diverse relation to the law. Prostitution and passionate friendship were both implicated within the structure of compulsory heterosexuality – both permitted sex between women, but provoked different kinds of disapprobation. Prostitution and pornography have reinscribed lesbianism within a phallocratic narrative as a prop (in both senses) to maintain the performance of heterosexuality. Still in a supporting role, though, props force a space, and even a brief analysis of these relations of power can disclose and facilitate fissures in a supposedly seamless heterosexuality quite exploitable to conscious intervention. These disputations on the appropriation of such figures by a centred culture rages on, as in the rather apposite phenomenon of lesbian chic, which yet occupies a similarly unstable space between the inside and the outside. Lesbian chic, as a fashion statement, can be read as the most contemporaneous example of the combined and somewhat contradictory discourses of the 'pure', white, upper-class lesbian and soft pornography. She is also femme pride offset against butch shame.[16] The lesbian has been 'inned' as a subversive gesture, but she has also been 'inned' as a process of reabsorption.

Rather than perpetuating the 'outlaw' model, recent queer theorists have argued for the centrality of homosexuality in Western culture. Work by scholars such as Eve Kosofsky Sedgwick, Jonathan Dollimore and Terry Castle has proffered a persuasive case for heterosexuality being dependent on the denial of an equally essential homosexuality. Heterosexuality and homosexuality together constitute a metaphorical see-saw, rather than the planet and orbiting moon model of centre and outside. The momentous energy consumed by heterosexuality's denial is said to count as testimony to the profound presence of homosexuality. Castle uses the metaphor of lesbian ghosting to indicate this diffuse, inextricable proximity. A ghost needs a body to (have) emanate(d) 'the real'. Perhaps shadowing is another poetic analogy for homosexuality: the body is always cast in some shade, being neither external nor intrinsic to it, but its mark is constantly adjusting to motion, and its purchase is relentless. Acts of same-sex are ubiquitous to the human subject, the naming of lesbianism is not.

It is the symbolic labelling and positioning of the lesbian, as an outlaw sign, which concerns me here. The spatial metaphor of inside/outside, like all binaries, is prone to both voluntary and unconscious de-construction and reinscription. Deconstructing binary antitheses such as centre and margin, of oppositions like inclusion and exclusion, inside and outside, subject and object, self and other, has become the bread and butter of postmodern cultural work. I continue to reproduce the binary system here not because I want to, or could, retain 'the heterosexual' or 'the lesbian' as singular units, monolithic and sealed. Our identities as lesbian are contingent on grids of meanings treacherous to tread, built on decades of non-consensual sexual regulation. Martha Gever in her article 'The Names We Give Ourselves'[17] describes how she is simul-taneously attracted and repelled by being a member of a caste, her ambivalence characteristic of the antilogy embedded in pride/shame. Boundaries are codependent; they only exist in relation to each other; furthermore, they are porous membranes, prey to destabilization and dissolution. In practice we shuttle between the stations of identity, our displacement sculpting new pathways, new challenges to a scarred centre. We cannot return to 'home', but we can continuously re-enter the margins and appropriate the structure of feeling, and through it the collaborative resistance we make there. The outlaw, like the hero, is a romantic figure generated from myth who has ascribed qualities which mutate according to context, and is thus contingent. In the examples I provide in the next section, the outlaw is conjoined with lesbianism in an attempt to elevate the outside to a pristine space, envisioned as open to new determinations. In my discussion of amazons and avengers, I aim to show how this outlaw space cannot be idealized as empty, how it is shot through with the grids of other(ed) meanings and yet still remains amenable to lesbian aspirations.

Out and proud: amazons and avengers

In lesbian culture there are a few lesbian warriors who distil the desires of the many; they are the folk heroes, fantasy figures who carry a multi-symbolic load of aspiration. The image of the warrior and the outlaw is a staple of pulp and classic lesbian fiction – for example, Katherine Forrest's *Daughters of a Coral Dawn* (1984), Ellen Galford's *Moll Cutpurse* (1985) and Monique Wittig's *Les Guérillières* (1971). Speculative tales of warrior women ruling ancient societies inspired the twentieth-century lesbian imagination. Anecdotal evidence of folkloric foremothers has fuelled a minor lesbian industry. Medusa the Gorgon, Pallas Athena, Minerva, Morrigu the Celtic Queen of War: heroic figures of female vengeance like these pervaded icons of lesbian desire, peaking around the 1970s and 1980s in cultural feminism. Whereas the more arriviste icons such as Diana Rigg are drawn from popular culture, long-standing examples are culled from the classics. The outlawed, reviled woman is an enduring trope of the heterosexual imaginary, from Eve onwards. The lesbian warrior is the idealized, heroic incarnation of Eve's revenge.

In order to understand the contemporary enchantment with the outlaw metaphor, we need to understand it as a resurgent image. Looking at the past thirty years of Second Wave feminism, we see how a previous generation of lesbians used this representation to mobilize as activist outsiders. The politics and culture of the lesbian feminists of the 1970s were galvanized by the deployment of a single, complex image – that of the amazon. Amazon warriors of antiquity are referred to in various detail by ancient Greek and Roman writers such as Herodotus,

Cleidemus, Plutarch, Plato, Isocrates, Demosthenes, Lysias, Aristides, Strabo, Ovid and Vergil, while hosts of artists and craftsmen depicted them in art.[18] Early amazons functioned as testing boards for male heroism and patriotism; the male conqueror would be victorious, his masculinity venerated by their defeat and exclusion. By the Middle Ages, with the spread of Christianity, amazons either transmuted into unnatural pagans of lust and uncontrolled sexuality or became hypostasized heroines emanating an androgynous, virginal chivalry. Joan of Arc – in English the term is evocative of archery and the Amazons' chosen weapon – became a versatile symbol of the latter in subsequent male-authored stories of her martyrdom.[19] The dreaming of the Renaissance also contrived real and imagined romantic voyages into the 'New World' – another 'outside' space – where travellers captured or were captured by, fantastic exotic amazons:

> Amazon women represented the transcendent, almost supernatural character of the many trials and challenges that lay ahead in regions awaiting discovery and exploration. Since the very, very brave, and the very, very great could trap them and tame them, Amazons represented most of all an affirmation of the strength and the ability of Western man to conquer and master these newfound worlds.[20]

Wars and legends of wars in Africa and America continued to see men subjugate the fabled Amazons, so in the sixteenth century they disappeared into obscurity. In the Enlightenment Amazons became opportunities for research, with the appearance of early anthropology that scrutinized matrilineal tribes and brought justification for the 'scientific' social theories of the nineteenth century, when the supersedence of (masculine) 'civilization' over 'mother right' was a logic of Social Darwinism. Famous twentieth-century rewrites of the Amazon myth include Charlotte Perkins Gilman's *Herland* (1915), Helen Diner's *Mothers and Amazons* (1930) and the first explicitly lesbian reincarnation in the life/biography of Natalie Clifford Barney. Barney made unequivocal the homosocial and homoerotic propinquities of the Amazon heritage.

The amazon combined the imagery of guerrilla warfare that suffused Movement politics of the late 1960s with the reification of female myths and archetypes endemic to cultural feminism, epitomized in the 1970s lesbian feminist journal entitled *Amazon Quarterly*. In *Daring to Be Bad: Radical Feminism in America 1967–1975* (1989) Alice Echols charts the emergence of radical feminism as a war against patriarchy, and its ascendance as a popular guerrilla movement. Its retreat into the creation of a female counter-culture, via the cultural feminism that supplanted it by the early to mid-1970s, meant the end of a directly confrontational challenge to gender conformity. She describes how radical feminists, influenced by the progressive Left and Marxist ideologies of the 1960s, saw gender as the fallacious imposition of arbitrary traits, based on specious notions of sexual difference intended to disempower women. Cultural feminists invoked the innate and superior differences of women over men. The dynamics of the two critiques diverge considerably – radical feminism contests a false, invested border between outside and inside – cultural feminism naturalizes the perimeter and celebrates being outside. Echols puts it acerbically: 'organize around your own oppression', soon degenerated into the narrower position, 'organize around your own interests'.[21]

Acts of urban terrorism evoke the underground political movements of the 1960s. The 1960s and early 1970s were the years of the Baader-Meinhoff Gang, the Angry Brigade, the Red Brigade, the Weathermen, the Red Army Faction, the New World Liberation Front – a web of many underground guerrilla movements were dropping *out* of bourgeois norms and forming quasi-militaristic cells to wage war on the Establishment. Although the phenomenon of the middle-class revolutionary has also been read as a convention which writers such as Doris Lessing, in *The Good Terrorist* (1986), have mocked, one woman – Patty Hearst – personified this conflict in the American imagination; to a turbulent white feminist resistance she was the quintessential amazon. To cynics she had been a psychologically unstable dupe. Endless examples of resistance from self-identified feminists in the USA can be provided from the histories of Redstockings, Cell 16, WITCH (Women's International Conspiracy from Hell), The Feminists, New York Radical Feminists, the Lavender Menace, the Radicalesbians, the Furies Collective and many more,[21] at the core of which there circulated a methodology of cultural 'zapping', drawing from the protest art movement 'Happening Art', a dramatic shock tactic effective in binding together members of the group in public theatre, and producing the dislocation of common sense, or ideological consensus. For example, one legendary action was initiated by New York Radical Women on 7 September 1968. A hundred activists from a number of cities converged on the annual Miss America pageant in Atlanta:

> they crowned a live sheep 'Miss America'. They paraded the sheep on the boardwalk to 'parody the way the contestants (all women) are appraised and judged like animals at a county fair'. Some women chained themselves to a life-size Miss America puppet to emphasise women's enslavement to 'beauty standards'. They tossed 'instruments of torture to women' – high-heeled shoes, bras, girdles, typing books, curlers, false eyelashes, and copies of *Playboy, Cosmopolitan,* and *Ladies Home Journal* – into a 'Freedom Trash Can'.... Peggy Dobbins sprayed Toni home permanent spray around the mayor's box in the auditorium... As the outgoing Miss America read her farewell speech, four or five women unfurled a large banner which read, 'Women's Liberation', and all sixteen women [who had infiltrated the audience] shouted 'Freedom for Women' and 'No More Miss America'.[23]

Significantly, the 1968 action is accredited with the most hackneyed cliché of Women's Liberation: the media widely reported seeing bra-burning. In fact this never took place, but the media understood what they were seeing in this synecdochical breast excision – the birth of the modern amazonian consciousness. Amazons, with their excised breasts, evince a particularly sexual fascination for lesbians too. The abscission of the breast also represents a refusal, or reinvention, of femininity. Scarification, piercing, branding, tattoo and similar body arts have a persistent cachet amongst subcultural groups; lesbians since the 1980s have ritualized their bodies thus.[24] Even Stephen Gordon in *The Well of Loneliness* carried the lesbian 'mark' of a facial scar.

In order to comprehend the mutability of the amazon myth consider two contemporaneous texts of the 1970s: Wonder Woman and Monique Wittig's *Les Guérillères* (translated in 1971). Whereas Wonder Woman is the apotheosis of post-Sexual Revolution hyperactive heterosexuality, a Marvel Comic blow-dried Super-Babe, perchance recoupable as a proto-feminist liberal (but more convincing as a cult camp queer hyperbole – a kind of Barbie With Wings), *Les Guérillères*, on the other hand, is a high cultural commemoration of a race of women warriors replete with the iconoclastic reproduction of feminist and Movement-based signifiers. Wittig uses the epic genre to depict a militaristic sexual dimorphism, a metaphor pertinent to the sex-war binaries of the 1970s. Amazons are plastic: they are moulded to the desires of the dreamer, whether she is a preadolescent girl pretending to zap her fears or a woman preparing to strike against the patriarchy. As existential outlaws they can be used to promote both the engagement of Radical Feminism and the separatism of Cultural Feminism. This ambiguity sustains their expedience for lesbians: in the 1990s *Tank Girl* exploited the same imagery-as-pleasure with postmodern post-politics.

Lesbian activists[25] were the self-conscious folk amazons of Peace Camps in the West during the early to mid-1980s, when the Cold War meant an escalating arms race[26] and a proliferating peace movement. Warrior woman, amazon and lesbian became coterminous both in the eyes of the protagonists and in the condemnation of the press. Cuttings from the period show 'angry women' collapsed into 'rabid lesbians' all too often. In Britain, at Greenham Common US Air Force Base in Newbury, Berkshire, the allegorical picture of a circle, often cited by cultural theorists to illustrate the containment of power, was organic and geographical – a twelve-foot fence kept the soldiers in and the women, camped by the gates, out. Incursions by lesbian guerrillas into the base became daily infractions, as the 'Other' refused to be contained – 'Breaching the Peace' in British law became the byword for breaking through the military's boundaries. The breaches were highly ritualistic, in recognition of the overdetermined symbolism of the (gendered) frontiers. In 1983 I went to Greenham Common on a freezing winter morning and met my mother, amongst tens of thousands of other women, so that we might fasten a mirror onto the fence, to reflect the base back in upon itself. The base disappeared into itself, in a spiral of its own repeating phallic solipsisms. As many hundreds of women were arrested over the years, legal discourse orbited around this conundrum: were the women who had encroached on government property outlaws, or were the Armed Forces illegally occupying common land which they had no right to colonize? Greenham women fought for their right of presence through the courts, years later overturning many of the original convictions of the Cold War. Who was in and who was out was the crucial, vexed foundational metaphor of these campaigns.[27] Battles at Greenham Common were repeatedly structured around the inside/outside metaphor. The women claimed the circle for themselves as a metaphysical symbol of power, like Wittig's diagrammatical circles in *Les Guérillères* or, more literally in one of her many uses, the warriors' 'rounded shields protect them',[28] and indeed like Wonder Woman's circular bracelet weapons, the circle, with its connotations of the female body, became a signal of powerful refusal. The circle is redolent with mythological and semantic notions of strength through closure; crucially its use instigates a new centre, a new interiority. Thus the lesbian is turned outside-in: she inverts the paradigm.

The Lesbian Avenger is a sublime combination of the late 1960s amazon/guerrilla, the 1970s lesbian feminist, the 1980s AIDS activist and the 1990s queer outlaw:

> The Lesbian Avengers is a direct action group using grassroots activism to fight for lesbian survival and visibility. Our purpose is to identify and promote lesbian issues and perspectives while empowering lesbians to become experienced organizers who can participate in political rebellion. Learning skills and strategizing together are the core of our existence.[29]

The Lesbian Avengers were *the* inspirational figures for the 1990s politically progressive North American lesbian. Their zaps combine humour with the exigency of a pressure group, beneficially inheriting the activist experience of ACTUP, Queer Nation and lesbian feminism combined. The excitement and popularity of this image responds, in part, to a nostalgic desire to return to the effective vanguard politics of earlier counter-cultural movements. But the image clearly articulates the needs and desires of the contemporary lesbian; it is an effective fantasy which symbolizes a specific iconic lesbianism, provoking a fantasy of enablement which dangles simultaneously a positive image and a knowing irony. The Lesbian Avenger tears down homophobia and erects the phallic dyke. Diana Rigg, chosen for the first publicity flyers, was the Avengers' iconic foremother. This founding image is lesbian camp for the 1990s; the fetishistic figure of this ironic idol contributes a knowing erotic ambiguity to the leatherized 1960s cult series. Diana Rigg, as the quintessential Avenger, is a queer top girl, lesbian chic with a sting. Postmodernist strategies of destabilization in popular culture have fashioned the outlaw into the phallic woman.[30]

The Lesbian Avengers perform urban warfare, as an attempt to colonize urban space through direct action. The politics of space are a frequent stimulation for Avengers for which there are many examples: an early suggestion for the New York chapter's first action was to parachute into Whitney Houston's wedding; on Valentine's Eve 1993 they staged a skate-in at the famous Rockefeller Center outdoor rink, skating arm-in-arm and kissing in front of amazed Saturday afternoon shoppers; on Valentine's Day they unveiled a statue of Alice B. Toklas standing by the municipal statue of Gertrude Stein in Bryant Park, a visual reminder of forgotten femmes and lesbian romance. The event climaxed with lesbian waltzing in the snow. In October 1994, a Brooklyn diner was occupied during Sunday brunch by two dozen lesbians canoodling and singing 'A Kiss Is Just A Kiss', after two dykes had been forcibly ejected the previous week when the owner saw one woman peck the other on the cheek. Actions like this extend to parallel non-Avenger organizations too, such as the women who bared their breasts on the New York subway in August 1994, informed by the Avengers' methods and amazonian tradition.[31] On the 1995 Dyke March down Fifth Avenue the action was reciprocated by hundreds of lesbians tearing off their T-shirts in protest at right-wing religious pressure on the Police Chief to arrest topless women.

The Lesbian Avengers were created in Spring 1992 by six New York women: Anne-Christine D'Adesky, Marie Honan, Ann Maguire, Sarah Schulman, Ana Maria Simo and Maxine Wolfe, all of whom had previous experience in building counter-cultural protest movements. The idea was to generate a new breed of grass-roots lesbian activists, a proactive, mature political organization which did not function purely on the level of critique; the organization would not assail other progressive movements. The group consolidated after the six, together with Kathryn Thomas and Debby Karpel, handed out 8000 fluorescent green club cards at that year's Pride which said 'LESBIANS, DYKES, WOMEN, WE WANT REVENGE AND WE WANT IT NOW!' The first meeting, at the New York Lesbian and Gay Center on 7 July, attracted fifty women. Their inaugural action was to picket one of the most conservative school districts, District 24, on the first day of school, in autumn 1992. The city had passed a multicultural curriculum that included discussion of lesbians and gay men, but the local state school board in Queens had passed an ordinance on sex education which excised all references to homosexuality. The Lesbian Avengers responded one morning by supplying a band dressed in Catholic school uniform to play outside the gate and sing 'When The Dykes Come Marching In' and 'We Are Family'. Volunteers, wearing T-shirts on which was printed 'I Was a Lesbian Child', handed out three hundred lavender balloons to the schoolchildren stamped with the words 'ASK ABOUT LESBIAN LIVES'. The action, as Sarah Schulman has observed, was emblematic: it confronted a taboo (lesbians and school), it was creative, humorous and colourful and it attacked right-wing homophobia.[32]

The first mass membership was culled from the Washington DC Dyke March of 24 April 1993. Over a million gays and lesbians had congregated that week for the largest civil rights march in history. Avengers marched wearing super-dyke action capes, and, in their now customary ritual, ate fire in front of the White House. The next day a small group crept into the House of Representatives and let off stink bombs, lifting up signs which said 'HOMOPHOBIA STINKS'. The subsequent development of chapters in dozens of US cities, and the 1994 advent of the London Avengers, has parallels with the franchising of name-brand stores – a local independent constituency agrees to operate within the original paradigm – lesbians come to profit from the consumption of an aspirant image which can be personally transformative. The New York Avengers have often provided 'start-up kits' to nascent chapters in other cities, including items such as T-shirts, graphics and handbooks. Women also join the Avengers for social and sexual needs, an agenda that the Left has only covertly recognized in its constituencies. By using five-dollar dances to fundraise, the Lesbian Avengers maintain a tight dependency on the ordinary lesbian community. Lesbian Avengers acquire skills, toys, a new identity and also get a girlfriend.

Lesbian Avengers, drawing on a dyke counter-discourse, have sprouted exponentially out of New York to all areas of the USA. At the end of 1994, there were chapters in thirty-five American cities across the continent. This marked colonization is a response to certain historical determinants: the model of AIDS activisms during the 1980s which, although it predominantly mobilized gay men, indicated to lesbians the efficacy of cell-based direct action groups; a new generation of twenty-somethings, having survived the relatively queer-tolerant environment of college, has hit the homophobia of the labour market; the pro-individualistic decade of the 1980s cedes to the new ethics and incipient communitarianism of the 1990s; the rise of lesbian chic in popular culture – as a reaction against the visibility of (male) homosexual sickness, repackaged in high cultural glamour – means that white, rich, assimilated lesbian readers can visualize themselves unambiguously as desired textual subjects. Avengers have captured the political sentience, indicated by lesbians who left earlier activist groups such as ACTUP and Queer Nation to join the Avengers. Resourceful drawing on post-1960s popular insurgency – such as the Freedom Ride through New England in autumn 1993 which 'involved people moving geographically to defend a community that they identify with when they are under siege'[33] – meant calling on a fund of resonating images of protest and modernizing them to suit contemporary anxieties and desires.

Central to the function of the classic outlaw hero are ideas of retribution and of witness, two profoundly Christian themes, which also speak to their specifically Western cultural location. These motivations are intrinsic to the Lesbian Avengers. A targeted act, a zap, an angry, swift and pointed presence in response to instances of homophobia, is the Avengers' preferred mode of attack. The Lesbian Avengers are motivated by the conviction that constituently defined articulations of lesbians can counter the negative imposed images and/or historical invisibility of lesbians in malestream society. Hart comments:

> That the *lesbian* might not be seen might mean that she is nowhere; but it might indicate that she is *everywhere*; and her more pronounced unidentifiability therefore phobically renders her invisibility omnipresent. Her very absence could thus make her implied presence even more terrifying.[34]

The identity of the oppressor is policed by the fear of contamination by the Other. The boundaries of white supremacist heterosexuality are fragile, and the consequence of denial is the constant fear of encroachment by an intangible and concomitantly enlarged threat. Diffusion does not necessarily produce defusion, and the indetermination of the enemy provokes instability at the centre. The efficacy of the Avengers is that their strikes are unpredictable, and are intended for maximum media effect. Shifting the terrain of political protest from the traditional municipal march to the news media format increases the public's perception of popular insurgency. In December 1992 when the Avengers shadowed the Mayor of Denver in protest at Proposition 2,[35] the Colorado State law that deprived its lesbian and gay citizens of any civil rights protection, pursuing him rowdily and doggedly throughout his two-day trade trip to New York, it must indeed have seemed that lesbians were everywhere. Media coverage was so successful that even Mayor Dinkins had endorsed the tourism boycott of the 'Hate State' by the end of the visit.

Early New York Avengers publicity used an icon of blaxploitation – Pam Grier wielding a machine gun – to advertise an autumn fundraiser, in which the effort to reappropriate may be falling into shades of grey.[36] Unintentional racism can be read into the figure of Pam Grier being juxtaposed next to text that includes the promise of 'GO-GO GIRLS' at the dance. A later flyer, for the New Year's Eve bash, precedes the image of Grier with the heading 'YOUR SEXUAL FUTURE REVEALED: HUNKY GIRLS!'. This is uncomfortably close to the historical deployment of blaxploitation images to connote exotic, unbridled sexuality. The effective war is over semiotics, foregrounding the instability of signs and presuming a 'knowing' reader.[37] An example of how vexedly multivalent this signifying can get is illustrated by the common white feminist trope of constructing black women as warriors. This works especially for dykes such as Audre Lorde, who called herself a warrior in *Sister Outsider*. The image collapses into a white colonialist reading predicated on the noble savage idea: the elevation and iconization, made possible because black women have been associated with excessive emotion and physicality, is founded on the discursive truth that the violence and rage of a black woman is so much easier to 'see'.[38]

I want to present the Avengers as an empowering symbol for contemporary lesbians, but recent schisms in the New York Avengers over the politics of race and class may augur more serious objections to praxis. Significantly, African–American lesbians in the Avengers contested the appropriateness of the 'Freedom Ride', calling attention to the thin line between honouring and capitalizing on a different struggle. The emigration of the Lesbian Avengers to Europe – in 1995 chapters existed in London, Berlin and Paris – also raises the issue of whether ventures formed out of US political traditions will transcend cultural differences and survive in variable social contexts. In London, the Lesbian Avengers' action on immigration laws insensitively failed to address how state xenophobia is so intransigently raced, falling into the rhetorical trap of middle-class entitlement. Generally, their American-style actions have produced a 'cringe factor' response in many British lesbians. The Lesbian Avengers' sexual politics may be 'out', but their race and class politics may still be largely 'in', which is less a comment on the group's intention and effort to create a multivalenced politic than an observation on the ineluctable snarls of single-issue activisms.

Almost contemporaneous with the emergence of the Avengers is the appearance of the 'zine warrior *Hothead Paisan: Homicidal Lesbian Terrorist* by artist Diane DiMassa. Hothead is a post-p.c. superhero, a dyke doing battle with the heteropatriarchy; she swings a double-headed axe with the caption 'No Guilt', striding the urban landscape with an Uzi strapped to her waist. Most 'zine culture is urban, young and generically rooted in the punk fanzines of the 1970s. 'Zine culture is popular protest art: the only technology required is use of the cheap and common photocopier. In Cultural Studies terms it is an authentic folk culture, where the means of production and distribution are autonomous, in the hands of the authors and artists. DiMassa alerts us to working-class typology in her use of 'paisan', an Italian–American version of 'homeboy', and indeed Hothead's behaviour rejects middle-class tactics of polite persuasion in favour of in-yer-face proletarianism. In this, the parody slides close to burlesque. Hothead combines the energy of Queer with lesbian feminism; her hybrid politics appeals to a range of lesbian subjects/readers as a vehicle for the articulation of a revenge fantasy, with its concomitant idealized empowerment. Hothead is the castrating bitch of men's paranoid nightmares. She is also the avenging amazon of women's expansive dreams. This phallic woman pickles her dicks in a jar.

Hothead is the animated progeny of Valerie Solanas's *SCUM Manifesto* [Society for Cutting Up Men];[39] from Vivian Gornick's Introduction (1970 edition), spatial metaphors are key:

> The fundamental vision of the *Manifesto* is that of the eternal feminist, the form is that of the decadent and emotionally *disconnected* twentieth century. The *Manifesto* speaks in the *voice of the lost* and grief-stricken child of the West of this moment. Savage and breathlessly icy, cruelly unforgiving with a world that has cheated it of its life, it is a *voice beyond reason, beyond negotiation, beyond bourgeoisie decencies*. It is the *voice of one pushed past the limit*, one whose psychological *bearings are gone*, who can no longer be satisfied with anything less than blood.[40] [my italics]

Valerie Solanas, notorious for shooting and nearly killing Andy Warhol in June 1968 for allegedly stealing her ideas, became a *cause célèbre* for radical feminists. Rage and fury characterizes this polemic, which includes such contemporary classic statements as men are a 'biological abortion', a 'walking dildo', 'an incomplete female'. Solanas's text pushes into hyperviolence, its excess seen as a necessary provocation for war. The *Manifesto* is a singularly vehement fume, but its scorching acerbity burns deeper for its wit:

> SCUM will conduct Turd Sessions, at which every male present will give a speech beginning with the sentence 'I am a turd, a lowly abject turd'.[41]

The historical conditions that produced this polemic tract for a revolution in 1968 provoked the visually parodic *Hothead Paisan: Homicidal Lesbian Terrorist* in 1991; the genesis for both is the violent rejection of heterosexuality. Angry women act out a particularly eroticized violence in the common imagination. This may be no more than the convention of sexualizing Woman – at the moment she is most intensely assertive, this is interpreted as sexuality (despite the fact that Solanas herself was vehemently anti-sex). The logical development of *The SCUM Manifesto* is a lesbian text. Contained within the image of the physical, violent woman is the lesbian. Associating excessive fury, and sex, with the figure of the lesbian underlines the configuration of an outlaw. Lynda Hart, drawing attention to the way female aggression connotes lesbianism, quotes Caroline Sheldon's study of mainstream cinema which argues that lesbians are inevitably portrayed as 'castrating bitches and sadists',[42] supposing that the reverse logic also applies – that the appearance of 'castrating bitches' presumes a subtextual lesbianism.

Recalling Wittig's claim that the lesbian is 'Not-Woman',[43] that renouncing the heterosexual matrix invokes a phantasmic lesbianism, it is also axiomatic that female violence, as a false discourse lying outside the boundaries of the discursive truth of passive femininity, is similarly unnatural. Paula Graham's essay in *The Good, the Bad and the Gorgeous* on Sigourney Weaver as Ripley in *Alien 3* is a coherent example of the way this phallic woman is lesbianized in popular culture, decentering the traditional subject/object relations of desire:

resistance is a condition of lesbian pleasure in the image of the female warrior. Lesbians resist female objectification (as the primary western form of exclusion and disempowerment of women) in order to act powerfully. One resistant strategy (among many) is to take up a 'phallic' viewing position. Having done this, a woman is excluded from the heterosexual order of desire... In order to desire a woman, she must objectify a woman – who, as a lesbian, will resist objectification. To stabilise this paradoxical tension, subjectivity may be disseminated across the subject and object positions.

When the lesbian spectator looks at the body of the female warrior, the female warrior is sexually objectified, but also identified with as 'phallic' (desiring) subject – opening up a lesbian subjective space.[44]

In Paula Graham's model, the lesbian spectator activates the implosive collapse of the inside/outside binary. The discursive construction of lesbian violence is synopsized in a semantic rupturing; thus the lesbian viewer, at least, emerges everywhere. Paradoxically, in the 1995 film version of Jamie Hewitt's 'zine character *Tank Girl* – a concatenation of Hothead, Ripley in *Aliens* and a fey Minnie the Minx – a lesbian reading is ubiquitous yet nowhere, simultaneously effaced by Attitude: 'Attitude is self-love in a void, denoting the projection of a non-specific, undirected anger as affect', Charlotte Raven wrote in the *Guardian*.[45] Iconographically the film reassembles a catalogue of Bad Girls commingling on a Liechtenstein; *Tank Girl* is a castrated Lesbian Avenger.

The bonds of outlawry

Early women's groups, like the Suffragists, came together under a rubric of anger, which was their stimulus to further political organizing. Within subordinated cultures, there appears to be a moment in the crucible of oppression when individual angers coalesce into affirmative group consciousness and action. Paradoxically, this response can occur due to growing visibility, liberalization *and* increased hostility – the former inducing the latter. The cost of popular exposure for lesbians is that we are now less likely to be able to pass. Lesbianism is more easily spoken. The codes of masculinity appropriated by butches, which could have been read as 'eccentricity' not many years ago, giving lead to the unarticulated suspicion of lesbianism, today often produce the direct verbal and physical assault. Queerbashing was undoubtedly rife in the 1940s and 1950s, but in other ways it was more possible to live a secret life.

The Lesbian Avengers, like any protest movement rooted in identity, seek to offer women validation for anger, to provide them with spheres of culture to *direct* their sense of outrage. Public discomfiture at the Lesbian Avengers is indicative of an established agitation regarding the phallic woman. In an interview at Brighton Arts Club on 3 February 1995, Schulman reiterated the anxious questioning of the mainstream press:

> 'Why are you so angry?' 'Will it lead to violence?' Schulman responds by being laconic: 'No: it's just a joke.'

Lynda Hart writes about how the lesbian is the shadow of women's aggression. Not only have dominant representations of lesbians relied on predatory and pathological deviance, but the masculinized woman and the female offender become one. Hart addresses the profound paranoia characterizing heterosexual patriarchy, relating it to the disavowal of homosexuality in Western culture. She explains how homosexuality is primarily signified by connotation, not denotation, that, in Roland Barthes' terms, it is a 'writerly text'. Connotation allows a kind of pluralism over meanings: it encourages a playful associative sport, a tension between differently inflected interpretations. Thus, with the Avengers, we see women acting together to wrestle with the disavowal of homosexuality, in re-presentation. The Lesbian Avengers' action exploits the paranoid fantasies of heteropatriarchy, in an ironic and very postmodern reversal of dominant fears. It is an act of revenge, its sharp subtlety resting on its pre-emptive status of being a joke. A joke punctures the priapic posturings of a despot, it is deflationary; simultaneously it reveals, ridicules and rewrites the text. A joke performs violence to the signifier; its elegance is in the fact that the damage is elusive and protected by that efficacious mechanism 'It's only a joke'. A joke establishes a resilient collusion between its participants. It is a cultural terrorist's weapon.

Any successful counter-culture organizes potential conscripts and promises a range of benefits: a stabilized identity, a functional role, a sense of communality and sameness. Anti-substance imperatives of the 1980s have meant that the Avengers' meeting, like a twelve-step programme,[46] provides an inclusive, structured, externally focused rendezvous for individuals to cement identities through relationships. A subculture has to be able to appear to satisfy the social and sexual desires of its recruits. bell hooks, writing in *Outlaw Culture: Resisting Representations* clarifies:

> In progressive political circles, to speak of love is to guarantee that one will be dismissed or considered naive. But outside those circles there are many people who openly acknowledge that they are consumed by feelings of self-hatred, who feel worthless, who want a way out. Often they are too trapped by paralysing despair to be able to engage effectively in any movement for social change. However, if the leaders of such movements refuse to address the anguish and pain of their lives, they will never be motivated to consider personal and political recovery. Any political movement that can effectively address these needs of the spirit in the context of liberation struggle will succeed. [47]

Groups like the Lesbian Avengers owe their success not only to the ostensible purpose of mobilizing anger and directing it back, but to the recognition that the process of revenge cements perpetrators' investment in new kinship affiliations. Lesbian Avengers benefit from the tortured history of a divisive Women's Liberation Movement by trying not to replicate the totem lesbian *qua* Woman. They also endeavour not to get trapped in the paralysing and insular ideological point-scoring which beset previous political campaigns, although this can be subtly intransigent. Basing education in the praxis of an action ensures members feel enabled rather than judged inadequate by intellectual debate; it should forge solidarity between differences, rather than regenerate the hierarchy of oppressions. Lesbian Avengers, like Amazons, are positive images mutable to the needs of their consumers, they bring together those outside the circle and kick back the shame associated with exile. It is too premature to speculate what interior or exterior conditions will see their demise – hopefully the outlaws will be assimilated as products of their own success.[48] This is seen as the see-saw determinism of society: the centre incorporates a threat, and is reshaped to throw out more dissidents to challenge and renew; these then recentre their outlaw identity by establishing communality, and in doing so regulate their own of/fence. The centre then incorporates the threat . . .

There is a class aspect to these spatial manoeuvres: white middle-class lesbians are most outraged by their exclusion. (And conversely, they are the ones most often invested in separatism, an extended notion of bourgeois privacy.) Perhaps there can only be revolt where there is expectation. The othered lesbian feels herself politely shrinking in response to a real or imagined attack, rather than expanding her space with self-righteous rage. The shape taken is an effect of power – theirs, yet she does not relinquish the hallucination that membership, through acquiescence, is still possible. This is the sad face of being an outlaw, wherein the cruelty of its perceived imposition, the ignominy of banishment, is felt. Ideally, shame can be understood on an empathetic level without incurring the brusque judgement of political ineffectuality or, worse, listlessness. For until pain is acknowledged it continues to immobilize. This is both the psychology and the selfishness of oppression. bell hooks reads this as a developmental process:

> [M]any of us are motivated to move against domination solely when we feel our self-interest directly threatened. Often, then, the longing is not for a collective transformation of society, an end to politics of domination, but rather simply for an end to what we feel is hurting us. This is why we desperately need an ethic of love to intervene in our self-centred longing for change. Fundamentally, if we are only committed to an improvement in that politic of domination that we feel leads directly to our individual exploitation or oppression, we not only remain attached to the status quo but act in complicity with it, nurturing and maintaining those very systems of domination.[49]

Shame, the abused hero and survival narratives

In this chapter so far I have examined heroic outlaws who embody and who arouse pride. I now want to offer an example of an heroic shame narrative, Dorothy Allison's *Bastard out of Carolina* (1993). Both *Stone Butch Blues* (1993) and *Bastard out of Carolina* represented the 'hit' heroic narratives of the mid-1990s, speaking to a cultural need for survival narratives which dealt with shame. *Bastard* is a white trash girl called Bone, from whose savage childhood springs a particular sort of outsider status which makes for a brittle life. But Bone, however pared down or broken, owns that indestructible persistence of a survivor. Allison's talent is that she neither glamorizes nor patronizes, giving the *appearance* of realism. Novels like *Stone Butch Blues* and *Bastard out of Carolina* are about becoming, about appropriating agency, about finding the heroic in oneself. Classic realism is criticized for its bourgeois mission to prove that the individual exists. This formulation ignores the studied attraction of the form for working-class writers; it assumes their technical and aesthetic ignorance. But these kinds of narrative rely on a central heroic structure – the reduction and rebuilding of the self – which functions as cultural space-making for the contemporary lesbian. The 1970s project to change the world has retreated into the 1990s project to change the self: the landscape to be appropriated is now internal. After two decades of the necessary ascendancy of pride, we need to gaze upon its corollary, shame; heroic narratives permit this by framing the story safely for the lesbian reader; she can dip into shame and be absolved by the heroic closure of the narrative.

In late-twentieth-century American culture, survival and recovery have become hugely important metaphors within lesbian and gay culture. The popular take-up of twelve-step programmes increases the narrativization of abuse in the ritualized confessional retelling and witnessing which structure meetings. It is clear that the production of the identity 'survivor' is analogous to the production of the identity 'gay'; both involve trajectories which reformulate time (the past) according to the needs of the present. In the case of sexual abuse, the connections are tighter. The rhetoric of 'coming out' of secrecy and shame suffuses both. Reclaiming a debased identity and reconstructing a new self as a survivor is replete with the symbolism of heroism. It is a movement of struggle, reappropriation and triumph. In surveying the literature of incest, Ann Cvetkovich has pointed out how lesbianism is disavowed, even in lesbian-authored texts, due to the taboo of suggesting a causal relationship. Instead, lesbianism becomes the unspoken subtext, and readers can recognize that 'incest narratives need not say 'lesbian' to be talking about lesbianism'.[50] In her analysis of *Bastard out of Carolina* Cvetkovich argues that Allison explores: 'the intimate connection between sexual trauma and sexual pleasure, and by implication the connections between incest, and, if not lesbianism explicitly, then perverse sexuality'.[51] In part this is insinuated by the novel, which leaves Bone at adolescence, prior to any direct evidence of sexual orientation, in the hands of her lesbian Aunt Raylene. It is a codified gesture to her lesbian future. It transposes Bone's incipient lesbianism onto her aunt, who in the final paragraph provides Bone with the comfort she has desired all along: 'When Raylene came to me, I let her touch my shoulder, let my head tilt to lean against her, trusting her arm and her love.'[52] This sensual affection is unavoidably erotic, and Bone's 'lesbianism' becomes her family's inheritance too. *Bastard out of Carolina*'s indictment of heterosexual masculinity codifies it as a feminist text, its reiteration of shame ('I lived in a world of shame'[53]) and its formula of heroic survival metonymically connote its parallel with lesbian narratives.

Outlaws, alienation and shame

Homophobia does not always provoke combat or heroism. It creates passivity, victimhood, depression and self-hatred. It produces an inexpressible weariness, a reluctance to engage, a cowardice which shames. On top of the shame imposed by the designation of deviance, there is a double shame, which berates the fearful inertia of the lesbian's defeat. The adage 'glad to be gay' in this circumstance is a bitter joke. I ritually avoid these feelings with rhetorical, habitual repetitions of the rubric of 'Pride', sneaking into the ghetto in order to assuage my estrangement. (I put my tie on just before I slope into the bar.)

For lesbians, shame sediments in our concept of Woman, specifically in the nexus of female sexuality. It is interminably difficult for women to resist experiencing some shame about our bodies, particularly around our genitals and sexual behaviours. Outlaw status simultaneously speaks sexuality and silences it, as the protagonist is defined and then delegitimated. Spatial metaphors mark the 'fallen' woman as an outlaw and she is cast from here to there (recalling the historical linkage of lesbianism with prostitution). An inversion of this process occurs when the lesbian who is out becomes 'Out'. If she is out*ed*, she is bounced from one form of internalized derision to another, more public; the gesture ensures she is spurned by both components of the hetero/homo binary. Her own motivations for 'coming out' can be, perversely, an attempt to get back 'in', to escape a private sensation of shame. In his essay, 'Emotions and Identity: A Theory of Ethnic Nationalism', Thomas Scheff describes how the experience of exclusion provides the motor for ethnic nationalism. He proposes the pride/shame hypothesis: 'Pride generates and signals solidarity, shame is an indicator and cause of alienation.'[54]

Scheff describes shame as the most social and reflexive of emotions because it always involves the consciousness of self from the point of view of the other. The self surveys itself. Shame and honour are conferred by others. He discusses Helen Block Lewis's research[55] into how most shame goes unacknowledged, and is usually bypassed or disguised as another disparate, vague feeling, hence 'one need not *feel* ashamed to be in a state of shame'[56] (and conversely, one need not *be* ashamed to feel shame). In shame, the self feels weak, powerless and fragmentary. Shame crucially involves feelings of exposure. Gershen Kaufman describes it as 'being seen in a diminished sense'.[57] The following passage from Scheff describes the dynamic:

> The most dramatic cues for both overt and bypassed states of shame in social interaction involve gaze direction… Overt, undifferentiated shame leads to furtiveness, looking down or away, with only an occasional sidelong glance at the other. A normal gaze involves turn-taking, first looking at the other, then away. Finally, bypassed shame results in continuous looking at the other, attempting to stare them down.[58]

The heterosexist gaze is a speculation which has a doubling effect – to include at the same time it casts out. It is an act of appropriation, owning and non-consensual classification replete with voyeurism. The heterosexist gaze is intended to mark us, the glance is a strike. The heterosexist gaze is a profoundly exposing stigmatization, and as an act of shaming its effect is to paralyse. The contradiction, of course, is that it is also a desiring gaze, a too-revealing repudiation. The idea of an outlaw depends on the conceptualization of an outer space, but the paradox of the perverse[59] is that it is constantly closing in, its near-intimacy an erotic enjambment. The cell's walls are porous, absorption is taking place, inside/outside closes in. Even if I look away, as the perpetrator enacts the gaze, his (or her) gaze is captured, polluted. Curiously, gazing is a sophisticated language of gay and lesbian communication, the nuances of various looks, lingering, direct, frequent or oblique, characterizing the preliminaries of street or bar interaction. The 'dyke stare', the eyes held by a stranger fractionally longer than decorously necessary, establishes a deft, brief and secret kinship, a mirroring, which colludes simultaneously to acknowledge and rebut shame.

Alienation results from the unending evocation of intense shame, as it leads to increasing feelings of abandonment. We see this in the horrendous statistics of gay and lesbian teenage suicide, which is a final detachment from affective ties. In another complex pattern, the pressure of relentless shame can also result in the idealization of another through the process of infatuation, a move caused by one's own sense of unworthiness, and a displacement or inversion of personal shame. It is a longing for inclusion. What Lewis and Adler have called 'Overt shame loops'[60] result in two routes: the inferiority complex or a striving for power. Scheff concludes that:

> Social connections can be either too loose, isolating the individual, or too tight (engulfment), suffocatingly so. By implication there must also be a high level of integration, neither too loose nor too tight. The Durkheim–Bowen approach implies an axis of integration with three main positions: isolation – solidarity – engulfment.[61]

He maintains that 'persons choose imagined communities over real ones when they feel desperately humiliated'.[62] This 'striving for power' is evident in the modern Lesbian and Gay Liberation movement, in the myriad of institutions we have formed. Their counterpoint is the thousands, perhaps millions, of people, who despite having a primarily homosexual orientation, dissociate from a public lesbian/gay identity, proclaiming those who do to be 'extremist'. The mechanism of isolation-solidarity-engulfment can also be read as a product of the pride/shame hypothesis in that it mirrors the experience of many of us whose entry into the lesbian or gay community facilitates such huge relief at the perceived end to alienation and ostracism that a fantasy chimera of home is fostered (maybe even festers). Early interactions often result in a period of infatuation with seemingly secure out lesbians, who are imagined to embody the assured, stable identity we lack. The initial solidarity we feel is akin to falling in love. As the relationship proceeds and tensions arise, real selves intervene and the disappointment is profound. Instead of withdrawing, bitter, hurt and overwhelmed, we would do better to appraise and own the measure of shame which drives us to compensate so needfully. Shame occurs when we internalize an ideal we are not able to meet, we become *a*shamed, punishing ourselves, and projecting this onto others whom we include in our failure. For example: butch-baiting, especially from other butches, is a product of this failure ('You aren't a real butch, Sally, because...'). An aspect of this is the competitiveness shame produces, a measuring of oneself against an internalized and projected ideal,[63] and a desire to make others fail in comparison to ourselves ('I'm butcher than you'). This is not about loving the diversity of butchness, this is about the idealization of an impossible category.

Shame as a centred identity has historical resonance in lesbian culture. Representations of the abjected stone butch abound in the middle-class cultures of lesbian feminism. She is recently being recast/reversed as a proud and honourable tradition.[64] The spectre of the 'too butch' persona has haunted lesbians, where butch is the distilled and visible embodiment of lesbian desire. This not only connotes sexual shame, but also represents the splitting off of shamed parts of the self. Stone butches seem to inhabit the sexual shadows of the lesbian corpus, cast there in an unacknowledged conspiracy of shame. The invocation 'For Shame!' enforces ejection from society, simultaneously conjoining its declaimants, conferring coveted membership of a branding elite. These structures of displacement can be read as an incessantly deferred and variable attempt to come to terms with one's own despised difference. These manoeuvres commonly display contempt, an affect closely allied to shame. We see this enacted against other political identities and groupings who would logically be our allies.

Eve Kosofsky Sedgwick has written about shame as 'Queer Performativity'. Shame results from the failure of contact, from the absence of recognition; it constitutes a break in social affection, recalling early intimacy with a parent figure whose disapproval seems to threaten our potential to thrive:

> shame and identity remain in very dynamic relation to one another, at once reconstituting and foundational, because shame is both peculiarly contagious and peculiarly individuating. Many developmental psychologists consider shame the affect that most defines the space wherein a sense of self will develop.[65]

Shame is about what one is, or is made to be; but it can also be a transformative experience. At the moment one is cast out, one enters a new space of definition and individuation, thus at the moment of othering this split forces a new self to rise and form. (Or fall and die.) The space of development is already substantially predetermined, but like the self, it is constantly in motion, and amenable to flux:

> *at least* for certain ('queer') people, shame is simply the first, and remains a permanent, structuring fact of identity: one that has its own, powerfully productive and powerfully social metamorphic possibilities.[66]

Lesbian sadomasochists – the self-proclaimed outlaws of the Lesbian Nation – are often understood to ritualize shame as part of a sexual scenario.[67] The vindication of lesbian sadomasochism has often been made in instrumentalist and therapeutic terms: that the knowing repetition of rhetorics of power, in domination and submission, can exorcise the implicit and exploitative presence of power in everyday existence, in a cathartic sacrament. This is a defence against the lesbian feminist excoriation of s/m as *irretrievably* shamed behaviour.[68] The temporary theatre of an s/m scene grants the participants – and especially the masochist – permission to be a spectacle, to be *seen*, to be the consummate focus of an erotic gaze via the extreme and scripted exchange of humiliation. I use the term exchange because the sadist, in conferring shame, is complicit in its execution (like any good top she must be able to take it, to give it correctly). The top is displacing her shame onto another, the bottom has her shame hypostasized and ideally dispersed ('hurts so good . . .'). The intense, desiring regard of the master, whose aim is to produce the masochist's most intense pleasure, reconnects her affect. Pat Califia makes the claim that sadomasochistic sex connects the participants more effectively through mutual recognition than does 'vanilla' sex:

> I could never go back to tweaking tits and munching cunt in the dark, not after this. Two lovers sweating against each other, each struggling for her own goal, eyes blind to each other – how appalling, how deadly. I want to see and share in every sensation and emotion my partner experiences, and I want all of it to come from me.[69]

The aim, so far as the masochist's pleasure is concerned, is to shatter and then rebuild the self, with the sadist as architect.[70] The masochist, whose function is to be fucked, is symbolically gendered as female and passive;

sexual shame is discursively intrinsic to her position. It is her subjectivity which is intended to be fragmented. At the moment she utters the safe word, though, she refounds a boundary and a self.

The s/m scene is often read as a theatrical construct: it has a certain distance, an alienation from the women's daily existence, which can stimulate a reflexivity, an 'acting out' in a Gestaltian sense. The formal, predictable repetition of the ritual of humiliation reinforces its supposed artificiality. The difficulty in proving whether there is a 'real' sexual subject behind the s/m scene who has, on returning to the mundane, been scoured of shame is taken up by Lynda Hart in 'Blood, piss, and tears: the queer real',[71] when she argues against 'accumulating testimonials about the 'truth' of our illusions', citing Derrida that 'there is no illusion as naïve as the illusion of unmediated experience'.[72] Hart proposes that our illusions – such as the one I supply here, that shame can be ritualistically rewritten in s/m scenarios – be continuously multiplied and traversed. The claim is not that scenes are intrinsically beneficial, but that they are potentially transformative forms. Hart, by focusing on sadomasochism's temporality, describes *where it can take you* :

> The scene takes place in what appears to be the 'present', but if it is a present indicative it is a performative one in which the 'I' is *ek-static* – being put out of its place.[73]

She continues: 'the bliss that is an ek-stasis is more like Nietzsche's "oblivion", an active forgetting'.[74] In remembering the originary moment, one connection that can be 'forgot' is the incipient moment of shame, loosening the affect and potentially redirecting it. So, if we follow Hart, then, for these lesbian sadomasochist protagonists, the scene can create a moment of remembering and forgetting, an interval of presence dependent on two desiring subjects meeting and breaking apart, re-formed. Both are changed by the operation of power. To what extent the ruling relations of power are fortified or disputed, whether each articulation shores up shame or dilutes it, will depend on many contexts, but the moment of instability is there.

Shame is a foundational moment in lesbian identity, and like most psychic structures its pattern is to repeat. We interminably reconstitute our lesbian pride out of shame. By addressing shame we can reforge the bond, not with the original parent, nor with the symbolic blaming parent – social opprobrium – but with each other. This *is* a survival issue: we can learn actively to forget the pain, panic and apathy of shame. The aim is not to commute shame magically into pride but to revision shame as facilitating a kind of agency or motility. A response based on empathetic identification leads to a kind of love which does not indulge victimhood, but listens to and affirms the individual's experience of cultural alienation as potentially disengaging from her dependence on heterosexist support.[75] Subjectivity or selfhood can then be predicated on the disavowal of heterosexuality, although this repudiation runs the risk of reification, it can also potentially liberate.

The language of contemporary criticism continues to evoke spatial positioning – liminality, hybridity – such concepts rightfully enrich the models, but as power enlivens the antithesized, oppositional paradigm of Self and Other, we must persist in dissolving it, by interrogating its incarnations. The desire for inclusion stems from a phantasm of an organic world. The profound grief and melancholia that attend lesbian identity (counterposed by jubilation)[76] evolve from the outlaw structure we claim to own. When we look to our own popular culture we can find the two sides of the pride/shame dichotomy being presented in the same popular representation: Hothead Paisan's Herculean hostilities are offset by intervals of anxious abjection. Hothead narratives personify the schizoid quality of this opposition, but whenever Hothead does sink into the depths of nihilism, she morphs into a superhero on return. Similarly, the lesbian cartoonist Alison Bechdel, whose series *Dykes to Watch out For* has had considerable commercial success, makes pride/shame one of her central thematic devices.

What Eve Kosofsky Sedgwick has called the 'irreducible incoherence' of homosexual identity – the contrariety of the minoritizing view on the one hand ('real' gays constitute a separate population) and the universalizing on the other (all men are queer, although some are more queer than others)[77] – is reducible to the inside/outside dichotomy on which pride/shame is predicated, as a transposition. Diana Fuss, writing in 1991, encouraged the reader to explore the dialectic of inside/outside to the point of 'critical exhaustion', at the same time reminding us that:

> The problem, of course, with the inside/outside rhetoric, if it remains undeconstructed, is that such polemics disguise the fact that most of us are both inside and outside at the same time. Any misplaced nostalgia for or romanticization of the outside as a

privileged site of radicality immediately gives us away, for in order to idealize the outside we must already be, to some degree, comfortably entrenched on the inside. We really only have the leisure to idealize the subversive potential of the power of the marginal when our place of enunciation is quite central.[78]

This admonition, rather than instigating resignation through its reorientation of the inside as the privileged site, should incite the reader to appropriate the kinds of knowledge growing out of her locatedness within different social positions, to allow strategic *cross*-identifications to drive a passage. The lesbian's place in culture is bounded by porous membranes, it is always already tentative, mutable, relative and transitory. Examining the structures of feeling emerging from this (dis)placement expedites a localized, specific politics. When the self is shattered into a kaleidoscope of splintered images, the transformation of personal experience into action depends on seeing in the many reflections empathetic identifications with kindred struggles. As a trope, the inside/outside dichotomy is a cardinal axiom of lesbian politics; simultaneously we understand that the mirror of the outside distorts and queers the picture.

I am attending the 1995 Pride March in New York: the five-and-a-half-hour-long stream of identity floats down Fifth Avenue, brandishing its coloured heraldry. It is dreamy, exciting, poignant. To a Brit the segmentation of the march seems also a tad peculiar: we have banners and the like, but the majority mess in together. New York Pride is producing a quandary – where can I join in? Gay Judges? Leather Lesbians? My friends spot a space, and we step out into the middle of the road in Greenwich Village; two Greek Canadians, two hyphen-Americans and one butch from Brighton sweep ecstatically forward. I take a photo of our exultant inclusion, a picture to incarnate the utopian moment of Pride. As I walk I can see quizzicality on the faces in the crowd: 'Who are they? What do they represent?' Seguing between a queer circus troupe and some ballet dancers, we are accidentally sequestered within the Performing Arts section of the march. Perfect. It is the euphoria of Pride that we do come together in such a visible statement of power, to reforge the bonds between us, to exorcise, abandon shame, to perform and rebuild our identities in a moment of ek-stasis. The Pride March, by definition, is a figure of identities in motion, moving through time and space. We do not claim to be the same, but to be kindred, some links in a chain.

Notes

1. Shane Phelan, *Getting Specific: Postmodern Lesbian Politics.* Minneapolis: University of Minnesota Press, 1994, p. 101.
2. This law made it illegal for local authorities to fund activities related to what the British government called 'pretended families' in the cause of 'promoting homosexuality'. The intention of the law – an attack by the Thatcher government against lesbians and gays to create a climate of homophobia – succeeded in this mobilization, but the law itself has never been tried in court; lawyers claim it is unenforceable.
3. Ruthann Robson, *Lesbian (Out)law: Survival under the Rule of Law.* Ithaca, NY: Firebrand Books, 1992, p. 57.
4. *Ibid.*, p. 185.
5. Homi Bhabha, *The Location of Culture.* London: Routledge, 1994, p. 151.
6. Such as Jagose, *Lesbian Utopics* (1994), Lynda Hart, *Fatal Women* (1994) and Teresa de Lauretis, *The Practice of Love: Lesbian Sexuality and Perverse Desire* (1994).
7. Sally R. Munt, *Murder by the Book: Feminism and the Crime Novel.* London and New York: Routledge, 1994, pp. 120–46.

8. Last night unto my bed methought there came
    Our lady of strange dreams, and from an urn
    She poured live fire, so that mine eyes did burn

At sight of it. Anon the floating flame
Took many shapes, and one cried: I am Shame
That walks with Love, I am most wise to turn
Cold lips and limbs to fire; therefore discern
And see my loveliness, and praise my name.

And afterwards, in radiant garments dressed
With sounds of flutes and laughing of glad lips,
A pomp of all the passions passed along
All the night through; till the white phantom ships
Of dawn sailed in. Whereat I said this song,
'Of all sweet passions Shame is loveliest.'

(Lord Alfred Douglas, 'In Praise of Shame', December 1894)

See further Ed Cohen, *Talk on the Wild Side.* London: Routledge, 1994. Thanks to Alan Sinfield for this point.
9. Lynda Hart, *Fatal Women: Lesbian Sexuality and the Mark of Aggression.* Princeton, NJ: Princeton University Press, 1994, p. 119.
10. Anna Marie Smith, 'The case of Jennifer Saunders', in Karla Jay (ed.), *Lesbian Erotics.* New York: New York University Press, 1995, pp. 164–80, p. 176.
11. Emma Donoghue, *Passions Between Women – British Lesbian Culture*

1668–1801. London: Scarlet Press, 1993, p. 50.

12. *Ibid.*, p. 78.

13. Michel Foucault, *The Archaeology of Knowledge*. London: Tavistock, 1972.

14. Terry Castle, *The Apparitional Lesbian*. New York: Columbia University Press, 1993, pp. 92–106.

15. Good historical examples include: Lillian Faderman, *Surpassing the Love of Men*. New York: William Morrow and Co., 1981; Carroll Smith-Rosenberg, 'The female world of love and ritual: relations between women in nineteenth-century America', *Signs: A Journal of Women in Culture and Society*, 1, Autumn 1975: 1–29; Martha Vicinus, 'Distance and desire: English boarding school friendships, 1870–1920', in Martin Bauml Duberman, Martha Vicinus and George Chauncey (eds), *Hidden from History: Reclaiming the Gay and Lesbian Past*. London: Penguin Books, 1991, pp. 212–29.

16. See Sue O'Sullivan, 'Girls who kiss girls – and who cares?', in D. Hamer and B. Budge (eds), *The Good, the Bad and the Gorgeous: Popular Culture's Romance with Lesbianism*. London: Pandora Press, 1994, pp. 8–95.

17. Martha Gever, 'The names we give ourselves', in Russell Ferguson, Martha Gever, Trinh T. Minh-Ha and Cornel West (eds), *Out There: Marginalization and Contemporary Cultures*. Cambridge, MA: MIT Press, 1990, pp. 191–202.

18. Abby Wetten Kleinbaum lists dozens of classical references in *The War Against the Amazons*. New York: New Press, McGraw Hill Book Co., n.d.

19. Joan of Arc carried a sexual and gender ambiguity that made her recoupable as a lesbian icon. She had a reputation as a virgin knight following her martyrdom at the stake in 1430. Rather than being read as a celibate, her abstinence from heterosexuality is co-opted into ambient sapphism. The charges against her read:

> The said Jeanne put off and entirely abandoned woman's clothes, with her hair cropped short and round in the fashion of young men, she wore shirt, breeches, doublet, with hose joined together, long and fastened to the said doublet by twenty points, long leggings laced on the outside, a short mantle reaching to the knee, or thereabouts, a close-cut cap, tight-fitting boots or buskins, long spurs, sword, dagger, breastplate, lance and other arms in the style of a man-at-arms.

> (Marina Warner, *Joan of Arc: The Image of Female Heroism*. Harmondsworth: Penguin, 1983, p. 149)

Sadly Warner rejects out of hand as 'totally inadequate' any reading of Joan as a lesbian, which she calls 'pathological' (p. 155). In a disingenuous denial, Warner describes various monachoparthenics (disguised female monks) as holy transvestites, virgins every one. According to popular lesbian rereadings, Joan renounced heterosexuality just as she abrogated Womanhood. Joan was executed as much for her transvestism as for her hearing of voices (a rather fascinating analogy for the whispering pull of counter-discourse). However, the various lesbian warriors of history are almost exclusively of a privileged socio-economic class; folkloric in origin, they often depend on chivalric and hierarchized codes of honour, their lesbianism often only a vaguely attributed rumour/wish. Thus occurs the customary binary structure of elevation/denigration: the woman who has the social authority to be able to represent others is heroized, the woman who is already othered is pathologized. A more sinister potential for Joan of Arc is illustrated in her appropriation by Jean Marie Le Pen's French National Front party, which has used the 'Maid of Orléans' as the symbol of Gaullist resistance. During the 1996 May Day parade, a young Catholic armoured horsewoman rode through the streets in a reincarnation of Joan of Arc (suggestively, Geraldine Guy 'prays to the saint every night'; *The Observer*, Sunday 5 May 1996, p. 20). The outlaw metaphor, encapsulated by Joan of Arc, is plastic and clearly appropriable by Fascism as well as by progressive political ideologies.

20. Warner, *Joan of Arc*, p. 98.

21. Alice Echols, *Daring to Be Bad: Radical Feminism in America 1969–1975*. Minneapolis: Minnesota University Press, 1989, p. 10.

22. See Echols, *Daring to Be Bad*.

23. *Ibid.*, pp. 93–5. Although hopefully one significant difference in a contemporary action would be a recognition that beauty contests are one of the few ways for working-class women to earn money and (limited) status, and therefore it would not depict the models targeted as mindless victims.

24. Although the mainstreaming of body arts in 1990s fashion can be seen as another example of the colonization of gay culture, it also indicates the diffuse boundaries of inside/outside.

25. Although in fact many of the Greenham women were heterosexual, their denotation and connotation as lesbians by all forms of media meant they were de facto symbolic lesbians. This was also enforced by the identity of 'political lesbianism'.

26. See Sally R. Munt, 'Imagery of Greenham Common Peace Camp'. Unpublished BA dissertation, University of Southampton, 1985.

27. And what about the lesbian Armed Forces personnel in the base? Were they in or out? The binary, under scrutiny, fragments.

28. Monique Wittig, *Les Guérillières*. Trans. David Le Vay. Boston: Beacon Press, 1985, p. 138.

29. Sarah Schulman *et al.*, *The Lesbian Avengers Handbook: A Handy Guide to the Revolution*. New York: The Lesbian Avengers, 1993.

30. The woman who appropriates the power of the phallus, to name, to act, to desire and be desired.

31. The group, Titi Liberation, has been campaigning independently for several years.

32. See Sarah Schulman, *My American History*. London: Cassell, 1995, p. 281.

33. *Ibid.*, p. 318. Organized to galvanize opposition to anti-gay legislation in Lewiston, Maine, the Avengers' bus travelled from New York through Boston, Northampton, Albany, Syracuse and Burlington, VT., ending in Lewiston two weeks before the vote.

34. Lynda Hart, *Fatal Women*, p. 93.

35. Recently overturned by the US Supreme Court.

36. Schulman *et al.*, *The Lesbian Avengers Handbook*, pp. 40 and 43. Ironically, this poster was designed by a black lesbian, but this does not define its reception.

37. The Avengers are not above appropriating more traditional methods too, such as the door-

knocking and leafleting campaign that volunteers ran in rural Idaho to galvanize protest against the proposed state-wide homophobic legislation (LACROP campaign, 1994). This tactic also resulted in previously isolated rural lesbians being contacted and mobilized into the activist lesbian community for the first time. It was effective recruitment.

38. As I write, three police officers are being tried for the murder of a British black woman, Joy Gardner, whom they suffocated by wrapping rolls of surgical tape around her mouth thirteen times and bound with leg restraints and a body belt with handcuffs to prevent her from moving, in an attempt at forced deportation. The descriptions of Gardner proffered by the defence caricature her strength to an incredible degree, in order to justify their – shall we say – overkill. The jury has been instructed by the trial judge to ignore any political or racial dimensions to the case, which he warned jurors 'it certainly does not possess'. Another example is Winnie Mandela, whose fall from the Western liberal pantheon is predicated on the preconception of her susceptibility to violence, as a black woman. Although the ANC dropped her first, the West was quick to concur.

39. Valerie Solanas, *The SCUM Manifesto*. New York: Olympia Press, 1968.

40. *Ibid.*, Introduction, p. xxiv.

41. *Ibid.*, p. 43. Sadly, the 1996 film production failed to capitalize fully on the satiric tendencies of SCUM, focusing rather on Solanas's tragic biography, with the hindsight of her death in poverty.

42. Caroline Sheldon, 'Lesbians and film: some thoughts', in Richard Dyer (ed.), *Gays and Film*. New York: Zoetrope, 1977, pp. 6 and 12, quoted in Lynda Hart, *Fatal Women: Lesbianism and the Mark of Aggression*. p. 76.

43. Monique Wittig, *The Straight Mind and Other Essays*. Hemel Hempstead: Harvester Wheatsheaf, 1992.

44. Paula Graham, 'Looking lesbian: Amazons and aliens in science fiction cinema', in Diane Hamer and Belinda Budge (eds), *The Good, the Bad, and the Gorgeous: Popular Culture's Romance with Lesbianism*. London: Pandora Press, 1994, pp. 196–217, pp. 217–18.

45. Charlotte Raven, 'Girl crazy', *Guardian*, Thursday 25 May 1995, Supplement, pp. 6–7.

46. British readers may not be familiar with the way these organizations have proliferated in the 'self-help' culture of 1980s and 1990s USA. In the UK the only widespread (and original) version is Alcoholics Anonymous, and its adjunct Al-Anon, a support group for friends and family of alcoholics.

47. bell hooks, *Outlaw Culture: Resisting Representations*. New York: Routledge, 1994, p. 247.

48. Although one would hope that *Tank Girl* is not the end of it.

49. hooks, *Outlaw Culture*, p. 244.

50. Ann Cvetkovich, 'Sexual trauma/queer memory: incest, lesbianism, and therapeutic culture', *GLQ: A Journal of Lesbian and Gay Studies*, 2 (4), 1995: 351–79, p. 385.

51. *Ibid.*, p. 388.

52. Dorothy Allison, *Bastard out of Carolina*. London: Flamingo Books, 1993, p. 309.

53. *Ibid.*, p. 113.

54. Thomas Scheff, 'Emotions and identity: a theory of ethnic nationalism', in Craig Calhoun (ed.), *Social Theory and the Politics of*

Identity. Oxford: Basil Blackwell, 1994, pp. 277–303, p. 286.

55. Helen Block Lewis, *Shame and Guilt in Neurosis*. International Universities Press, 1971.

56. Scheff, 'Emotions and identity', p. 90.

57. Gershen Kaufman, *Shame: The Power of Caring*. Rochester, VT: Schenkman Books Inc., 1992, p. 8.

58. *Ibid.*, p. 291.

59. Jonathan Dollimore, *Sexual Dissidence: Augustine to Wilde, Freud to Foucault*. Oxford: Oxford University Press, 1991.

60. The phrase belongs to Lewis, *Shame and Guilt*, and Alfred Adler, *The Individual Psychology of Alfred Adler*. New York: Basic Books, 1956.

61. Scheff, 'Emotions and identity', p. 298.

62. *Ibid.*, p. 301.

63. Lacanian feminism is centrally concerned with this problem for women.

64. See Leslie Feinberg, *Stone Butch Blues*. Ithaca, NY: Firebrand Books, 1993; Judith Halberstam, 'Male identified women', Paper given at *InQueery, InTheory, InDeed, The Sixth North American Lesbian, Gay, and Bisexual Studies Conference*, Iowa City, 17–20 November 1994.

65. Eve Kosofsky Sedgwick, 'Queer performativity: Henry James' *The Art of the Novel*', *GLQ: A Journal of Lesbian and Gay Studies*, 1 (1), 1993: 1–16, p. 5. Sedgwick pursues the debates on shame in *Shame and Its Sisters*, edited by Eve Kosofsky Sedgwick and Adam Frank (Durham, NC, and London: Duke University Press, 1995), which is a reader of Silvan Tomkins' theories of affect. I intend to take up these ideas more fully in my next book, *Shame, Subjectivity, and the Self* (forthcoming).

66. Sedgwick, 'Queer performativity', p. 14.

67. Some lesbian sadomasochists would argue that in fact s/m practice ritualizes *humiliation* in order to reinscript states of shame, the difference being that whereas shame is perceived as an ontological state, humiliation is transitory and contextualized, but can arguably release the former.

68. See works by Sheila Jeffreys, e.g., *Anticlimax*. London: The Women's Press, 1990; *The Lesbian Heresy*. London: The Women's Press, 1994.

69. Pat Califia, *Public Sex: The Culture of Radical Sex*. San Francisco: Cleis Press, 1994, p. 163.

70. Although the top is herself implicated:

    The top does not merely wait on the shore, dispassionately observing the descent and resurgence of the bottom. Nor does she simply facilitate that movement. She takes and is taken there by and goes and comes there *with* the bottom.

    (Lynda Hart, 'Blood, piss, and tears: the queer real', *Textual Practice*, 9 (1), Spring 1995: 55–66, p. 64.)

71. *Ibid.* Hart takes up this subject in her book, *Between the Body and the Flesh: Performing Sadomasochism*. New York: Columbia University Press, 1997.

72. *Ibid.*, pp. 63 and 62.

73. *Ibid.*, p. 63.

74. *Ibid.*

75. Needless to say: not all narratives will be the same, nor can they be assimilated.

76. I am not trying to formulate lesbian identity here as a manic/depressive state (!), but to characterize the psychology of outlaw status.

77. Eve Kosofsky Sedgwick, *The Epistemology of the Closet*. Hemel Hempstead: Harvester Wheatsheaf, 1991.

78. Diana Fuss, *Inside/Out: Lesbian Theories, Gay Theories*. New York: Routledge, 1991, Introduction, p. 5.

5

The Lesbian Nation

'So, that was my role in the growth of Queer Nation,' Troy
Ruby told me, chomping on a cigarette. 'One minor character in
a minor movement. *Queer* did get old very fast, nowadays only
academics take it seriously. But *Nation* managed to live on in
many fond conversations. Transgender Nation, Alien Nation,
Reincar Nation. And all along the line no one noticed how much
that word echoed with the secret store of nostalgic desire for
normalcy, normalcy, normalcy. Those apple pie, warm kitchens
and American flags that are trapped somewhere back there
between the hypothalmus and the frontal lobe. Someplace in the
Central Drawer where *One* Nation Under *God, Indivisible,
With Liberty and Justice For All* resonates eternally. And that is
why *Nation* is ultimately such a comforting word. And that is
how I became an American poet.'[1]

*In 1994 I spent six months living in New York. For the first time
the fact of my Englishness is forced upon me as it is often the first
topic of conversation with American lesbians I meet. Invariably,
they read me as upper-middle-class, which is what Englishness
seems to mean in American cultural representation. Passing in a
class context is something I would never manage in England (my
accent is distinctively Northern and working-class), and the
ability creates an uneasy self-consciousness, of whiteness and of
fraudulence. I had gone to America naïvely expecting the Lesbian
Nation still to be intact. Instead I am confronted by my own
exile.*

The idea of the Lesbian Nation developed from the lesbian feminisms
formed in the USA during the 1970s, its most famous encapsulation
appearing in Jill Johnston's eponymous *Lesbian Nation: The Feminist
Solution* written in the three years 1970–2, and published in 1973. The

idea of the Lesbian Nation, as I intend to examine it here, is of a utopic community and a fantasy of autonomy, which offered a kind of heroic narrative for the lesbian feminists of the 1970s. The idea of a Lesbian Nation provided a rhetoric of empowerment, and most significantly a cognitive space, for women experiencing *dis*placement from American culture. Further, as an imagined community, it was a metaphor of movement, of aggregation, of transit and progress to a *state* of belonging. The Lesbian Nation provided the sense of a bounded, shared identity of resistance which was conceptualized in relation to other political protest movements of the 1960s, notably the black Civil Rights Movement, drawing from the longing of other excluded identities for their place in American society.

It has become formulaic in the 1990s to patronize the 'excesses' of 1970s lesbian feminism; I hope to avoid that here by attempting a critical but fair appraisal of one of its most structuring totems. The liberal academic consensus on nationalisms is to bipolarize movements into 'good nationalisms' and 'bad nationalisms', which depends on the perceived relative social power of disenfranchised/dominant minority groups.[2] To be trite, a nationalist agenda proposed by white supremacists is not accorded the same legitimacy as, say, one originating from Native American tribes. There is a degree of liberal relativism, not to mention nascent hypocrisy here. A certain romanticization of oppression is evident in the knee-jerk tendency to laud any territorial claim arising from marginalized groups, which often masks dominant historical discourses of regulation and displacement hovering in the wings, such as in the connotative 'reservations'. Ideologies of race or ethnicity often compound the nationalist controversy, as they provoke the question of how that identity is being defined, specifically who is to be included and who is to be excluded – and who will be displaced. Any nationalism has a historical and ideological complexity which needs to be examined separately for just cause and expression. (The obvious subsequent problem is to consider who can be elected to examine.) Lesbian nationalism became a mobilizing force; the impetus for its ideology can be understood as the counterpoint to years of felt exclusion and invisibility. But we may also wish to consider who was excluded from lesbian nationalism, what were the limits of its historical roots and ideological liaisons, what were its inadvertently destructive effects and whether its agenda can ultimately be read simply as either radical or reactionary. We may also be able to distil the analogy of lesbian nationalism to comment on the idea of the bounded lesbian identity itself.

Nations and nationalism

> Nations as a natural God-given way of classifying men, as an inherent...political destiny, are a myth; nationalism, which sometimes takes pre-existing cultures and turns them into nations, sometimes invents them, and often obliterates pre-existing cultures.[3]

Nations as we know them are social artefacts, belonging to a particular, recent, modern historical period. Nations appear under certain technological and linguistic conditions, and are inherently unstable, due to the contingency of those conditions. Nationalism is defined above by Ernest Gellner as primarily to mean 'a principle which holds that the political and national unit should be congruent'.[4] However, there are fissures within nationalism, as Eric Hobsbawm points out:

> First, official ideologies of states and movements are not guides to what is in the minds of even the most loyal citizens or supporters. Second, and more specifically, we cannot assume that for most people national identification – when it exists – excludes or is always or ever superior to, the remainder of the set of identifications which constitute the social being. In fact it is always combined with identifications of another kind, even when it is felt to be superior to them. Thirdly, national identification and what it is believed to imply, can change and shift in time, even in the course of quite short periods.[5]

Already the idea of nationalism becomes complex and contingent on numerous competing discourses. For a nationalist ideology to form there must be some general functional prerequisites: firstly there must be an emergent 'specialised clerical class', as Gellner called it, 'a clerisy',[6] which forms an intellectual culture. Education is key to this development, producing a shared culture and technological skills of communication. Nationalism is the 'consequence of a new form of social organization, based on deeply internalised, education-dependent high cultures'.[7] Crucially, Gellner's formulation of nationalism depends on the establishment of a common culture, one which is proselytized by the middle class. Perversely this culture is one appropriated in the name of the 'folk', i.e. the putative working class. Its symbolism draws heavily from a selective and idealized representation of the working class. It is repackaged and delivered back to 'the people' in a stylized and romanticized summons to authenticity. Genuine folk traditions only manage to survive artificially, preserved in the form of heritage culture:

> nationalist ideology suffers from pervasive false consciousness. Its myths invert reality: it claims to defend folk culture while in fact it is forging a high culture; it claims to protect an old folk society while in fact helping to build up an anonymous mass society.[8]

Secondly, despite the fact that nationalism preaches a historical continuity with the past, paying homage to the 'folk culture' it has bowdlerized, it operates by using a form of nostalgia which is intrinsically new and commensurate with the demands to amalgamate and reformulate 'the nation' according to contemporary criteria. In its 'narcissism of self-generation',[9] 'its self-image and its true nature are inversely related';[10] nationalism is an ahistorical and homogenizing process. In 1882 Ernest Renan gave his now famous lecture 'What Is a Nation?' in which he observed: 'the essence of a nation is that all individuals have many things in common, and also that they have forgotten many things'.[11] Thirdly, Ernest Gellner defines nationalism as a *sentiment* produced when the political and national unit is incongruent:

> the feeling of anger aroused by the violation of the principle, or the feeling of satisfaction aroused by its fulfilment. A nationalist *movement* is one actuated by a sentiment of this kind.[12]

If we understand nationalism as a sentiment, a feeling of exclusion which is articulated as a protest for inclusion, we must necessarily examine that feeling and the ways in which it is echoed and reproduced as an act of language, becoming in Foucault's words a 'discursive formation', a political structure, inventing the 'nation' where one previously did not exist.

We also need to conceive of how nationalism appears as a narrative, a story, which inscribes its readers through a mechanism of identification, through interpolating sentiment. Nations are imaginary constructs that depend on a range of cultural fictions to maintain their mythic existence. Geoffrey Bennington highlights this connection:

we undoubtedly find narration at the centre of nation: stories of national origins, myths of founding fathers, genealogies of heroes. At the origin of the nation, we find a story of the nation's origin.

Which should be enough to inspire suspicion.[13]

He continues to stress, 'the idea of the nation is inseparable from its narration'.[14] Thus we need to approach any examination of the occasion of nationalist sentiment with the tools of narrative analysis, to see how nations, as fictions, involve the curiosity and evoke the commitment of a reader, and ask why this particular story captures her/his intricate social imagination, at this specific fork in history.

Nation space

It seems axiomatic to claim that 'nation' is a spatial metaphor. Any thought of nationhood implies the construction of a bounded space, a place which has borders and frontiers, which contains a centre and margins. The edges of a nation attempt both to enclose and of course to exclude. The borders of a nation are better perceived as membranes, permeable boundaries which permit communication with, and sometimes infusion by, the other. The nation has to have something to delineate itself against: meaning is created by a process of differentiation, and 'nation' as a concept contains its own degeneration, as those boundaries bleed.

In considering the nation as a space from the point of view of the Other, the most cogent theorization appears in Homi Bhabha's work, specifically in his essay 'Dissemination: Time, Narrative, and the Margins of the Modern Nation',[15] from which I wish to take some significant premisses. Firstly, Bhabha speaks movingly of the gathering of scattered peoples: 'The nation fills the void left in the uprooting of communities and kin, and turns that loss into the language of metaphor.' Here we have the sense of nation as an expression of grief for something which has been lost and is consequently longed for. Interestingly, the nation is for Bhabha what heterosexuality is for Butler – the site of loss and melancholia.[16] The nation also embodies the desire of the exile – Bhabha lyrically invokes us to realize 'how fully the shadow of the nation falls on the condition of exile'.[17] The nation from this perspective is not 'here' but 'there', a desired object, representing a projected yearning for a perfectly consolidated self, paradoxically beyond the self. Perhaps we might think of this nation as externalizing the dream of integration. Interestingly, the profundity of this yearning can only be revealed metaphorically, in that sense linguistic expression is itself displaced in a 'figure of speech'. So, the grief of unbelonging, of migrancy, is fixated by its own antithesis, a fantasy of transcendence and immanence.

Secondly, Bhabha poses the question of representing the nation as a temporal process, a 'national time-space'. The people are not simply a series of historical events, an origin or a national past, they also exist contemporaneously as signs of the present:

> The scraps, patches and rags of daily life must be repeatedly turned into the signs of a coherent national culture, while the very act of narrative performance interpellates a growing circle of national subjects. In the production of nation as narration there is a split between the continuist, accumulative temporality of the pedagogical, and the repetitious, recursive strategy of the performative.[18]

In writing the nation there is a temporal tear between the need to marshal the present and perform the past. According to Bhabha this results in the splitting of the national subject, hence:

> the problem is not simply the 'selfhood' of the nation as opposed to the otherness of other nations. We are confronted with the nation split within itself... The barred Nation It/Self, alienated from its eternal self-regeneration, becomes a liminal signifying space that is *internally* marked by the discourses of minorities, the heterogeneous histories of contending peoples, antagonistic authorities and tense locations of cultural difference.[19]

Thus 'the difference of space returns as the Sameness of time'- in an attempt to cohere diverse people into one horizontal nation, history must be read as one homogenous tradition. Bhabha is drawing attention to the instability of the nation, arguing that any notion of the people will emerge in narrative ambivalence, fluctuation and disjunction, in the 'abyss of enunciation'[20] produced by this rupture. He then argues that 'from the liminal movement of the culture of the nation... minority discourse emerges... minority discourses that speak betwixt and between times and places'.[21] A nation is ineluctably comprised and shaped by what it defines itself against from its own *inside*. The imagined nation of nationalism is fantasized as intact, impregnable, unitary, constant and monolithic; as a material entity the nation space is ruptured, it is mutable, temporal, limited and precarious, haunted by its own division.

Nationalism and sexuality

Corporeal metaphors are unavoidable, as the nation is often depicted as a vital body, with a heart, lungs, mind and extremities, concomitant with the fantasy of the bounded sealed body. Nations can be 'healthy' or 'diseased', depending on one's rhetorical viewpoint. Nation/bodies have lives – they are born, get old and die. Metaphors of contagion assail the nation/body. Nations, like bodies, are also sexed. 'Nationalisms', as Anne McClintock underscores 'are from the outset constituted in gender power'.[22] Despite the fact that citizenship has historically been denied to women, who in law have paradoxically been rendered stateless, as the editors of *Nationalisms and Sexualities* have pointed out, in the rhetoric of war there is a deeply ingrained 'depiction of the homeland as the female body whose violation by foreigners requires its citizens and allies to rush to her defence'.[23] This rape analogy depends on the trope of nation-as-woman, but more specifically on the patriarchal construction of the nation as Mother, the dutiful angel who nurtures and protects the propagation of the national culture. By implication, then, nations are metaphorically incestuous, for who, if not 'men', impregnate the Mother – who is at once the ground (grammatically) and the figure? The rape metaphor, which invokes not so much loss as incorporation, produces melancholia.[24]

In this heterosexist and perverse construct, then, the men impregnate the 'soil' of the nation with their potent seed. Critics have observed how often liberation movements also employ this same predicate, 'women's bodies can become cyphers in the imaginings of male resistance fighters'.[25] In the erotic fervour of nationalism, heterosexual desire foments the ardour of the activist. Geraldine Heng and Janadas Devan have this to say regarding the politics of nationalism which led to the Republic of Singapore:

> A sexualised, separate species of nationalism, in other words, was being advocated for women: as patriotic duty for men grew out of the barrel of a gun (phallic nationalism, the wielding of a surrogate

technology of the body in national defense), so would it grow, for women, out of the recesses of the womb (uterine nationalism, the body *as* a technology of defense wielded by the nation).

They conclude: 'Women, and all signs of the feminine, are by definition always and already anti-national.'[26] I am reminded of the poignancy of Virginia Woolf's asseveration in *Three Guineas* (1938), 'As a woman I have no country'.

Building on Homi Bhabha's work that I have outlined briefly above, R. Radhakrishnan takes up the question of the juxtaposition of nationalism with feminism, asking specifically, 'Why is it that the advent of the politics of nationalism signals the subordination if not the demise of women's politics?'.[27] Most of the contributors to this volume (*Nationalisms and Sexualities*) see feminism in antipathy to nationalism, and Radhakrishnan offers an argument as to why: observing the dichotomous structure of inside/outside that nationalism (in this case Indian nationalism) deploys, Radhakrishnan argues that this produces a false and repressive resolution of its own identity, through an anti-feminist, even mysogynistic, gesture. This recalls Bhabha's temporal splitting, contemporary experience versus historical tradition:

> The locus of the true self, the inner/traditional/spiritual sense of place, is exiled from the processes of history while the locus of historical knowledge fails to speak for the true identity of the nationalist subject. The result is a fundamental rupture, a form of basic cognitive dissonance, a radical collapse of representation. Unable to produce its own history in response to its inner sense of identity, nationalist ideology sets up Woman as victim and goddess simultaneously. Woman becomes the allegorical name for a specific historical failure: the failure to co-ordinate the political or the ontological with the epistemological within an undivided agency.[28]

So, Woman occupies the place of the split subject of nationalism. Women (standing in metonymically for Woman) are blamed for the failure of the masculinist fantasy of a coherent spatial subjectivity. This framework of nationalism is cast in a heterosexual bipolarism.

Nationalism claims a privileged narrative perspective: as Mary Layoun puts it, 'Narratives of nationalism propose a *grammar* of the nation – the 'correct' or orderly use and placement of the constituent elements of the nation'.[29] She describes how the rhetoric of nationalism-as-narrative persuades and convinces its audience of the efficacy and desirability, the 'naturalness' of its terms. But she identifies a momentary gap, a space, between the rhetoric and the grammar, allowing flexibility which can favour an articulate manoeuvre to be spoken. Despite the formulations of nationalism as a patriarchal narrative, it seems an essentialist mistake to imbue it with intrinsic masculinity, positioning women as solely intransigent passive victims of male agency. The disjunction between the mythic level and the material level of the experiential (although this distinction is never absolute) suggests that women must be more than semen receptacles for the nation/body. Layoun herself provides examples of this slippage in the fiction of the Palestinian writer Sahar Khalifeh, which recasts the patro-centric nationalist narrative. Two other examples in the same volume deserve a closer look. First, Joyce Hope Scott's essay on black nationalist fiction records the role black women played in the movement as early as the eighteenth century, in the benevolent and mutual relief societies, into the 1830s in the anti-slavery societies and continuing with relative vocalness and centrality within the Harlem Renaissance and the Black Arts movements. Against this she contrasts the summons to female subordination in the 'phallocentric and patriarchal vision of Black Power',[30] which returned women to the margins in the 1960s. Second, Ketu Katrak analyses Ghandi's *Satyagraha* independence movement for a strategy which deliberately deployed 'feminine' tactics of passive resistance. Ghandi did mobilize vast numbers of women for the nationalist agenda, and Katrak invokes their momentous struggle. However, Katrak also critiques the way this potentially feminist direction is undermined by Ghandi's reinscribing of female sexuality according to a selective use of religious precepts, stating that a woman can only be pure by renouncing sex. In both these essays the authors do not take the view that nationalisms can be unproblematically adopted for feminist political purposes. However, they do focus on ideological interstices that adjust to feminist practices.

In mapping out the field of nationalism it is essential to refer to the research that posits the homoerotic rather than heterosexual affiliations of nationhood. George Mosse's history of sexual norms in modern Europe, *Nationalism and Sexuality*, argues that our present notions of middle-class morality and 'respectability' are rooted in nineteenth- and twentieth-century ideologies of nation. Mosse substantiates Ernest

Gellner's claim that the consolidation of middle-class norms leads to the imposing of those norms on the rest of society in the name of 'the nation'. Specifically, he argues how nineteenth-century bourgeois idealizations of virility came to be sublimated as nationalist virtue, manliness and male beauty, symbolizing the nation's spiritual and material vitality. The 'back-to-nature' movement in England and Germany depended on the neoclassicist romantic revival of Greek models of (male) citizenship and the naturalization of nudity. The covert homoeroticism abeyant in this cult of the body was made explicit by figures such as Edward Carpenter in England and the poet Stefan George in Germany. Both men inspired a following, one from the political Left, the other from the Right. Edward Carpenter was a utopian socialist who espoused a return through nature to a true community of men. A reformist homosexual, he believed that nudity, 'the gospel of individual regeneration',[31] would abolish discrimination. Carpenter was particularly interesting for his romanticization of the land and of working-class labour, both factors that reoccurred in lesbian nationalism.

It is Nazi Germany that provides Mosse with an example of established homoerotic nationalism. The naked Greek youth distilled the aspirant imagery of the Third Reich, clearly a raced symbol, as well as sexed. As Mosse comments: 'a beautiful Jew was a contradiction in terms'.[32] The Nazis built upon the nineteenth-century concept of the *Männerbund*, passionate male friendship formed primarily among élite youth, emphasizing nature and physical strength grounded in a brotherhood of leaders. According to the historian Hans Blüher, homosexuality in the *Männerbund* represented spiritual principles – heroism, leadership and communality. Mosse comments on how the distinction between homoeroticism and homosexuality became blurred:

> The rediscovery of the human body combined with the exclusively male nature of the early youth movement did raise the spectre of homoeroticism, even homosexuality. Those who tried to recapture their own bodies as well as nature from the hypocrisy as well as artificiality of bourgeois life, as they saw it, also wanted to find refuge in a true community of affinity. They began to perceive the nation as such a community. Moreover the nation helped spiritualize their new sensuality...[33]

Within the intellectual Stefan George's circle, homoeroticism was seen as the principal agent of national renewal. Mosse concludes:

> The dynamic of modern nationalism was built upon the ideal of manliness. Nationalism also put forward a feminine ideal, but it was largely passive, symbolizing the immutable forces which the nation reflected. As a living organism, filled with energy, nationalism tended to encourage male bonding, the *Männerbund*, which by its very nature presented a danger to that respectability the nation was supposed to preserve. Such bonding had been reinvigorated by the rediscovery of the human body at the *fin de siècle*. The male eros tended to haunt modern nationalism.

Such formulations are redolent of the works of critics such as Eve Kosofsky Sedgwick (1991), Jonathan Dollimore (1991) and Terry Castle (1993), all of whom locate homosexuality as proximate, even central, to Western culture. I am not proposing that homosexuality is the 'closet' secret of nationalism, but indeed, because the homoeroticism of the *Männerbund* led eventually to Hitler's *Reichszentrale* police,[34] the purging of homosexuals during *Kristallnacht*, Paragraph 175 and the pink triangle, I am obliged to Sedgwick's claim that gay proximity leads to gay panic:

> I argue that the historically shifting, and precisely the arbitrary and self-contradictory, nature of the way *homosexuality* (along with its predecessor terms) has been defined in relation to the rest of the male homosocial spectrum has been an exceedingly potent and embattled locus of power over the entire range of male bonds, and perhaps especially over those that define themselves not *as* homosexual, but *as against* the homosexual. Because the paths of male entitlement, especially in the nineteenth century, required certain intense male bonds that were not readily distinguishable from the most reprobated bonds, an endemic and ineradicable state of what I am calling male homosexual panic became the normal condition of male heterosexual entitlement.[35]

If we take this model in relation to nationalism, it is feasible to argue that the pervasive, visceral heterosexuality of most nationalisms is the manifestation of a kind of panicked response to the elemental structure of homoeroticism it is compelled towards and concomitantly desperate to repudiate. It is with these contradictory characteristics of nationalism in mind that we turn to lesbian nationalism.

The lesbian nation

So far in this book I have explicated some of the expedient and instrumental identities appropriated and explored by a subculture as forms of spatial resistance. I have described how lesbians can take up space in the urban (post)modern world, how they envision that space-taking and enable themselves through the politics of identity and agency. I have spelled out the necessity for utopian models and described the motivating relationship between icons and lived identities. Now, I wish to examine lesbian identity expressed as a form of nationalism. Lesbian citizenship is located in space and time and self-consciously lived as a form of process, of relational movement. Like other oppressed cultures, lesbians hold fast to a dream of commonality and unification. An ethic of solidarity and commitment informs many liberation movements, and the drive for the 'rightful' colonization of 'their' space – the desire to occupy their perceived constituency – fuels the imagination and the movement of radical struggles.

Several writers have explored spatial metaphors as a way of articulating lesbian occupation, including Gloria Anzaldúa in *Borderlands/La Frontera* (1987), Minnie Bruce Pratt in 'Identity, Skin, Blood, Heart' (1984), and Cherríe Moraga in *Loving in the War Years* (1983). Some have written about the lesbian presence in the city as a locale which makes lesbian identification possible.[36] Ideas of a lesbian nation first appeared as a result of lesbian feminism, in the 1970s: Jill Johnston's project, in The *Lesbian Nation* (1973), was to assemble the sentiment of radical and lesbian feminism into one metaphor, and then to claim the inauguration of a radical state, as a form of political mobilization. Her brief introduction in 'Remarks' indicates her affiliation with nationalist ideology: the first sentence contains a brisk injunction to create a monolithic meaning 'This book *should read...*' [my italics]; it is a text originating from '*middle* unconscious post-war America'; it purports to be a 'true explanation' of 'collective memories' of an archetypal past, with a summons to 'constantly [return] to a [point] of origin'; finally Johnston invokes 'the return to the harmony of statehood and biology through the remembered majesty of women'.[37] Homogeneity through nostalgia, naturalized truth claims and a heroic utopianism – these precepts are not unique to lesbian radicalism. The book is a series of micro-texts that segue through rhetoric, fiction, diary entry, stream of consciousness, spontaneous prose and cultural myth-making, held together by the dominance of the author's voice. In parts a parochial journal through New York Bohemia, the book is a record of white bourgeois radicalism *circa* 1970–2. The narrative builds up a story of failed heterosexuality, descent into madness (the mental exit to another space), personal illumination, political indictment and reconstruction of the hero-protagonist into lesbian feminist consciousness; in structure the book resembles a *roman à thèse* (see pages 18–22).

Johnston argues that prior to the Radicalesbians,[38] 'There was no lesbian identity. There was [only] lesbian activity.'[39] The narrative is a treatise of the move from personal experience to structural analysis, in line with the rhetoric of various liberation movements of the 1960s. Centrally, the political collectivity is formed around the expressive practices of identity, distinguished by the culmination of experience: 'My case was a paradigm for a revolutionary consciousness.'[40] The first shift is to claim an identity (lesbian), the second is to form an affinity group based on that identity ('the community') and the third is to define an enemy ('man as my natural enemy');[41] the fourth is to declare secession:

> I did have a goal or an objective and that was somehow to buy up a lot of space and establish a chain of lesbos on the mainland and invite the lesbian population and … just forget about the men.[42]

The fifth is to begin to colonize: 'All women are lesbians';[43] and finally reproduce: 'The order for the day for all women immediately is *psychic* parthenogenesis.'[44]

A call to parthenogenesis makes sense if we understand the psychic project of the book as an attempt to interrupt the real and metaphorical invasion of female body space, in a rejection of the permeated and 'besieged female'[45] of heterosexist culture. Noticeable in Johnston's text is the repetition of the dualistic image of the violated/inviolate woman, 'Nature is woman, man is the intruder'.[46] The book continuously invokes the threat of the invaded woman, and its call to separatism can be read as an attempt to seal the boundaries of an imagined woman's body. In particular the last chapter is awash with imagery of the 'intact' or 'violated' female, where the most articulated argument for the lesbian nation occurs. There is a metonymic replacement of the female body for the lesbian nation. The body imagery is not unlike that appropriated by other nationalist cultures, and similarly figurations of rape are invoked to produce outrage as a stimulus for warfare and separation. However, whereas in conventional nationalist ideology the female nation body is the passive possession of contesting forces, in Johnston's book the female nation body prefigures Wittig's *The Lesbian Body*[47] in an intense eulogy to the actively desiring woman, an attempt to destroy the binary grammar of (male) subject/(female) object. Johnston, like Wittig, recovers the Amazons as contemporary models of agency and autonomy, a gesture which recalls the recourse to antiquity and classical myths evident in other nationalisms. The active principle of the warrior woman does not merely replace soldiers with their female counterparts though – the female agent acting on the feminine groundspace of nature creates a lesbian text that is able to expose the erotics of nationalism and transform the linear antipathy of the traditional (heterosexist) configuration. Hence Amazon society 'turns around on itself in its own image',[48] in the circular mantra:

I am a woman who is a lesbian because I am a woman and a woman who loves herself naturally who is other women is a lesbian a woman who loves women loves herself naturally this is the case that is herself is all woman is a natural born lesbian...[49]

The textual solipsism posits Woman as an exclusionary category. Johnston's model is further circumscribed by its class- and race-specific denotation – it is clear from the text's dismissal of existing 'old gay' cultures that, using Gellner's formulation, this nationalism is addressed to a clerisy, to a white, middle-class and educated audience. The congruency of its preferred identity is at the expense of a fissured subjectivity, loyal to disparate oppressions. The 'temporal tear' that Homi Bhabha speaks of is here evident in the tendency to create 'Year Zero' in lesbian political identity, oblivious to the personal history of lesbians active in pre-Stonewall gay life. The past being performed is not their past, rather the nationalism being espoused here is selectively open mainly to the youth. Integral to this lesbian nation is the propensity to fracture and forget along the lines of its incompatible discourses. By mimicking nationalism, Johnston has preordained the split of Woman into the competing identity groups which characterized the feminist movement from 1973 to 1983. The centre could not hold.

The utopian rights movement of lesbian feminism was able both to mimic and subvert nationalism. The cultural feminist[50] nationalism of the 1970s was predicated on an ideological and material separatism which led to the creation of 'Wimmin's Land' throughout the USA, its real existence merely a shadow of its powerful symbolic effect. By positing the category of Woman as individuated, no longer dependent on the qualifier 'Not-Man', the conceptual space of Woman as autonomous was squeezed open. The ideology of separatism, lived as an incarnation of the idea of the lesbian nation, dominated lesbian culture in the 1970s. It is to the lived experience of the lesbian nation I now turn.

Utopianism and separatism in the 1970s

The lesbian nation of the 1970s constituted discursive space rather than geographical space. There was no prior land to claim, and a predominantly anarchic movement meant there was no state to make. Lesbian nation was an imagined space, envisioned as the symbolic rupture of women from men – or more specifically – 'patriarchy',[51] as Mary Daly put it: 'Patriarchy is the homeland of males; it is the Fatherland; and men are its agents'.[52] Even if the impetus for separatism was contained within a binary, the establishment of lesbian space did create more freedom to centre the category Lesbian/Woman, providing manoeuvrability within that cypher to align an identity.

There was a vitality in radicalism in the 1970s which is hard to reflect upon now without nostalgia or cynicism. Even in the 1990s we can still appreciate the legacy of lesbian activism in the feminist social infrastructure it produced: rape crisis helplines, battered women's shelters, women's centres, well-woman clinics, retreat centres, all these and more, staffed mainly by lesbians, are the material result of the vision for a safe, utopic space for women to separate and affirm their identity. To be a lesbian and a separatist was to be endowed with the kudos of having made the total commitment to feminism, and separatist communities became the elected conscience of the (lesbian) nation. Dana R. Shugar[53] makes the point that separatist groups were the first amongst white feminists to tackle 'competing' oppressions, even if they did often attribute them to a common cause (sexism). Shugar has analysed the political outcomes of separatism:

Creating a binary other in the figure of men compelled separatists to place all their collective conflicts outside the practice of women themselves. And while some of the opposition women faced did indeed come from external sources, much more of it came from conflicts among collective members themselves... Construction of a demonic, binary other thus ironically provided the impetus toward female community and made the success of that community impossible.[54]

Indicative of this is Shugar's observation that despite the numbers of black women living in separatist communities, in the period 1960–90 not one fictional utopia was written by a woman of colour, nor was there envisioned a utopia for women of colour, i.e. the separatist imaginary was *white*. Blame/victim culture was not left behind with the men; however, it osmosed through into the heart of the collectives themselves circulating in a soup of sick reductionism. ('The most destitute black woman in the world can still be raped by a black man' was one of many offensive edicts I can remember.) Shugar again: 'women's conceptions of an always-oppressive patriarchy took away any effective method through which they could claim responsibility for their own destructive behaviours'.[55] Similarly, despite the romanticization of poverty and of manual labour and trades, and despite the ethnic working-class style adopted by members as fashionable (the infamous 'downward mobility'), the practices of the separatist collectives remained securely middle-class, not least in the way that they were highly literate and mannered. The daily praxis of talk, analysis, meetings and discussion reinforced a verbal culture where self-articulateness was valued, and leaders carried authority through their discursive sophistication. The appropriation of working-class jobs was accompanied by middle-class attitudes to work, in the expectation that these skills would be recognized, rewarded and professionalized. Significantly, that staple of working women's employment – cleaning – never attracted the same cachet.

Ernst Bloch has named the quintessential utopian principle, or 'anticipatory consciousness', 'hope', which when embedded can provide the 'spiritual survival' of a people.[56] This principle of hope had material effects in the form of a national movement inspiring many thousands of women. 'It is possible to understand the utopian text as a determinate type of *praxis*', wrote Frederic Jameson in 1977.[57] Here he wishes to discriminate between the representation of utopia as a static, timeless, image and utopian method, which operates to deconstruct the binary oppositions – and hence divisions – of contemporary society. The utopian process is thus a mechanism of movement, a production of functional radical principles. The utopian discourse of lesbian nationalism in the 1970s can be seen to have resulted in utopian *practices* which did have some positive material effect on woman's everyday lives. The first phase of lesbian separatism can be read as an anticipatory consciousness of hope which produced a range of utopian practices, the most crucial of which was the movement away to form an identity which was not dependent on men; this was, in Jameson's terms, the attempt to break down the binary. The second phase, which was the reconstruction of Lesbian/Woman, floundered. Lesbian nationalism became a discourse of exclusion; in a desire to place and fix the meaning of this identity, the hope died.

Angelika Bammer has analysed feminist utopianism of the 1970s, and concluded that in order for utopianism to succeed it must be grounded in history, acknowledging the real conditions of the world it desires to relinquish. In nationalism we have observed the tendency to reconstitute historical events as myth and nostalgia. Both utopianism and nationalism therefore propose a temporal leap: one creates a mythical 'future', the other a mythical 'past'. Pragmatic utopianism, or utopian process, is the unfolding of the 'latent potential in the here and now';[58] in Jameson's formulation it refuses temporal and spatial polarities and the temptation of exclusion in favour of heterogeneous utopian impulses, tactically driven. Bammer's argument is that 'utopia' as a fixed place and time is inherently conservative. She wishes to replace what we might call an archetype with a *prototype*, a working model which is fashioned by diverse and changing needs. This resists the rejection of the 'old' for the 'new', as a prototype is not fully formed, but a potential moulded from the two. A further contravention of binaries is proposed by Bammer in the way she argues that the 'their world/our world' thinking of the 1970s has been pragmatically reconceptualized to envision change in concrete and incremental ways, in the form of the 'partial utopia'.[59] Thus, rather than viewing the lesbian nation as a revolutionary replacement of the heteropatriarchy, we might see it as a series of radical incursions which widens the fissures of an already cracked edifice. One contemporary remnant of 1970s lesbian nationalism is the Michigan Womyn's Festival, which has grown exponentially during the 1980s and 1990s to include many thousands of dykes each summer. This arguably 'temporal utopia' is regarded by women as a short, safe, rural retreat from a beseiging culture. But, as others have shown,[60] arguments over who can gain entrance to the Festival arise periodically, forcing the participants to redraw the map of 'womyn' each time. Despite the strife generated over, for example, sadomasochism and transgenderism, 'Michigan', as it is colloquially and fondly known, appears to manifest an ethos of inclusivity which mutates to surpass (or assimilate) prejudice. A full study of Michigan remains to be undertaken, as it is a fascinating and anachronistic blend of lesbian ideologies.[61]

Borderlands/La Frontera (Gloria Anzaldúa, 1987)

The configuration of bounded categories such as race, nation, sexuality and identity is an inheritance of nineteenth-century imperial obsessions with naming, containing and blaming. The scurry to secure ambiguity and fix contradiction can also be read as expressive of a fear of the unknown and the different, that can be banished to the non-discursive or extra-symbolic. There is a contrary semiotic action evident here: difference is positioned as either supra or underrepresentable. In effect it becomes a slippery character indeed. In relation to nationalism, we have seen Mosse's attempt to locate a nexus of sexuality, race and gender concerns historically in the nineteenth century. Judith Raiskin has drawn attention to the twin Victorian doctrines of evolution and degeneration to remind us how those 'hybrids' who crossed so-called 'natural' boundaries of race or sex were classified and reviled as deviant and regressive. A healthy nation, according to the ideology of eugenics, was racially and sexually homologous. But Raiskin points out that even in the nineteenth century homosexual rights activists such as Edward Carpenter were advocating 'intermediacy' as 'a revolutionary step forward, not a degenerate state'.[62] Raiskin refers to Carpenter in order to locate the contemporary work of Gloria Anzaldúa within a tradition of radicalism which has appropriated the conceptions of biological essentialism, transforming this conflation of racial/homosexual degeneracy and reworking it into the language of a strategically essentialist reverse discourse. Anzaldúa calls this emerging space the 'mestiza consciousness'.

Borderlands/La Frontera was published in 1987 and has itself functioned as a crossover text in the Anglophile academy, occupying the borderlands of canonized yet 'racially marked' feminist theory. As Raiskin identifies, Anzaldúa draws on her model for the 'New Mestiza' from the work of Mexican nationalist writer José Vasconcelos, who in 1925 proposed that instead of racial purity the ideal nation should be based on 'constructive miscegenation' or 'hybrid progeny', a patriotism dependent on the inversion of nineteenth-century fears of degeneration. But Anzaldúa rewrites his model of a unified Mexican nationhood based on heterosexual reproduction as a queer consciousness 'experienced through the body'[63] – in Anzaldúa's case, a lesbian body, one predicated on active, plural ambiguity, not the passive, prescribed female body of conventional nationalism.

Borderlands has been designated a postmodern lesbian text, a designation which has its own colonialist affect. Anzaldúa, in tandem with the postmodern destruction of secure 'truth' categories, sees the mestiza consciousness as potentially destabilizing the givens of national belonging – the social and sexual fixities of citizenship. She envisions a new space, a national consciousness that frees the self to wander, secure in spiritual belonging. The dispossessed begin to occupy space not confined to the binaries of inside/outside but transcending the material altogether. She describes the Borderland as a state of psychic unrest, which, like a cactus needle in the flesh, has to be excised by the process of writing. 'Nudge a Mexican and she or he will break out with a story',[64] she announces at the start of one chapter, and then proceeds to explain the necessity of performative narrative in the making of tribal cultures. However, in contrast to traditional nationalist narrative, this myth-making is not so much nostalgic as an intentional and *recognized* evolvement based on experience:

> When I write it feels like I'm carving bone. It feels like I'm creating my own face, my own heart – a Nahuatl concept. My soul makes itself through the creative act. It is constantly remaking and giving birth to itself through my body. It is this learning to live with this *la Coatlicue* that transforms living in the Borderlands from a nightmare into a numinous experience. It is always a path/state to something else.

In Anzaldúa's book the body is as much a metaphor as anything else; she stresses that the mestiza consciousness is not literal, but a transformative affect which permeates all spatial relations, collapsing 'here' and 'there'. Thus 'home' is loosened from place, to become a state of mind.

By replacing 'truth' with 'fiction', superseding 'place' with 'motion' and by disposing of the fixed body and replacing it with 'queer consciousness', Anzaldúa deconstructs the old ideal of identity as a totalizing essence. In another essay she writes:

> 'lesbian' is a cerebral word, white and middle class, representing an English-only dominant culture, derived from the Greek word *lesbos* … 'Lesbian' doesn't name anything in my homeland.[65]

Hence, Lesbian Nation, in her formulation, becomes redundant too:

> As a *mestiza* I have no country, my homeland cast me out; yet all countries are mine because I am every woman's sister or potential lover. (As a lesbian I have no race, my own people disclaim me; but I am all races because there is the queer of me in all races.)[66]

Anzaldúa rejects the confrontational stance which was intrinsic to lesbian nationalism in the 1970s as limited by its reactive status, and hence dependent on the definitive manoevres of the oppressor. Anzaldúa repudiates anger and rage on similar grounds, those emotions that fuelled and then splintered much of lesbian feminism. She also rejects separatism as anything but one transitory potential among many, preferring instead a 'continual creative motion that keeps breaking down the unitary aspect of each new paradigm':[67]

> *La mestiza* constantly has to shift out of habitual formations; from convergent thinking, analytic reasoning that tends to use rationality to move toward a single goal (a Western mode), to divergent thinking, characterized by movement away from set patterns and goals and toward a more whole perspective, one that includes rather than excludes.[68]

Anzaldúa is prevented from being fully inscribed within Chicana culture because of her queerness, and she is excluded from dominant white lesbian culture because of being Chicana. Rather than fragment down into another single enclosed identity position, she chooses instead to read her multiple and *simultaneous* identities as bridges (like Lorde), within herself and connecting others. Anzaldúa took the fault-lines of lesbian feminism which formulated an identity based on exclusion and articulated how that vision was *de facto* raced as white and classed as bourgeois; as Phelan points out, she emphatically rejects ontological separatism, which reifies absolute incompatibilities. This is not pure voluntarism, but an attempt to integrate (not merge) different aspects of the self already present and lived from day to day. It is an indictment of the postmodern equivocation that prevents political engagement; it also challenges the postmodern trivializing of the fractured self: these differences are not collapsible into an indeterminate malaise. Drawing upon the black feminist critiques of the preceding decade which refused single-issue identity politics, Anzaldúa presents a new utopia based upon process, positive engagement, fluidity, ambiguity and above all inclusivity. Her desert 'mestiza consciousness' flowered into Queer Nation.

Queer Nation

Queer Nation was first started in New York in April 1990, primarily by people involved in AIDS activism who also wanted to respond politically to a number of bashings of lesbians and gay men in the East Village. So, its origin in part was in the desire to defend space. Queer Nation coalesced around a new generation who were both angry and ironic. It assembled around an anarchist aesthetic which mobilized a 'cultural happening', a momentary incursion into the domain of representation. It wanted to create actions which would have maximum media effect, and its main target was heterosexuality. It aimed to challenge the national, public discourse of sexuality, and in that Queer Nation's anthem was 'We're here! We're Queer! We're fabulous! Get used to it!' Anti-assimilationist in intent, Queer Nation's exhibitionist agenda was self-consciously to shove the homosexual into America's face.

The divide between the younger Queer Nation and the older Lesbian and Gay Liberation Movement seemed profound. The former saw older lesbians and gays (as one critic put it – the over-35s) as capitulating to capitalism and defeated by their own rigid identity politics. The latter patronized Queer Nation and accused it of risking the civil rights gained since the 1960s by alienating a largely liberal public, and of glossing over material inequalities in people's experience of queerness. At issue was the deconstruction of identity *per se*: Queer Nation celebrated liminality, alternative practices, sexual freedom, subversion and ambiguity. It opened the doors to the marginalized and excluded, especially those who were transgendered, bisexual and/or sadomasochist who had borne the brunt of the exclusionary practices of the 'mainstream' movement during the sex wars of the 1970s and 1980s. Pleasure, and individual desire, was the celebratory incentive of this new federation of queers. Queers did not share an identity, only an opposition to the discipline of normalization. Rather than basing a nationalist movement on exclusion and on the scrutiny of who should belong, Queer Nation reversed the parameters and focused on the inclusion of anyone who felt 'different', although crucially sexually different.

Queer Nation practised a form of cultural terrorism on the American nation by incursions into the public realm of sexuality which attempted to 'queer' the nation body. This had the effect of disclosing the hetero-normative hegemony at the same time as it attempted to camp it up. Its intent was to make the nation a space safe for queers, not just in the sense of being tolerated, 'but safe *for* demonstration, in the mode of patriotic ritual'.[69] Queer Nation was a spatial politics of queer embodiment, as Lauren Berlant and Elizabeth Freeman argued:

> This emphasis on safe spaces, secured for bodies by capital and everyday life practices, also finally, constitutes a refusal of the terms national discourse uses to frame the issue of sexuality: being queer is not about the right to privacy: it is about the freedom to be public.[70]

Queer Nation inverted the liberal division of society into public/private space to which lesbians in particular had been confined. The public spectacle of queer sexualities being performed was intended to make heterosexuality estranged, to displace it to the margins and centre the formerly deviant queer. As a strategy of inversion it was risky, but the desire to territorialize aggressively was a reverse colonization and a felt response to a hundred years of restraint: 'queers are thus using exhibitionism to make public space psychically unsafe for unexamined heterosexuality'.[71] Its assertiveness in taking up public space gave Queer Nation an incipient masculinity it was never able to shake.

Despite the well-meaning attempt to welcome social diversity into the Queer Nation, the phenomenon remains perceived today as a white, middle-class eruption of *sexual* discontent. The quintessential protagonist is still the muscular white boy in a 'Queer as Fuck' T-shirt. Steven Seidman has commented on this:

> This very refusal to anchor experience in identifications ends up, ironically, denying differences by either submerging them in an undifferentiated oppositional mass or by blocking the development of individual and social differences through the disciplining compulsory imperative to remain undifferentiated.[72]

In its rush to affirm a new political moment Queer Nation, like many nationalisms, refused and 'forgot' the complex lessons of history, and broke apart over the same social divisions evident in Lesbian Nation and other single-issue projects. Seidman makes a hypothetical remark which I think bears further attention:

> Queer Nationals hope to avoid the self-limiting, fracturing dynamics of identification by an insistent disruptive subversion of identity. Yet... their subversive politics presupposes those very identifications and social anchorings. *Is it possible that underlying the refusal to name the subject (of knowledge and politics) is a utopian wish for a full, intact, organic experience of self and other?* [my italics]

By choosing to consolidate around the rubric of 'queer', young activists were organizing around what they perceived to be the end of shame. But the renunciation of shame involves its invocation. Queer Nation outlaws tried to reinvent the lesbian and gay identity as separated and individuated from shame. But here we hit Seidman's cycle of presuppositions: secession was necessary in order to break the (Gay) Pride/Shame binary, but this was predetermined on a loss. That loss, the grief of denunciation, persisted in resurfacing as the utopian desire for an anchored identity – the past kept breaking into (Queer) Nation Time in the fissures of the future. A Queer identity was fixed in romantic undifferentiation, but the present reality of inequality and regret kept breaking through. In a piece on 'Women as Queer Nationals' in *Out/Look* Maria Maggenti makes a similar point; bemoaning the loss of the agency of the Lesbian Nation of the 1970s she attends a Queer Nation meeting and senses:

an underlying desire, an unspoken yearning it seems, to be accepted instead of liberated. I go home that night worried. How are lesbians ever going to be able to define ourselves in this group, in this decade, in this world?[73]

In bemoaning the need for a young lesbian participant to find her home, she concludes with a fantasy refrain for the new nation:

And I want to tell her to grab her female friends and run, run out into the rainy street shouting with power and anger and glee, shouting and dancing her way to some unknown place, some undiscovered continent, some still-unnamed territory.[74]

American lesbians are still 'lighting out for the territory'.[75]

Imagined communities and lesbian citizenship

If we interpret the utopian desire of lesbian nationalism to be, as Homi Bhabha puts it, 'being in the beyond', it is to inhabit an intervening space with a wish to 'touch the future on its hither side',[76] an understandable desire for lesbians snared by a homophobic present. As any critic of science fictional narrative will point out, though, visions of the future are based on an extrapolation of the present, which, whilst attempting to abandon the present, will also be reinscribing it through a mechanism of selective projection. Despite a powerful revolutionary optimism, both Lesbian Nation and Queer Nation were caught by the very political embeddedness they were trying to escape, by a syntax of forgetting which returned as the race and class politics they were attempting to repress, in the hierarchical name of a sexual 'greater good'. Nationalism was an understandable temptation to lesbian and queer women, appearing to offer them a place of belonging, but as a result of the predetermined tendencies of the discourse of nationalism, both Lesbian Nation and Queer Nation were undone by a historical past which refused to be subsumed by homogenization. Nationalisms are caught between an imaginary past and an imaginary future, both being adjunctive to the imaginary realities of the political present. By appealing to the entrenched interest group rhetoric of US politics, American lesbians seized the imagery of nationalism only to discover that the implicit 'nostalgic desire for normalcy, normalcy, normalcy'[77] unravelled the radical impetus for future structural change, spinning them around and returning them to the mainstream political context. Lesbian Nation and Queer nation were specifically American nationalist formulations, their allure specific to the ideologies of the land of mixture, polyglot opportunity, individual freedom and ethnic rights.[78]

Benedict Anderson observes how nations, nationality and nationalisms are notoriously difficult to define. However, the wish for them originates from a fear of meaninglessness and death – in the lesbian context we can interpret nationalist desire as arising from a historical invisibility contingent on a dea(r)th of signification; lesbians wanted to put themselves on the map. Conversely, they wanted to disappear from it too, the separatist impulse wanting to remove lesbians from the cartography of heteropatriarchy. Their tenacity to maintain the myth of the Lesbian Nation can also be understood as a longing to rebuild familial origin, having been made outcasts from the mythical heterosexual nation family. The seduction of nationalism lies in its promise of an 'imagined community', 'conceived as a deep, horizontal comradeship',[79] a mental image of communion powerful in evoking 'love, and often [a] profoundly self-sacrificing love'.[80] As Bhabha points out, though, whereas it is possible to bind people together in nationalism in the name of love, 'the ambivalent identifications of love and hate occupy the same psychic space', and hence there must be other people left to target with latent aggression: 'the paranoid projections outwards return to haunt and split the place from which they are made'.[81] Benedict Anderson explains how nationalisms arise from the 'outsider within', and we have seen how the Lesbian Nation constituted a similar toehold in dominant culture, whose unacknowledged complicity fuelled a divisive exclusion of 'other others'. Thus nationalisms reproduce a cyclical inclusion and expulsion based on a need to fix identity in place – literally and metaphorically.

Lesbian feminism set itself an impossible task, to constitute a categorical identity – the lesbian. The move was stimulated by a fantasy of autonomy that was inflected by American ideologies of liberal individualism. This reverse discourse was bound to risk counter-reification. 'What a lesbian is' too quickly became 'what a lesbian is not', and divergencies and differences rapidly became excluded from categorization. Nationalisms, like individualisms, are the inventions of modernity. An essentially Marxist model of revolution is a macro-narrative promising to seek total social change. Ironically, class undermined the lesbian feminist revolution by marking it as an activity affordable only by the middle-class women desirous of, and able to afford, the totalizing gesture of separatism. In a conceptual parallel, black feminist theory has shown how middle-class academic feminist theory often forecloses and subjugates real differences between women by invoking 'our' unified differences in deference to a hardly disguised transcendent lesbian or feminist subject. Shane Phelan[82] argues that the problem is not with separatism *per se*, but with the terms of the separatist identity, based as it is on a metaphysical and essential gender incompatibility. Separatism also imposes a categorical unity from within, which is twinned with an excessively paranoid fear of deviation.

Phelan is unequivocal on queer nationalism, which 'provides nothing new, and recycles much that is better left to decompose'; she adds, 'the nationalist version of queer reanimates the problems of lesbian feminism in its cultural feminist versions without resolving them':[83]

> To the extent that queers become nationalist, they will ignore or lose patience with those among them who do not fit their idea of the nation. This dynamic in nationalism will always limit its political usefulness. The only fruitful nationalism is one that has at its heart the idea of the nonnation – the nation of nonidentity, formed not by any shared attribute, but by a conscious weaving of threads between tattered fabrics. And at that point, why speak of nations?[84]

Perhaps because 'nation' carries the romantic rhetorical appeal that 'community', in its nebulousness, has lost. But even 'community' is a dangerous idea in modernity; even though it is read as in antithesis to the state (and is therefore potentially anti-nationalist), community has been 'firmly entrenched within the logic of the same',[85] a victim of identitarian politics which presume that common action must be based in a shared identity.

Recently critic-activists of community and nation have turned to ethics, specifically invoking the concept of love.[86] But, as Jeffrey Weeks asks, 'What do we mean by love? It is difficult to 'love' humankind, except as a metaphysical flight'.[87] Certainly the love generated by nationalism is at least in part a response to the experience of aggression, in a desire to foreclose it.[88] In a historical moment characterized by the homophobia produced by AIDS, and in the general misogynistic milieu, a call to love is an heroic narrative invoked to sustain our spiritual survival; it is a working mestiza consciousness, inflected by the utopian hope that we will be able to create bonds across differences:

> Love in its broadest sense, based on care, responsibility, respect and knowledge, is not an escape from a life without meaning, but a recognition that we make our individual lives meaningful through our involvements with (our love for) others.[89]

Whereas nationalism can foster the love of the same, it also provokes a movement against others; it is insufficient for recognizing our interdependence and need for others. We need an heroic desire that acknowledges and includes our commonalities and our differences and refuses to homogenize conflict. We need an heroic desire that eschews nations and embraces the specifics of people's real material needs. We need to replace the now increasingly vacuous term 'community' with a concept that will invigorate people temporarily and contingently to vitalize the radical process, and create safe spaces for lesbians to live. Love is a contentious term to invoke, a discomforting concept within an academic work, as it is associated with unanalysed feeling and imaginary enchantment. We need to deromanticize love and begin to acknowledge its presence openly, for lesbians and gays do love each other, practically and emotively, in the weaving interstices of our daily lives together. We have constructed an elaborate ethics of care that we check and refine and reference, that we measure ourselves and others against. Many lesbians now spend inordinate amounts of time in therapy learning to love, and yet we scorn this intimacy amongst those to whom we belong. I cannot help but suspect that shame is a negative player in this, an effect of melancholic displacement and repudiation, and that it is conceivable that the pride/shame dichotomy can be commuted into love. Love is recognition, empathy and action. A call to love is not an invitation to easy sentiment, it is to arouse that most arduous and perceptible of practices.

In Edward Said's essay 'Reflections on Exile' he describes the heroic literature of exile as merely an effort to overcome the crippling sorrow of estrangement and loss. These are the conditions of nationalism. But exile is a solitary experience, a sense of being outside a group: 'Exiles feel, therefore, an urgent need to reconstitute their broken lives, usually by choosing to see themselves as part of a triumphant ideology or a restored people'.[90] Clearly, the pride/shame dichotomy is in evidence here. The exile is in the position of being banished, s/he becomes 'eccentric', and seeks to compensate...

[But] because *nothing* is secure. Exile is a jealous state. What you achieve is precisely what you have no wish to share.

Conditions of exile create envy and destructiveness, and a defensive retrenchment. Elements of the Lesbian Nation can be seen to have perpetuated this and caused its implosion. But exile, as my earlier comments on shame show, can also fracture the self and permit new formations to erupt and new connections to configure. As we understand from molecular science, it is the moment of separation which allows new elements to appear. Love can only arise out of this conjunction if first we are able to recognize the emotional profundity of our loss of that chimera: social belonging.

Notes

1. Sarah Schulman, *Rat Bohemia*. New York: Dutton/Penguin Books, 1995, pp. 111–12.
2. During the 1990s, with the growth of nationalisms and the resurgence of Fascism in Europe, there is even more of a wish to try and distinguish between the radical and the oppressive discourses of nationalism.
3. Ernest Gellner, *Nations and Nationalism*. Oxford: Blackwell, 1983, pp. 48–9.
4. *Ibid.*, p. 1.
5. Eric J. Hobsbawm, *Nations and Nationalism Since 1780*. Cambridge: Cambridge University Press, 1990, p. 11.
6. Gellner, *Nations and Nationalism*, p. 8.
7. *Ibid.*, p. 48.
8. *Ibid.*, p. 124.
9. Homi K. Bhabha, *Nation and Narration*. London: Routledge, 1990, p. 1.
10. Gellner, *Nations and Nationalism*, p. 125.
11. Ernest Renan, 'What is a nation?', reprinted in Bhabha, *Nation and Narration*, pp. 8–22, p. 11.
12. Gellner, *Nations and Nationalism*, p. 1.
13. Geoffrey Bennington, 'Postal politics and the institution of the nation', in Bhabha, *Nation and Narration*, pp. 121–37, p. 121.
14. *Ibid.*, p. 132.
15. Homi Bhabha, 'Dissemination: time, narrative, and the margins of the modern nation', in *The Location of Culture*. London: Routledge, 1994, pp. 139–70.
16. Thank you to Sarah Chinn for this connection. See Judith Butler, *Gender Trouble: Feminism and the Subversion of Identity*. London: Routledge, 1990.
17. Homi Bhabha, 'Dissemination', p. 141.
18. *Ibid.*, p. 145.
19. *Ibid.*, p. 148.
20. *Ibid.*, p. 154.
21. *Ibid.*, pp. 155 and 158.
22. Andrew Parker, Mary Russo, Doris Sommer and Patricia Yaeger (eds),

Nationalisms and Sexualities. New York: Routledge, 1992, Introduction, p. 17, footnote 19.

23. *Ibid*., Introduction, p. 6.

24. Thank you to Lynda Hart for this observation.

25. See Parker *et al*., *Nationalisms and Sexualities*, Section VI, pp. 366–446.

26. Geraldine Heng and Janadas Devan, 'State fatherhood: the politics of nationalism, sexuality, and race in Singapore', in Parker *et al*., *Nationalisms*, pp. 343–64, pp. 348–9 and 356.

27. R. Radhakrishnan, 'Nationalism, gender and narrative', in Parker *et al*., *Nationalisms and Sexualities*, pp. 77–95, p. 78.

28. *Ibid*., p. 85.

29. Mary Layoun, 'Palestine women, national narratives', in Parker *et al*., *Nationalisms*, pp. 407–23, p. 411.

30. Joyce Hope Scott, 'From foreground to margin: female configurations and masculine self-representation in black nationalist fiction', in Parker *et al*., *Nationalisms and Sexualities*, pp. 296–312, p. 299.

31. Edward Lewis, *Edward Carpenter: An Exposition and an Appreciation*. London, 1915, p. 67. Quoted in George L. Mosse, *Nationalism and Sexuality*. Madison: University of Wisconsin Press, 1985, p. 63.

32. *Ibid*., p. 139.

33. *Ibid*., p. 57. This middle-class rebellion from middle-class life also has parallels with Sexual Liberation and the (white) student resistance cultures of the 1960s and 1970s.

34. Formed in 1934 for the state persecution of homosexuals.

35. Eve Kosofsky Sedgwick, *The Epistemology of the Closet*. Hemel Hempstead: Harvester Wheatsheaf, 1991, p. 185.

36. See Gloria Anzaldúa, *Borderlands/La Frontera*. San Francisco: Aunt Lute Press, 1987; Minnie Bruce Pratt, 'Identity, skin, blood, heart', in Elly Bulkin, Minnie Bruce Pratt and Barbara Smith (eds), *Yours in Struggle: Three Feminist Perspectives on Anti-Semitism and Racism*. New York: Long Haul Press, 1984, pp. 9–64; Cherríe Moraga, *Loving in the War Years*. Boston: South End Press, 1983; on the city see Elizabeth Wilson, *The Sphinx in the City*. London: Virago Press, 1991.

37. Jill Johnston, *The Lesbian Nation*. New York: Touchstone Books/Simon & Schuster, 1974, p. 11.

38. See Johnston, *The Lesbian Nation*, Ch. 3, 'The lesbian outlaw'.

39. Johnston, *The Lesbian Nation*, p. 58.

40. *Ibid*., p. 75.

41. *Ibid*., p. 92.

42. *Ibid*., p. 76.

43. *Ibid*., p. 90.

44. *Ibid*., p. 258.

45. *Ibid*., p. 254.

46. *Ibid*., p. 190.

47. Monique Wittig, *The Lesbian Body*. Boston: Beacon Press, 1986 (1983).

48. Johnston, *The Lesbian Nation*, p. 262.

49. *Ibid*., p. 266.

50. Cultural feminism was predicated on the opposition 'Man equals culture' (negative) versus 'Woman equals Nature' (positive) – early indications of this position are evident in Johnston's The *Lesbian Nation*.

51. I deploy the term reluctantly, as a shorthand for the complex matrix of sex/gender oppression.

52. Mary Daly, *Gyn/Ecology: The Metaethics of Radical Feminism*. Boston: Beacon Press, 1978, pp. 28–9.

53. Dana R. Shugar, *Separatism and Women's Community*. Lincoln: University of Nebraska Press, 1995.

54. *Ibid*., p. 181.

55. *Ibid*., p. 89.

56. Quoted in Angelika Bammer, *Partial Visions: Feminism and Utopianism in the 1970's*. London: Routledge, 1991, p. 3.

57. Frederic Jameson, 'Of islands and trenches: naturalisation and the

production of utopian discourse',
Diacritics, 7 (2): 6.

58. Bammer, *Partial Visions*, p. 159.

59. See *ibid.*, pp. 161–2.

60. See, for example, Ann Cvetkovich, 'Sexual trauma/queer memory', *GLQ*, 2 (4), 1995: 351–78.

61. I, however, am not the one to do it. I'm arachnophobic and I've hated camping since I was forced to go as a Girl Guide, aged eleven.

62. Judith Raiskin, 'Inverts and hybrids: lesbian rewritings of sexual and racial identities', in Laura Doan (ed.), *The Lesbian Postmodern*. New York: Columbia University Press, 1994, pp. 156–72, p. 160.

63. Raiskin, 'Inverts and hybrids', p. 162.

64. Anzaldúa, *Borderlands/La Frontera*, p. 65.

65. Gloria Anzaldúa, 'To(o) queer the writer – *Loca, escritora y chicana*', in Betsy Warland (ed.), *Inversions*. London: Open Letters, 1991, pp. 249–64, pp. 249–50.

66. Anzaldúa, *Borderlands/La Frontera*, p. 80.

67. *Ibid.*, p. 80.

68. *Ibid.*, p. 79.

69. Lauren Berlant and Elizabeth Freeman, 'Queer nationality', in Michael Warner (ed.), *Fear of a Queer Planet: Queer Politics and Social Theory*. Minneapolis: University of Minnesota Press, 1993, pp. 193–229, p. 198.

70. *Ibid.*, p. 201.

71. *Ibid.*, p. 207.

72. Steven Seidman, 'Identity and politics in a "postmodern" gay culture', in Warner, *Fear of a Queer Planet*, p. 133.

73. Maria Maggenti, 'Women as queer nationals', *Out/Look*, Winter 1991: 20–3, p. 23.

74. *Ibid.*

75. For example, the women who set up Camp Sister Spirit in Mississippi in the early 1990s as women's land based on lesbian feminist ideals. Camp Sister Spirit has been continuously harassed by locals since its inception.

76. Homi Bhabha, *The Location of Culture*, p. 7.

77. Schulman, *Rat Bohemia*, p. 111.

78. By comparison, Lesbian Nation and Queer Nation had no political currency in the UK, a country largely cynical of nationalist movements and still bitterly aware of the National Socialism of World War II.

79. Benedict Anderson, *Imagined Communities*. London: Verso, 1991, p. 7.

80. *Ibid.*, p. 141.

81. Bhabha, 'Dissemination', in *The Location of Culture*, p. 149.

82. Shane Phelan, *Identity Politics: Lesbian Feminism and the Limits of Community*. Philadelphia: Temple University Press, 1989.

83. Shane Phelan, *Getting Specific: Postmodern Lesbian Politics*. Minneapolis: University of Minnesota Press, 1994, p. 153.

84. *Ibid.*, p. 154.

85. *Ibid.*, p. 82.

86. See, for example, Phelan, *Getting Specific*.

87. Jeffrey Weeks, *Invented Moralities: Sexual Values in an Age of Uncertainty*. Oxford: Polity Press, 1995, p. 173.

88. Conversely, as I have already pointed out, foreclosing aggression (if that were possible) would make 'love' impossible.

89. *Ibid.*, p. 184.

90. Edward Said, 'Reflections on exile', in Russell Ferguson, Martha Gever, Trinh T. Minh-Ha and Cornel West (eds), *Out There: Marginalization and Contemporary Culture*. New York/Cambridge, MA: The New Museum of Contemporary Art/MIT Press, 1990, pp. 357–66, p. 360.

6

Lesbians and Space

The stimulus for working on this book originally came out of the experiences in Nottingham I describe in 'The Lesbian Flâneur' (Chapter 2 in this volume). As a coda to this, a few months later I was browsing in the small lesbian and gay section of the city's 'alternative' bookstore, when a stream of neo-Nazis wearing Afrikaaner swastikas broke in and trashed the store, badly beating three people, including one woman on crutches. Two of them came straight for me and my girlfriend, both visible dykes. In that moment we became (butch) 'bodies that matter(ed)', straightforward, easily read signs, and targets for a hostile attack. How can the same space, in an instant, a freeze-frame, be transformed from 'gay space' to 'homophobic space'? What happened to me in the bookshop has also become internalized homophobic space, and a threat to the lesbian identity I invoke, as I think about my vexed positioning as a police witness. I have examined the effects of modern lesbian identity, caught in the structural nexus between outside and inside. These denotations are contextual and temporal and subject to social forces. As a result of this attack, inhabiting urban space changed for me; living my lesbian identity in a social space such as the city has never felt so emphatically endangering. Why do I do it? Why do I risk myself? Can this kind of very real geographic and historical event have anything to say about abstract social relations? In this book I have considered strategies for thinking about space as a positive concept for lesbians. It is an academic way of enacting the old pagan ritual of carrying a smoking sage branch through the rooms of a new home, to make the space welcoming and safe. I needed to enact this gesture mentally after the attack in Nottingham, to make my real and imagined spaces safe again. I wanted to escape a fearful present by bringing hope back into it.

Models of space and spatial identities, urban and urbane wanderings, form a web of ideals, travels, movements, dependent on, and relating to, ideologies of belonging and immanence from both dominant and counter-cultural formations. Where are all these lesbians going? Is it too late for envisioning a home, or is stasis equivalent to death? Who belongs in social spaces, and what are the criteria for membership? Who is excluded? In the lesbian home, is it really a case of 'families we choose' – and who, in this case, are 'we'? Lesbians are adept at constructing survival strategies. Our being in this world exacts a cost, and our identities mutate to incorporate and resist that cost. Parallel configurations like the binary of heterosexual/homosexual and kindred structures such as inside/outside are unstable and exceedingly contingent. In my own experience of attack, at the moment when the internalized homophobia – the shame – coheres within my subjectivity as the abject, the dominant relations of location break down, when a new, resistant self can arise, shifting the spaces around it and within.

The epoch of space

In the three years I have been writing this book a plethora of new publications in Lesbian and Gay Studies concerned with spatial relations have appeared, a tautological testimony to the argument that space is central to theorizing about identity. Michel Foucault, as perhaps the hero of Queer Theory, can be said to have stimulated our thoughts on the subject:

> The present epoch will perhaps be above all the epoch of space. We are in the epoch of simultaneity: we are in the epoch of juxtaposition, the epoch of the near and far, of the side-by-side, of the dispersed. We are at a moment, I believe, when our experience of the world is less that of a long life developing through time than that of a network that connects points and intersects with its own skein.[1]

Lesbian identity is currently focused on its own cultural intersections, a spatial primacy which bears out Foucault's observations. Within cultural theory as a whole, space has been 'mapped', 'explored', 'contested' and 'colonized', as a metaphorical way of understanding the varied and multiple material effects of oppression and domination. Much of this theoretical work has been generated by those for whom concerns about space are ultimately concerned with making some, in the 'place' of politics. Emerging from critical and cultural studies is the embodiment of Foucault's project:

> A whole history remains to be written of spaces – which would at the same time be the history of powers (both terms in the plural) – from the greatest strategies of geophysics to the little tactics of the habitat.[2]

Self-evidently, places are being read as the locale of politics, and modalities of space are appropriated as the favourite exegetical structure to interpret power. Foucault also described the spaces that 'claw and knaw [sic] at us',[3] breaking open the desire for belonging and for a relief from displacement. It becomes clear how invested spaces are with emotion; the stakes are fraught with the intensity of longing, as though the self can somehow be 'homed', rested and resolved. This pursuit of ontological peace, the place for 'us', in which 'we' can dwell, is of course only to be reached by climbing over the rainbow. Spaces and identities are constantly morphologizing, and the force of the longing for a space in which to live can only be a rhetorical metaphor. As with desire, which is only ever satiated with the onset of another desire, so with space: as soon as we get there our presence changes it and we desire to move on.

Space is historically associated with Being, implying a kind of fixity and stasis, as opposed to time, which is conceived of as becoming, of active progress. Traditionally the former is gendered as feminine and hierarchically subsumed under the masculine march of history. Space/Time is aligned with a series of antithetical binary opposites such as passive/active, feminine/masculine. As Elizabeth Grosz has illustrated, however, this binary is to be deconstructed; space is not passive, fixed or absolute, but a relational concept which depends on the position of objects contained within it: 'Space makes possible different kinds of relations but in turn is transformed according to the subject's affective and instrumental relations with it'.[4] There is a certain contingent coherence afforded by the subject's temporal movement through space, which becomes constituent of it, and thus also a constituent of history (time) and politics. Grosz uses the example of the body, which through a perception of itself as a spatial entity is able to manifest and manipulate its corporeality. To paraphrase Grosz, 'a body is what a body can do',[5] and this 'doing' depends on its activity in space. She continues to argue that lesbian (and gay) lifestyles produce lesbian bodies, which are derived from the sexual practices that fashion the body itself. The formation of the lesbian is thus dependent upon her interactivity, in the way that she brushes against others; she is constitutive of them as they are constitutive of her. What I like about this idea is the sheer reproductivity of lesbian desire, and in the power with which this endows the lesbian touch. So, it matters less what we are than what we do. Lesbian energy, lesbian technologies, infect the spaces we inhabit, and those motions are pebbles in a pool; they produce lesbian effects which echo, reverberate, generate, multiply and magnify our presence, and consequently dislocate heterosexuality. Homophobia deploys strategies of containment which are intended to diminish these effects. What this struggle indicates is the provisionality of space.

What Doreen Massey has called 'power-geometry'[6] also gestures to the instability of spaces, which are imbued with partiality. Not only is space contested, but any space is always contingent on the space next to it, and so positionality is dependent upon relations of proximity. The awareness of this proximity is best illustrated by Eve Kosofsky Sedgwick's now classic work on the closet, the defining structure of twentieth-century (male) homosexuality:

> Living in and hence coming out of the closet are never matters of the purely hermetic; the personal and political geographies to be surveyed here are instead the more imponderable and convulsive ones of the open secret[7]

– the open secret of homosexuality, lobbed into containment by its paranoid proximity to heterosexuality, in a failed attempt to define itself as impermeable. This denial of homosexuality is predicated on its projection into a no-space, the closet, which abuts onto heterosexuality with the intrinsicality of a founding wall. What we see here is the erroneous and hopeless struggle to keep spaces 'pure', which can only originate from the panicked realization of multivalency upon which the 'open' secret is predicated. The splitting mechanism operated by heterosexual polar logic tries to exclude the homo, making him (or her) the abject and the locus of shame. It is a deconstructive move which introduces instability. Despite the feverish retrenchment into binaries, as Diana Fuss points out:

> The fear of the homo, which continuously *rubs up against* the hetero (tribadic style), concentrates and codifies the very real possibility and ever-present threat of a collapse of boundaries.[8]

Spaces are not only gendered, and sexed, they are also moralized. Spatial boundaries are moral boundaries which expel the abject, due to the perception of difference as defilement. Thus we are constrained by a subjectivity A that repels not-A. Conversely, definition is also accorded by mutual denial, by asserting the not-A. This routine abhorrence of ambiguity occurs in the two spaces A and not-A. Selves are formed in the erection of boundaries; individuation is a consequence of this manoeuvre. Maintaining the purity of the self involves the splitting off of 'good' and 'bad' objects, an anxiety based on the idea of self as an essence and loss of self as a defilement. We can see how this procedure is grounded in the masculine reification of insulate segregation, singularity and autonomy. bell hooks has drawn attention to how this construction is also raced, in that whites invest in an aetiology of sameness, defining any others as not-white.[9] David Sibley, drawing from post-colonial theory, has written about the making of Western culture in which 'civilization' was defined against mapping the defiled, the (moral) deviation of non-European cultures.[10] Identity emerges through (the denial of) difference, through what Ernesto Laclau has called the *constitutive outside*.[11] This admiration for detachment is also, perhaps inevitably, a prerequisite for domination.

Crowded spaces

To escape this binary antithesis, black and Asian theorists have been the most instrumental in conceptualizing alternatives: Homi Bhabha has talked about 'being in the beyond', in an intervening space he calls the Third Space. The Third Space disrupts meaning, referentiality and enunciation: it is an in-between space which foregrounds hybridity, disarticulating the consensus on signification and meaning predicated on the sovereign notion of self/other:

> the importance of hybridity is not to be able to trace two original moments from which the third emerges, rather hybridity to me is the 'third space' which enables other positions to emerge.[12]

Bhabha invests the boundary with importance as providing the genesis of presence. He describes 'being in the beyond' as 'touch[ing] the future on its hither side',[13] as part of a revisionary time which rebounds as a space of intervention in the here and now. The iterative time of the future is a becoming-space where the 'in-between' becomes utterable, and can return and be reiterated in the interstices of the present. Post-colonial critics have used their writing to invent this new space, which allows the supplementary to emerge. Trinh T. Minh-ha argues how displacement allows the invention of resistant forms of subjectivity:

> Displacing is a way of surviving. It is an impossible truthful story of living in-between regimes of truth… Strategies of displacement defy the world of compartmentalization and the systems of dependence it engenders.[14]

And Gayatri Spivak comments similarly 'the deconstructivist can use herself (assuming one is at one's own disposal) as a shuttle between the center (inside) and the margin (outside) and thus narrate a displacement'.[15] Displacement of the other is able to become displacement of the centre. Signalling from the periphery is a precarious gesture which can provoke the centre into swallowing or spitting you out, but it remains forced to respond. All these models propose that some agency or energy is enacted by exclusion, that force generates its own reaction. But outside and liminal spaces are not only reactive, they are also proactive, they facilitate their own dynamism. Thus 'where I stand' can be rearticulated as a position of marginal resistance, reinventing space as a frontier site where political mobilization occurs. Identity politics become not just deconstructive of mechanisms of exclusion, but strategically reconstructive of the spatializing which assigned them there. Thus activists have argued for the construction of new spaces which are not reducible to the antithetical binary of inside/outside, including for recognition of the excluded middle – in bisexuality perhaps.

However, the outside is a busy place, and the margins are crowded and even these spaces are contested by a range of disparate others; because all spaces abut onto other spaces, the excluded are expected to compete for existence with each other. Identities are the battleground here, and tactically identities have depended on formulating moments of arbitrary closure in order to facilitate struggle. Because identities are always processual, this closure can be seen as strategic and contingent, for example, when the state invokes laws against lesbian and gays, provoking many to identify as such for the first time as an intentional strategy of resistance, to strengthen the first line of defence. This is a territorial act. When Fredric Jameson called for 'a new kind of spatial imagination'[16] he was arguing for a perception of the spatial as invested politically and historically in power, and the vocality of the cultural subaltern has inscribed this onto the perceptions of the cultural mass.[17]

In revising the simple binary of inside/outside space a fundamental tactic is the attempt to decentre the oppressor: Prathiba Parmar insists that creating identities as black women is not done 'in relation to', 'in opposition to' or 'as a corrective to' but 'in and for ourselves'.[18] bell hooks elaborates on the crucial distinction between ascribed marginality and chosen marginality:

> It was this marginality that I was naming as a central location for the production of a counter-hegemonic discourse that is not just found in words but in habits of being and the way one lives. As such, I was not speaking of a marginality one wishes to lose – to give up or surrender as part of moving into the centre, but rather as a site one stays in, clings to even, because it nourishes one's capacity to resist. It offers the possibility of radical perpectives from which to see and create, to imagine alternatives, new worlds...
>
> I want to say that these margins have been both sites of repression and sites of resistance...
>
> This is an intervention. A message from that space in the margin that is a site of creativity and power, that inclusive space where we recover ourselves, where we move in solidarity to erase the category coloniser/colonised. Marginality is the space of resistance. Enter that space. Let us meet there.[19]

What hooks is advocating is spatial praxis as political intervention, a concept first deployed by Henri Lefebvre.[20] She encourages us to reflect upon where we are, and to reflect back that marginalization. Crucially, this activity is established in the way we live our lives, not just in the political grand gesture but in the minutiae of existence. It depends on having a consciousness and an intent; we need to know (in Foucault's sense of the power/knowledge axis) where we are coming from – as Foucault said of power, it is productive and exercised from innumerable points.[21] The strategies and modalities of agency thus become nomadic terrorist interventions to destabilize and reform the centre. The issue of *relative* agency remains, though: when hooks invokes the margins as a space of refusal, one has to question how much choice in this placement there actually is.

hooks draws our attention to the margin, which is not unlike Foucault's structure of heterotopias, which he saw as:

> something like counter-sites, a kind of effectively enacted utopia in which the real sites, all the other real sites that can be found within the culture, are simultaneously represented, contested, and inverted.[22]

Heterotopias are kinds of mirrors to utopias, a counterpoint of the real to the unreal, in which the utopic glance returns to reconstruct the real, in a new way of seeing. Heterotopias are the conceptual space in which we live, six principles of which are identified by Edward Soja:[23] i) they are found in all cultures, although no type is universal; ii) they change over time, they have a genealogy as well as a geography; iii) they are dynamic places where many different, incompatible spaces/sites may intersect; iv) they can occur at particular temporal and spatial axes; v) they presuppose systems of territorial opening and closing which make them subject to the disciplinary technologies of power; vi) they function in relation to the spaces around them, either through the creation of an illusion or out of the sensibilities of compensation. Heterotopias are simultaneously and paradoxically here and nowhere; perhaps they can best be described as an enabling idea which permits the imagination to reconfigure space, rather than affording a real place we can actually go to. Heterotopias allow a slippage of meaning in common to Bhabha's Third Space; they:

> make it impossible to name this and that... because they shatter or tangle common names, because they destroy syntax in advance, and not only the syntax with which we construct sentences but also that less apparent syntax which causes words and things... to 'hold together'... [heterotopias] desiccate speech, stop words in their tracks, contest the very possibility of language at its sources; they dissolve our myths, sterilize the lyricism of sentences.[24]

It is this juxtaposition that produces a kind of space play, out of which can emanate new languages, new subjectivities, in a new kind of semiotic.

Spatial practice

Perhaps a more grounded suggestion for daily spatial praxis can be found in Pierre Bourdieu's *habitus*. Habitus is the practice(s) of everyday life, particularly to be found in the body. For Bourdieu the body is a kind of mnemonic device upon which culture is habitually inscribed. So, in Bourdieu's habitus, the bodyspace re-enacts its placement – according to social taxonomies such as gender and sexuality – in social frameworks. Bhabha talks about the *locality* of culture, something which is lived in the specificities and corporealities of individuals' lives. It is important to stress the tangibility, perhaps even the nearness, of these theorizations, in the fact that they rub up against us, become us, in our particular daily lives, in our mannerisms, in our deportment, in our sexual responses, in the diaphanous but ordinary dispositions of our days. In this matrix of inter-implication, Elspeth Probyn has this to say:

> The singularity of queer desire may reside in the ways in which it puts the body, bodies, and bits of bodies to work hyphenating connections. The momentum here is rhizomatic, with stems of images carrying both their roots and shoots; the image constantly turns itself inside out. Or, as Foucault puts it in one of his rare comments on lesbians, 'sexual relations are immediately transferred into social relations and the social relations are understood as sexual relations'.[25]

As Grosz has said before her, we need to 'look at lesbian relations and if possible, all social relations in terms of bodies, energies, movements, inscriptions'.[26] Thinking so locally – so personally – prevents us from disassociating ourselves from these potentially distantiating theories of space. It also reminds us that the fashionable rhetorics of fragmentation need not come down to our lives being lived as so much circling space dust. We need models of habitation which respect the somatic and affective integrity of our existence.

It is my conviction that we need to theorize spatial relations as something we can ordinarily inhabit, and I wish to question the propensity to romanticize these spatial metaphors to the point of meaninglessness, or to assign an unproblematic agency which has somehow been freed from the mechanics of rejection which constituted its originary moment. Another such culprit is to be found in the reification of 'difference', which, whilst useful in the past as a counterpoint to homogenizing elements of centrist projects, has now degenerated into new kind of fetishism. 'Difference' clouds the specificities and the singularities of how we live our lives. Models such as Homi Bhabha's Third Space and hybridity have a tendency to be applied as though any kind of displacement or instability, like 'difference', is an end in itself, and intrinsically progressive.[27] I disagree with the conviction of Queer activists who argue that destabilization is all – this is to reinstate a (false) binary which sees the dominant as monolithic and change as intrinsically progressive, an irony revealing how much this advocation is in fact reinvesting Enlightenment principles. An example of the disjunction between how we *should* think and how we *do* think came to me in a conversation after a Queer Theory seminar I attended the other week: driving home in the car, four of us who had been at the seminar were discussing whether we really believed that sympathetically 'queer' straights understood and shared 'our' struggle (two lesbians and two gay men). Initially our response was yes, but on the issue of 'do we trust them?' our response was no. What this tells me is that after six years of queer mobilization, if the theory does not fit how we feel, then there is something wrong with the theory. I know this is contentious, in different respects (the primacy of 'feelings', the constructions of 'us', etc.), but despite this I remain convinced there is an important point, that gays and lesbians still wish to protect 'their' space of homosexuality. My intuition is that this guardianship is not reducible to theoretical naïvety, rather, it is politically astute. Instead of embracing the spatial metaphor of hybridity we need to recall that spaces are constructed in time, and that we have histories, as well as spaces, to inhabit. We need to temper our infatuations with new formulations of space and expansion/productivity with memory.

This is concretized for me when I pause with the thought that I have not always been a lesbian. My upbringing in Huddersfield as the child of working-class parents and the ten years I spent as an Evangelical Christian[28] are not overtly integrated into my lesbian present. I moved to Brighton in 1985 to be a postgraduate, and hence embark on a professional career, and to be a lesbian. At the time, these two decisions were conscious reaches for security, but I was unaware until recently how commodified my lesbian identity has become as a consequence. Both these worlds offered conditions I aspired to, and I have learned to inhabit a purchase in both. Both are constructed by migrancy and in exile from my cultures of origin. I have keenly, desperately, cunningly, sneaked into the world of professional lesbianism, where I am only passing, because of my class. I remain attentively cognizant of my precarious footing here, guarded and watchful of 'my space'. This thing I call 'my space' is a portable self, sometimes reducible to my body, often extended, in order of priority, to my house, my car and my office. The only public or social location where I do not, in one form or another, police my lesbianism is the bar. Despite my presence within a certain subculture, I, like many lesbians, police my own space for the presentation of my lesbianism. I never talk about it when I visit Huddersfield, home of my ageing father, dead mother and disabled brother and home of my working-class past. In middle-class lesbian environments, even with my most intimate friends, I have learned to censure behaviour that might make them read me as 'common'. Until I was thirty-four, I was terrified my father would 'find out' about my lesbianism; I remain anxious in Brighton that my working-class pain of non-belonging will be 'found out'. Actually I think neither group really wishes to know. (Neither do I tell people I like to watch *Songs of Praise*.) I do not want to undervalue the very real friendship and love conferred on me by both, and I do have a gay friend who understands some of these complexities, but I also want to address the fact that I have no space where those two conjunctions, lesbian and working-class, connect. They have not consolidated into anywhere I can live. Doubtless in part because my desire to 'home' my lesbian identity has repeatedly felt like a coercion to transcend my class, I have never known a working-class lesbian community. I did have a working-class girlfriend once, another butch, who left me for my (rich) ex-girlfriend. (Despite the pathos, I am laughing as I write this, as I realize the mutual identifications were probably too much to bear.) Brutally: I escaped my class to become a lesbian. I juggle with these feelings of being a traitor, an alien, a stranger, a migrant, an exile, an impostor; I am the enemy within who wants what you have (and you). Even writing this in my book produces feelings of embarrassment and usury as I accuse myself of using my class credentials[29] to manipulate my argument. My lesbian pride becomes an exchange for my class shame. Aspiration, as a cruel cipher of loss, still drives my lesbian present.

This fragmentation is partly explained by the Americanization of identity politics, which has had a profound effect in Britain on how we compartmentalize and homogenize lesbian and gay identity.[30] Secondly, it is a reflection of how bourgeois exigencies become normalized, for example in not talking about money. Thirdly, the hegemonic silence about class is a reaction against the vituperative self-justifications actioned in the name of lesbian feminism in the early 1980s. Fourthly, my family had known I was a lesbian for a decade, they just did not want to talk about it; my talking about it, in my 'talk, talk, talk', is read by them as a tactless reminder of my 'talkie' profession. There are a number of structural explanations. There is one arena, though, in which I suspect these taxonomies reside: my butchness. My butchness makes me indiscreet; its visibility alerts those around me to my lesbianizing of space. My butchness makes me appear like one of those 'tough-looking, promiscuous women who are into roles' that frequent the homophobic hinterlands of the middle-class appetite for secrecy, privacy and a quiet life. This is my habitus – the way my body is inscribed by my origins and my way of life. My butchness takes the bar into the home; it does not just reflect my class, it constitutes it in that space.

This narrative could be reduced to a working-class heroic of suffering and survival, but this would miss the complexity of the time/space nexus which contains it. I appear to be arguing a contradiction, that we should politically consolidate under the signifier 'lesbian' and subsume within it the perhaps incompatible histories that precede it. Yet there are aspects of the self which refuse this, and remain other-to-the-self. This is at least due to the ways in which we are able to read some aspects of subjectivity more easily than others, the ones that call to us through social signification, which resonate within us through recognition and direct our desires. There is a space we can occupy already waiting, and we squeeze into it. The residues, the bodily excesses, run the risk of being turned into the defiled and the abject. I have in mind a more therapeutic reconciliation, which reintegrates history and is fully present in its occupation and movement, a recovery of the self which authenticates experience without reifying it, and examines and produces desire in a critical way.

Heroic space

According to my heroic interpretation, the lesbian's movement through time and space is an act of her professed belief in an imagined community, one in which there is full citizenship for her. Our visual statement to a predominantly heterosexual world is a constant invoking of this utopianism (complete with its corollary dystopianism, in that a visible queer is also an invitation to queerbashers). Becoming a lesbian is a perpetual expression of hope, it is an active intervention of optimism, a profession of belief in social transformations. Space is an important concept here. As I have argued, identities are produced, expressed and authenticated by and through space. Understanding 'real' and metaphorical spatial structures helps us to discover new sites of presence and resistance. Some famous, fabulous spaces, such as New York, Paris and Berlin, have been constitutive of modern gay and lesbian identities. Social spaces teach us something about the relations of domination and subordination around us, and also that the penetration of queer space by Nazis creates a simultaneously homophobic and queer zone. Spaces, like identities, are rarely discrete.

Metaphors of movement chronicle the lesbian imagination. Sometimes movement is chosen, sometimes imposed. Prior to the Stonewall Riot in New York in 1969, and the consequent formation of the modern Lesbian and Gay Liberation Movement, imposed narratives of lesbian movement were usually inexorably regressive – a path of destruction to despair and death. Post-Stonewall our reconstructed myths of movement have been deliberately and self-consciously progressive. The classic lesbian journey, in the coming-out story, is from isolation to inclusion, an idealized trajectory of self-realization. It follows the footpath of all those hundreds of thousands of Westerners since World War I who made the geographical shift – the heroic journey – to the gay and lesbian homeland, the city. The imagination and experience dialectically constitute the lesbian subject. The imagination is of paramount importance in a heterosexual world which effaces our experience, by rendering us absent. We hardly have the luxury of positive reinforcement or of defining our own manifestation in culture. We need to, and we do, fantasize about the *possibility* of homosexual behaviour, before acting on our desires. Somewhere, we believe, there's a place for us.

The desire to integrate the self is itself heroic, not in the traditional trajectory which appropriates others, but in a revised way which brings the self to itself, moving/journeying through space and in time. And so I return to Zimmerman's concept of the multivalent self which concerned us in Chapter 1. Remembering that the multivalent self is constituted in motion (and hence in space) and in history (time), we see the multivalent self as a desire for interaction without self-loss or abnegation. The multivalent self is not an essence, as it is subject to the changes and spaces through which it moves, but it does honour the singularity of each particular trajectory. Because it becomes the other at its edges, it cannot reproduce the oppression of the subject/object dichotomy. The multivalent self leans into a distinctive context, altering the parameters of that context, aware of the motion it generates and the echo it receives. The spaces of the self expand and contract in a dynamic relation to its environment, in a relationship of reciprocity. Elements of the multivalent self 'move' it, and form it, and are constitutive of the body, like habitus; for example, in Ed Cohen's cogent description of gayness this alignment between the self and the body is the epitome of ethical activism:

> You see I *feel* there *is* something 'different' about the body: I *believe* feeling is the difference that bodies make, a difference that *moves* people to action. As far as I can tell political movements are engendered by personal and political (e)motions that impel people – in the parlance of the old 'New Left' – to put their bodies on the line. If we want to consider what it is that moves people to act together often in the face of manifest danger or violence in order to transform their collective life-worlds, then we must begin to take seriously the notion that political movements cohere only to the extent that they express and make meaningful the shared *feeling and knowledge* that things ought to and can become different than they are – i.e. to the extent that they touch and move people who touch and move each other... By advocating an understanding of political movements as embodied processes, then, I want to suggest both that bodies do make a (political) difference and that difference is often a matter of (e)motion.[31]

For the sake of political efficacy we need to relinquish disembodiment and its corollary splitting as the primary metaphors of subjectivity (except as a way of understanding how to avoid it). We should investigate instead how we can formulate models of integration, as a route to agency. This is an imaginative project which recognizes we can never achieve 'wholeness' (nor would want to), but we can try to inhabit the present with all sides of ourself open to interaction. Discomfort with ourselves can then be something to explore as it abuts against someone else, to work out the specificities of why we 'do not fit', and to respond sensitively and ethically to bridge the gap. (We do this constantly in our intimate relationships.) Leaning into the experience of others is not always an equal exchange, and we need to temper our leaning with another necessity to stand still and listen, acknowledging that the specificities of the self also require humility, allowing others to lean into us. Certain spaces of the self can expand or contract due to the exigencies of the context. We need to nurture our power to seize space too.

Heroic journeys are predicated on a lack and this motivates the desire of the hero. I do not wish to reproduce the taxonomy desire/lack, I would rather suggest that this desire for the self is predicated on a desire to reproduce the self as a spatial presence, as something that moves and changes for itself, for the pleasure of moving and changing and materializing, in the field of power. Thus we can begin to theorize an energy which is not ephemeral and disconnected from the self but that arises from it and multiplies within the public sphere, becoming its own entity, innovating and moving for the sake of connection, of embodiment. This expansion can displace the homophobic, especially when the spaces blend together to form entire communities of resistance.

Space and time

Foucault's assertion that we are living in an epoch (time) of space contains an interesting paradox: that we cannot theorize space without time. To try to extract space from time is to commit a conceptual delusion. Whilst contemporary cultural theory has enthused about space, it has often failed to address its temporal context with the same vigour, being given to interpret space as a kind of static void, deprived of political content. In part, this can be interpreted as a clumsy effect of the postmodernist reproach to appeals to inevitable Progress, with its implied link to a monolithic Politics (the Marxist March of Time... Come the Revolution). Time, it appears, is not on our side. The present, too, is troubled: Fredric Jameson, for example, sees the postmodern as characterized by a spatiality of 'chaotic depthlessness'.[32] Within the endless proliferation of the commodified present, past and future have been subsumed to the apparently voracious desire to have things *now*; it is a fairly terrifying simultaneity. If history itself can only be read as a relativized fiction, it is therefore no longer to be trusted. If the real is only a realm of representation – what are we fighting for? These crude aphorisms are taken to be the *Zeitgeist* of the *fin de siècle*. One can see why space has become so attractive to lesbians living in a culture which, in so many ways, generally and zealously craves to get some, from the local to the global. But, as I have tried to indicate, space without time is a disabled concept, so, briefly and finally, I want to contextualize my thoughts on space with a model that incorporates time.

The flâneur – the hero of lesbian desire – is not just a figure of space, she also embodies time. A moving body occupies space, but these spaces are not fixed moments with individually recoverable co-ordinates, they are acts of duration, of space-in-time. The restless spaces of the flâneur are fluctuating, rippling and relational, her wandering is not concerned with closure, there is no purpose to it, it is movement for the sake of its own pleasure; in the modernist sense of time it is not productive.[33] It is not to be interpreted, it is to be done, to be written, not read. The flâneur has succeeded in being (spatial) and becoming (temporal), by expressing duration, a concept of Bergson's which is elaborated by Ann Game:

> A moving body occupies successive positions in space, but the process by which it moves from one position to another is one of duration which eludes space (Bergson 1950: 111). Motion itself, the act, is not divisible, only an object is; space which is motionless can be measured but the motion of bodies cannot. Movements cannot occupy space, they are duration... To think of a body occupying points in space is to do so from a perspective outside the body, not from the perspective of the moving body. To be *in* the body is to be in time.[34]

There is a particular meaning of time being deployed here, one that is experienced as a body in motion, which in Bergson's formulation is a kind of creative evolution. As Game discusses it, this evolution is a process without an end, it is a proliferation of experience without finality or conclusion, it is a kind of infinite differentiation without negativity or denial. As she says, Bergson's theory of time is compatible with positive desire, reproducing itself for its own sake, moving for pleasure. There is an attitude of openness which infuses it. It is an entering of time, rather than a measurement of it. This is to deconstruct the binary of time/space, where they collapse to form a moving present; it is 'space that it is lived and is transformed by imagination'.[35] The lesbian configurations I have discussed in *Heroic Desire* deploy this imagination as a form of creative evolution.

The spaces of the lesbian flâneur are not fixed or empty, they are constituted through her motion, she moves them, and is moved by them, in an (e)motional way. She has found a way to embody the present. Her imaginative present has a relation to the past and to the future, both of which are constantly remaking the present, in a process of synthesis. This present is in an important sense utopian: utopian desires attempt to change the present by integrating possible futures; the quality of hope transforms that present. The recognition that possible futures are latent within the present simultaneously enables her to belong and become. This is not about predicting a future, neither does it resort to a myth of inevitable progress; it is about animating a kind of optimism, Bloch's anticipatory consciousness. Utopias are not fixed entities or static spaces; they generate utopian thinking, or speculations, the reader's own projection of and response to desires for a better present. These desires are never 'utopian' in the derogatory sense of too distanced to be real, they are very real and express a yearning, a movement towards possibilities. Roland Barthes, whose work is presently enjoying a critical renaissance, understood utopias as intrinsic to creative resistance:

> For me the ideal takes on a very precise form which is that of utopia. I have a utopian imagination and very often when I write, even if I'm not referring to a utopia, if, for example, I'm analysing particular notions in a critical way, I always do this through the inner image of a utopia: a social utopia or an affective utopia.[36]

Barthes' political critique was intentionally conceived as intrinsic to the evocative and homoerotic style of language he deployed; his vision for utopia was concurrent with the writerly creation of his homosexuality; his energy and his ability to move people depended upon his personal and affective engagement with them, through his style. The performative self needs a performative language, one that can go beyond the parameters of meaning, that is infinitely expansive. Barthes conjoined space with time in his yearning for utopian futures; similarly, his work brought back those utopias to the present, by sharing his poetic imagination, his passion, his euphoria, his sense of wonder, with the reader. Barthes equated the concept of utopia with the novelistic, or even more broadly, Text, so:

> At the centre of Barthes' understanding of the utopia is the writer's permanent commitment to *writing* the world, by which he means an act of conceptualization, understanding, complicity and projection... Barthes believed that present-day language is the

intractable site of social division, so that the liberation of the one could not be thought without that of the other... the figure of utopia necessarily embraces both content and form.[37]

For us, we need to write lesbian texts where we can live, supplanting division with a diffuse, erotic attachment: we need to inhabit our own fictions.

Utopian desires lean into potential futures, and in doing so those futures elaborate the present and create moments of transition. For the lesbian to put herself into the present is a utopian act, and that present constantly moves forward, in disruption and realignment. If we reconsider Althusser's definition of ideology – 'Ideology represents the *imaginary* relationship of individuals to their real conditions of existence'[38] – we can conceive how necessarily compelling this re-visioning of the present, in opening up potential futures *and spaces*, becomes. Monique Wittig expresses this succinctly in the penultimate lines of *Les Guérillères* (1971): MARGINS SPACES INTERVALS/ WITHOUT PAUSE/ACTION OVERTHROW.[39] It is an imperative to be constantly moving, since movement induces change in time *and* space. Thus, with reference to identity politics, where we stand is less consequential than how we move. The body which moves to touch another in the spirit of reception rather than intrusion materializes the utopian habitus as an 'approach toward'. The challenge to 'touch and move people who touch and move each other' is about living in the localized present with hope; effective political engagement depends on it. Touching is an act of emotional gentleness, a gesture of trust which is also open to the return touch, the willingness to allow my body to imprint your body, and yours to imprint mine.

Notes

1. Michel Foucault, 'Of other spaces', *Diacritics*, Spring 1986: 22–7, quoted by Edward W. Soja, 'Heterotopologies', in Sophie Watson and Katherine Gibson (eds), *Postmodern Cities and Spaces*. Oxford: Blackwell, 1995, pp. 13–34, p. 17.
2. Foucault, 'Of other spaces'.
3. *Ibid*.
4. Elizabeth Grosz, *Space, Time, and Perversion*. New York: Routledge, 1995, p. 92.
5. *Ibid*., p. 214.
6. Doreen Massey, 'Power-geometry and a progressive sense of place', in J. Bird, B. Curtis, T. Puttnam, G. Robertson and L. Tickner (eds), *Mapping the Futures*. London: Routledge, 1993.

7. Eve Kosofsky Sedgwick, *The Epistemology of the Closet*. Hemel Hempstead: Harvester Wheatsheaf, 1991, p. 80.

8. Diana Fuss (ed.), Introduction, *Inside/Out: Lesbian Theories, Gay Theories*. New York: Routledge, 1991, pp. 1–10, p. 6.

9. bell hooks, *Black Looks: Race and Representation*. London: Turnaround Press, 1992.

10. David Sibley, *Geographies of Exclusion*. London: Routledge, 1995.

11. Ernesto Laclau, *New Reflections on the Revolutions of Our Time*. London: Verso, 1990.

12. Homi Bhabha, 'The third space', in Jonathan Rutherford (ed.), *Identity, Community, Culture, Difference*. London: Lawrence and Wishart, 1990, pp. 207–21, p. 211.

13. Homi Bhabha, *The Location of Culture*. London: Routledge, 1994, p. 7.

14. Trinh T. Minh-Ha, 'Cotton and iron', in Russell Ferguson, Martha Gever, Trinh T. Minh-Ha and Cornel West (eds), *Out There: Marginalization and Contemporary Cultures*. New York: The New Museum of Contemporary Art/MIT Press, 1990, pp. 327–36, pp. 331–3.

15. Gayatri Spivak, 'Explanation and culture: marginalia', in Ferguson *et al.*, *Out There*, pp. 377–94, p. 381.

16. Fredric Jameson, 'Postmodernism, or the cultural logic of late capitalism', *New Left Review*, **146**, 1984: 53–92.

17. As I write this, in the wake of the 12 July 1996 Protestant Orangemen's triumphalist marches through the Catholic housing estates of Northern Ireland, two days' rioting by Nationalists marks the end of the peace process. The Loyalists' violation of space, safeguarded by the British government, cuts through the homes of Irish Catholics, barricaded by British troops. The effect has been that diverse, often antagonistic, Catholic political and cultural groups have opened up and coalesced to form temporary lines of force. The terms of this battle are entirely spatial, in fact both sides could be termed marginal, but each interprets its orientation to Britain and to Ireland in different ways.

18. Prathiba Parmar, 'Black feminism: the politics of articulation', in Rutherford, *Identity*, pp. 101–26, p. 101.

19. hooks, *Black Looks*, pp. 149–52.

20. Henri Lefebvre, *The Production of Space*. Oxford: Blackwell, 1991.

21. Michel Foucault, *History of Sexuality: Volume One*. Harmondsworth: Penguin, 1984, p. 94.

22. Michel Foucault, 'Of other spaces', p. 24.

23. Edward W. Soja, 'Heterotopologies', in S. Watson and K. Gibson (eds), *Postmodern Cities and Spaces*, pp. 13–34.

24. Michel Foucault, *The Order of Things*. New York: Vintage, 1980, p. xvii.

25. Michel Foucault, *Foucault Live*. New York: Semiotext(e), 1989, quoted in Elspeth Probyn, *Outside Belongings*. New York: Routledge, 1996.

26. Elizabeth Grosz, 'Refiguring lesbian desire', in *Space, Time, and Perversion*, p. 182.

27. Subsequent to writing this point, I came across Alan Sinfield's article which makes this criticism more thoroughly: Alan Sinfield, 'Diaspora and hybridity', *Textual Practice*, 10 (2), Summer 1996: 271–93.

28. Some would say this explains a lot…

29. Although 'parading' my working-class identity could be read cynically as an attempt to promote my non-centrist position and earn political credibility, rarely are the actual experiences of marginalization or oppression taken seriously by those who are counting points.

30. See Sinfield, 'Diaspora and hybridity'.

31. Ed Cohen, 'Who are we? Gay "identity" as political (e)motion', in Diana Fuss (ed.), *Inside/Out*. London: Routledge, 1991, pp. 71–92, pp. 84–5.

32. Fredric Jameson, *Postmodernism; or, the Cultural Logic of Late Capitalism*. London: Verso, 1991, quoted in Doreen Massey, *Space, Place, and Gender*. Cambridge: Polity Press, 1994, p. 251.

33. I am indebted to Ann Game's observations about the flâneur here, from Chapter 7, 'Places in time', of her *Undoing the Social: Towards a Deconstructive Sociology*. Milton Keynes: Open University Press, 1991.

34. *Ibid.*, p. 95.

35. Ann Game, 'Time, space, memory, with reference to Bachelard', in Mike Featherstone, Scott Lash and Roland Robertson (eds), *Global Modernities*. London: Sage Publications, 1995, pp. 192–208, p. 200. She is referring to H. Bergson, *Time and Free Will*. Trans. F. L. Pogson. London: George Allen & Unwin, 1950.

36. Roland Barthes, 'Sur l'astrologie', in *Roland Barthes: Oevres Complètes*, ed. Eric Marty, Volumes 1–3. Paris: Seuil, 1993–5, pp. 443–9.

37. Diana Knight, *Barthes and Utopia: Space, Travel, Writing*. Oxford: Clarendon Press, 1997, p. 271. This book provides a useful and detailed account of Barthes' use of Utopia, but it is unfortunately marred by the author's (probably unconscious) squeamishness on the subject of his homosexuality.

38. Louis Althusser, 'Ideology and ideological state apparatuses', in *Lenin and Philosophy and Other Essays*. Trans. B. Brewster. New York: Monthly Review Press, 1971, pp. 127–87, p. 162.

39. Monique Wittig, *Les Guérillères*. Boston: Beacon Press, 1971, p. 143.

Index

Acker, Kathy   44
Africa   5, 38, 103
agency   9, 16, 39, 54, 118,
    167–8
AIDS   3, 65, 109, 152, 157
alienation   17, 38–9, 45–6,
    48, 119–27
Allen, Paula Gunn   22
Allison, Dorothy: *Bastard
    Out of Carolina*
    117–19
Althusser, Louis   78, 179
amazons   96, 102–14, 116,
    145
America, *see* USA
America, Miss   105
Anderson, Benedict:
    *Imagined
    Communities*   156
androgyny   56, 64, 72
Anzaldúa, Gloria:
    *Borderlands/
    La Frontera*   23,
    143, 149–52
Aristotle: *Poetics*   8–9
avengers   96, 102–14

Bammer, Angelika   148–9
Barnes, Djuna   37
Barney, Natalie Clifford
    103
Barthes, Roland   115, 178–9
Bastard Out of Carolina, *see*
    Allison
Baudelaire, Charles   32, 34
Baudrillard: *America*   48
Bechdel, Alison: *Dykes to
    Watch out For*   125
Benjamin, Walter   32, 35,
    39, 41, 48
Bennington, Geoffrey
    135–6
Bergson, Henri   177
Berlant, Lauren   153
Bersani, Leo   78, 81
Bhabha, Homi   96, 136–7,
    139, 145, 155–6, 166,
    169–70
Bildungsroman   17
binaries   13, 78, 96, 101,
    163–5
    homo/heterosexuality   3,
    101, 119, 163

idealization/denigration
    16, 96–122
inside/outside   42, 86,
    126, 139, 167–8
pride/shame   96–7,
    117–19, 123–5, 154,
    158–9
subject/object   5, 175
Birtha, Becky   22
bisexuality   69, 153, 167
black   15, 17, 24, 38, 40,
    166
    feminism   24, 152, 157
    women   5, 15, 23–5, 111,
    140, 147, 168
Blakeley, Johanna   90
Blankley, Elyse   37
blaxploitation   111
Bloch, Ernst   147–8, 178
body, the   65, 151, 164,
    170, 175, 177
    butch   54–94, 162
    lesbian   62–8, 164
    of the nation   138–45
    transsexual   58
bonding   114–15
Bourdieu, Pierre   169–70
Brighton   30–1, 49, 56, 126,
    171
Brummell, George Bryan
    ('Beau')   33
butch   16, 30–1, 54–94,
    172–3
    body   54–94, 162
    definitions of   54–5
    drag   42–4, 54, 71
    stone   54, 73–6, 122
Butler, Judith   60, 78, 83,
    85, 90, 136
Byron, Lord   16, 100

Califia, Pat   123
Campbell, Joseph: *The Hero
    with a Thousand
    Faces*   9–10
capitalism   47–8, 72, 152–3
Caprio, Frank: *Female
    Homosexuality*   65–7
Carlyle, Thomas: *On Heroes*
    12
Carpenter, Edward   141,
    149
Castle, Terry   100, 101, 142

Certeau, Michel de   49
Chauncey, George   39–40
Christianity   9, 75, 103,
    110, 171
citizenship   138, 150,
    155–9, 173–4
city, the   37–41, 48–9
civilization   103, 166
class   37–40, 71, 97–8, 132,
    135
    middle   97, 100, 117,
    141, 157
    working   14–17, 39–40,
    112, 171–3
closet   165
Cohen, Ed   175
colonialism   38, 84, 111,
    150
'coming in'   15, 99–102,
    119
'coming out'   14–15, 119,
    174
community   15–16, 157–8
    imagined   155–9, 173–4
cross-dressing   36, 55,
    70–71, 89
Cvetkovich, Ann   118

Daly, Mary   146
dandy, the   32–4, 36, 39, 71
de Lauretis, Teresa   81–4
de Lynn, Jane: *Don Juan in
    the Village*   41, 44–8
denigration, *see*
    idealization/denigration
desire   10–11, 26, 73, 80–2,
    88, 95–6
Devan, Janadas   138–9
dichotomies, *see* binaries
difference   170–1
dildoes   64, 82
DiMassa, Diane: *Hothead
    Paisan*   112–13, 125
Dollimore, Jonathan   101,
    142
Don Juan in the Village, *see*
    de Lynn
Donoghue, Emma   98–9
Dyer, Richard   8, 20
Dyke Marches   108
dystopias   35, 48, 173

Echols, Alice   104
Ellis, Havelock   64

Ellison, Ralph: *Invisible Man* 38
erotic, the 23–4, 80–2
essentialism 23, 57, 85, 149–50
eugenics 65, 149
Eve 102
exile 158–9

Farwell, Marilyn 11–13
Fascism 18, 71
Feinberg, Leslie: *Stone Butch Blues* 16–18, 21–2, 24, 74, 117–18
femininity 43, 56, 105
feminism 70, 85, 102–4
  cultural 102–4, 106, 146
  radical 104–6, 112–13
  see also lesbian feminism
femmes 42–3, 55–9
fetish, the 80–4
fiction 6–13, 16–18, 102
flâneur, the 30–49, 177–8
  textual history of 31–41
folk tales 6–8, 17, 102
Foucault, Michel 25, 49, 70, 74, 96–7, 99, 135, 163–4, 168–70, 176
Freeman, Elizabeth 153
Freud, Sigmund 21, 35, 68–70, 79
Frye, Northrop 9
Fuss, Diana 125–6, 165

Galford, Ellen 102
Game, Ann 177
Gay Pride 47, 108, 126
gaze, the 31–2, 42–3, 120
  homophobic 58–9, 65, 120
Gellner, Ernest 134–5, 141, 145
gender 39, 56–60, 72
  dysphoria 69, 83
George, Stefan 141–2
Gever, Martha 101
Ghandi 140
ghosting 82, 101
Gibson, Gloria 4
Gide, André 9
Ginsberg, Ruth 24
Girls, Visions and Everything, see Schulman
Gomez, Jewelle: *The Gilda Stories* 15
Graham, Paula 113–14
Grahn, Judy: *Another Mother Tongue* 54–5
Greenham Common 106–7
Greenwich Village 37–41, 45, 126

Grosz, Elizabeth 84–5, 88, 164, 170

habitus 169–70, 173, 175
Halberstam, Judith 89
Hall, Radclyffe: *The Well of Loneliness* 14, 55, 64, 75–6
Harlem 37–40
Hart, Lynda 97, 110, 113, 115, 124
Heng, Geraldine 138–9
heroes 1–29, 173–6
heroines 2–3
heterotopias 169
Hill Collins, Patricia 5
Hirschfeld, Magnus 62–3
Hobsbawm, Eric 14, 23, 134
homo/hetero binary, *see* binaries
homophobia 72, 74–5, 78, 119, 157, 162
  discourses of 20, 25
  gaze and 58–9, 65, 120
  internalized 7, 28, 90, 119
homosexuality
  panic and 78, 87, 142
  theories of 60–70
hooks, bell 116–17, 166, 168–9
Hothead Paisan, see DiMassa

idealization/denigration 16, 96–122
identity 4–6, 15, 20, 23, 172, 179
ideology, definition of 179
inversion 61–4
invisibility 59, 98

Jameson, Fredric 147–8, 167–8, 176
Jeffreys, Sheila: *The Lesbian Heresy* 81
Jews 17, 46–7
Joan of Arc 55, 103, 128–9
Johnston, Jill: *Lesbian Nation* 132, 143–5
Julien, Isaac: *Looking for Langston* 38

Katrak, Ketu 140
Kerouac, Jack 45–6, 47, 48
King, Katie 54
Klapp, Orrin E. 8, 13
Krafft-Ebing, Richard von 61–3
Kristeva, Julia 90

Lacan, Jacques 83, 88
Layoun, Mary 139–40

Lesbian and Gay Liberation Movement 3–4, 121, 152, 174
Lesbian Avengers 107–16
Lesbian Nation 22, 123, 132–3, 151, 154–6, 159
lesbian/ism
  chic 54, 100–1, 109–10
  citizenship 143, 155–9
  feminism 70–1, 102, 112, 122, 143–6, 156
  flâneur 41–9
  nation 132–59
  nationalism 133, 141, 143–6, 151, 155–9
  phallus 80–4
  see also butch
Lesbian/Woman 146, 148
Lesbos 1, 37, 151
LeVay, Simon 68
liberal humanism 9, 22
Lister, Anne 55, 99–100
Lorde, Audre 22–4, 26, 111, 151
Loulan, Jo Ann: *The Lesbian Erotic Dance* 57–8
love 156–9
Lynch, Lee: 'The Swashbuckler' 41, 44, 48, 55

McClintock, Anne 138
Maggenti, Maria 154–5
Mannerbund 141–2
marginality 13, 39, 166–8
Marxism 35, 104, 156, 176
masculinity 16, 34, 56
  appropriation of 54, 59, 70
  female 68, 84, 87
Massey, Doreen 165
medical
  language 63–8, 99
  practice 60–1, 63
'mestiza consciousness' 149–52, 158
metaphors, spatial 136–7, 143, 164, 170–6
Minh-ha, Trinh T. 167
Moers, Ellen 33–5
Moraga, Cherríe 143
Mosse, George 140–2, 149
Mother 83–4, 138
myths, *see* folk tales
Mytilène 37

narcissism 33–4, 70, 86
Nation 142
  see also Queer Nation; Lesbian Nation
nationalism 133–43, 155, 158

ideology and 134–5, 140–1, 143
lesbian 133, 131, 143–6, 151, 155
sexuality and 138–43
Nationalisms and Sexualities 138–9
Navratilova, Martina 55, 71–2
Nazism 18, 65, 141–2, 174
Nestle, Joan
'Stone Butch, Drag Butch, Baby Butch' 41–3, 48
A Restricted Country 59, 79–80, 82
'The Bathroom Line' 79–80, 82
'New Woman' 34, 50
New York 37–49, 126, 132, 143
nostalgia 20–1, 47
Nottingham 30–1, 162
nudity 141

oppression 3, 24, 117, 133
Other/other 24–5, 43, 81–4, 96–8, 125
outlaw 12, 14, 71, 95–131

parables 19–20
Paris 32, 34, 37
Parmar, Prathiba 168
parthenogenesis 144
patriarchy 104, 146
peace movement 106–7
penetration 74, 76, 85–7
penis envy 70, 80
Perkins, Muriel Wilson 68
phallic woman 107, 113–15
phallus, the 66–7, 80–4, 87
Phelan, Shane 95, 157
postmodernism 13, 24, 35, 71–2, 176
Pratt, Minnie Bruce 89, 143
pride 7, 96–7, 117–19
pride/shame 96–7, 101, 117–19, 123–5, 154, 158–9
Probyn, Elspeth 170
Propp, Vladimir 7
Prosser, Jay 74
prostitution 34–6, 84, 100, 119
prototypes 148

Queer/queer 3–4, 18, 71–2, 112, 150–7, 163, 171
flâneur 36–41
Queer Nation 132, 152–6

race 39–40, 84, 133, 166
racism 98, 111

Radhakrishnan, R. 139
Radicalesbians 104, 144
Raiskin, Judith 149–50
rape analogies 76, 138, 145
realism 16–22
Renan, Ernest 135
Rigg, Diana 102, 107
Robson, Ruthann 95–6
roman à thèse 17–22, 144
romance 10, 158
Rubin, Gayle 56, 59, 71
Russ, Joanna 2

sacrifice 9, 75, 86
sado/masochism 123–4, 149, 153
Said, Edward 158
sameness 81
Sand, George 36
Scheff, Thomas 119–21
Schulman, Sarah 41, 45–7, 108–9, 115
Girls, Visions and Everything 41, 45–7
SCUM Manifesto 112–13
Section 28 95, 127
Sedgwick, Eve Kosofsky 59, 101, 122, 125, 142, 165
Seidler, Victor 24–5
Seidman, Steven 154
self, the 11, 24–5, 80–1, 125, 173
multivalent 2, 5, 16, 22–26, 174–5
separatism 146–8, 151, 157
sexology 60–9, 72, 84, 97, 99
sexuality, nationality and 138–43
shame 76, 79, 87, 117–27
see also pride
Showalter, Elaine 34
Shugar, Dana 146–7
Sibley, David 166
Smith, Anna Marie 98
Social Darwinism 103
social types 8, 13
Soja, Edward 169
Solanas, Valerie 112–13
Somers, Margaret 4
space 43, 136–8, 162–81
discourses of 166–9
heroic 173–6
models of 47, 162–3
time and 176–9
spatial practice 170–3
Spivak, Gayatri Chakravorty 23, 167
stereotypes 6–8, 13
Stone Butch Blues, see Feinberg

'Stone Butch, Drag Butch, Baby Butch', *see* Nestle
Stonewall Riots 1, 4, 11, 14–15, 27, 145, 174
subjectivity 167, 173
Suleiman, Susan 19–20
Sullivan, Andrew 81
survivors 117–19, 124
'Swashbuckler, The', *see* Lynch

Tank Girl 106, 114
toilets 44, 76–9
transsexuals 83
female to male (FTM) 58–9, 89

Ulrichs, Karl Heinrich 61
urning/urningin 61
USA 32, 38–9, 77, 118, 132
Americanization 172–3
politics of 104, 155
sexology in 65, 68
utopias/utopianism 17–21, 25, 35, 147–9, 178–9
and heterotopias 169

vampirism 15, 66–7
Vasconcelos, José 149
Vivien, Renée 37
voyeurism 34, 41–2, 120

Waldby, Catherine 87
warrior, the 102, 112–14, 144–5
Weeks, Jeffrey 157
Wheeler, Wendy 21
white 15, 38–40, 117, 132, 166
middle class 110, 147, 151–2, 154
Wigley, Mark 43
Wilde, Oscar 33–4, 36, 50, 97
Wilson, Edward O. 68
Wilson, Elizabeth 21, 35–6, 39
Wittig, Monique 12, 81, 105–7, 113
Les Guérillières 102, 105–7, 179
Lesbian Body 145
Wolff, Charlotte 64
Woman 12, 23, 34, 70, 74–6, 87, 116, 139, 145
Women's Movement 25, 64, 104–5, 116
Wonder Woman 105, 107
Woolf, Virginia: *Three Guineas* 139

Zimmerman, Bonnie 11–12, 15, 17, 22, 24, 174